Born in Tasmania in 1931, **Lloyd Robson** was educated at the University of Tasmania, the University of London and the Australian National University. He was appointed to the Department of History at the University of Melbourne in 1964. Both as a teacher and writer he always achieved much. His earlier books included *The Convict Settlers of Australia* (1965) and *The First AIF* (1970). Volume 1 of his *History of Tasmania* was published in 1983 and won the *Age* Book of the Year prize for non-fiction. Dr Robson died of cancer in 1990, a few months after submitting the manuscript of Volume 2, which was published in 1991.

Michael Roe's life has had an odd complementarity to that of Lloyd Robson. He too was born in 1931, but in the suburbs of Melbourne. He was educated at the University of Melbourne and completed his doctoral studies at the Australian National University. In 1960 he took up a position at the University of Tasmania. Like Dr Robson, he stayed at the university of his first appointment throughout his entire professional career, retiring as Professor of History in 1996. Over those years he wrote many articles and several monographs, the last being *Australia, Britain and Migration 1915–1940* (1995).

King Island

Bass Strait

Three Hummock
Island

Robbins Island

Hunter Island

Mt Cameron
West

Smithton

Stanley

Table
Cape

Burnie

Tewkesbury

Mt Bischoff

Waratah

Mt Heemskirk

Zeehan

Mt Zeehan

Trial Harbour

Queenstown

Strahan

Hells
Gates

*Macquarie
Harbour*

Sarah Island

Arthur   *River*

Heemskirk R

Pieman

Cradle
Mt

Mesan

River

Mt
Dundas

Linda

Mt Lyell

Henty

King

Franklin R

Teepookana

*Frenchmans
Cap*

Gordon

River

Mt Field
West

Olga R

Davey R

*Lake
Pedder*

Port Davey

South West Cape

Maatsuyker
Island

Emu Bay

Penguin

Ulverstone

Leith

Devonport

Wesley Vale

Riana

Leven

Latrobe

Wilmot

Sheffield

Mt
Gog

Beaconsfield

Frankford

Deloraine

Hagley

Meander River

Miena Dam

Arthurs Lake

Lake St Clair

*Lake
King William*

Lake
Sorell

Tarraleah

Russell
Falls

Forth

Tamar R

Leonardsburgh

Port
Dalrymple

Bell Bay

Launceston

North Esk R

*Norfolk
Plains*

Longford

*Great
Lake*

Waddamana

Ouse

Derwent

River

+ Mt Reid

New Norfolk

Claremont

Glenorchy

Mt Wellington

Geeveston

Huon

HOBART

Scottsdale

Derby

Ringarooma R

Blue Tier

St Helens

South Esk

Ben Lomond R

Mathinna

Fingal

Avoca

Campbell Town

Macquarie

Ross

Oatlands

Triabunna

Richmond

Sorell

Sullivans Cove

Risdon

Boyer

West

Waterhouse
Island

Cape
Portland

Flinders Island

Tinkettle Island

Woody Island

Cape Barren
Island

FURNEAUX

Guncarriage
Island

ISLANDS

Clarke Island

Lottah

*Oyster
Bay*

**FREYCINET
PENINSULA**

Schouten
Island

Maria
Island

**FORESTIER
PENINSULA**

Eaglehawk Neck

**TASMAN
PENINSULA**

Point Puer

Port Arthur

*Adventure
Bay*

Bruny
Island

South East Cape

N

0   20   40   60   80   100
kilometres

A SHORT HISTORY
of TASMANIA

———————— • ————————

LLOYD ROBSON

Updated by

MICHAEL ROE

WITHDRAWN

Melbourne

OXFORD UNIVERSITY PRESS

Oxford Auckland New York

OXFORD UNIVERSITY PRESS AUSTRALIA
Oxford New York
Athens Auckland Bangkok Bombay
Calcutta Cape Town Dar es Salaam Delhi
Florence Hong Kong Istanbul Karachi
Kuala Lumpur Madras Madrid Melbourne
Mexico City Nairobi Paris Port Moresby
Singapore Taipei Tokyo Toronto
and associated companies in
Berlin Ibadan

OXFORD is a trade mark of Oxford University Press

National Library of Australia
Cataloguing-in-publication data:

Robson, L. L. (Leslie Lloyd). 1931–1990.
A short history of Tasmania.

{2nd ed.}.
Bibliography.
Includes index.
ISBN 0 19 554199 5.

1. Tasmania - history. I. Roe, Michael, 1931 - .
II. Title.

994.6

Text and typesetting by
Derrick I Stone Design
Map drawn by Cart Deco Cartographics
Cover design by Anitra Blackford
Printed through Bookpac Production Services, Singapore
Published by Oxford University Press
253 Normanby Road, South Melbourne, Australia

Contents

11/12/97

Preface

Any short history by its nature demands a certain boldness in presentation and selection of material and themes: stern experts will doubtless bring careful study to bear on areas judged to demand more attention, in their judgment. The nature of the writing of history in and about Australia has changed and is changing very rapidly in comparison with the work produced in the period to around the early 1960s, and it is in the nature of analysis of the past for fashions to come and go and fresh insights be offered.

All written histories reflect the experience and assumptions of the writer, and to that extent any historical work will reveal to the perceptive reader a good deal about the times in which the history was written, and possibly disclose more about the writer than he might expect. The author is willy-nilly a standing target but this is as it should be if our understanding of the past is to enrich and broaden our knowledge of the present. There are no holy custodians of the past, gifted with the ability to call the shots in the present and future. The world around us has always been dissolving and differences of opinion about what is significant should lead to further constructive work in the field.

The overall theme of this Short History is the establishment in Van Diemen's Land/Tasmania of part of that restless society which has emerged from Europe since the seventeenth century and spread itself across the globe, suffused with the ideology of Christianity and increasingly equipped with powerful technology.

The pattern is largely that of colonialism, conceived in terms of the exploitation which the word evokes, and the essential duality of the colony/state in its relationship to the colonising authority. The implications of the term 'colonist' are everywhere in the history of the

British Empire and Sir Keith Hancock's felicitous term 'transplanted Britons' is nowhere more evident in Australia than in the case of the island state.

Tasmania developed as a stereotype colony and the interlocking of British and colonial interests dominate its history. The economy of the colony and state for nearly all its past since European settlement was steered by the needs of the metropolitan authority established in London. In political terms, Tasmania sought to emulate British parliamentary practice and procedure, except that whereas the second House of Parliament in Britain had its wings clipped in the Edwardian period, the Legislative Council of Tasmania continued to set the parameters of political action to such an extent that its conduct came to be judged as not remarkable.

All this was aided greatly by Tasmanians' perception of their weak and isolated position out on the very edge of the Empire. This was the principal factor which sharpened loyalty to Britain, so that the great European civil wars which commenced in 1914 and in 1939 inevitably drew Australia (and hence Tasmania), as an economic and cultural dependency, into those conflicts in the same way as other dependencies and trading partners were involved.

Yet there developed in the island some indications of a local character and style, not a little associated with the important fact that the colony/state was an island, the inhabitants of which were always, like all islanders, suspicious of outsiders and a little envious of the wider world and its preoccupations and developments. At the same time, the rugged landscape of Tasmania led to regional identity and interests.

The violent and bloody origins of European settlement in Tasmania have only recently come to be explored in terms of how Tasmanians see themselves, and it is to be hoped that this Short History may go some way further towards an understanding of the past and, therefore, of the present and future, both for Europeans and for Aborigines. If we perceive the past refracted through a distorted lens, we falsify our present perceptions and react to false resonances of the past.

I wish particularly to thank my publishers for their initiative and tactful silences, especially Louise Sweetland and Sarah Dawson. Janet McKenzie employed editorial skills of a high quality, and the Department of History at the University of Melbourne helped greatly with financial assistance. Geoffrey Stilwell at the Allport Library and Museum of Fine Arts in Hobart was, as ever, an invaluable source of information, as were Barbara Valentine and Margaret Glover. Jeff Scrivener at the Morris Miller Library, University of Tasmania, greatly assisted me by so readily making available material embodied in theses, full details of which will appear in Volume 2 of my *History of Tasmania*.

Lloyd Robson
1985

Preface to the second edition

While much briefer than his two-volume work on Tasmania, Lloyd Robson's *Short History* has almost comparable value. It gave greater scope to the poetic side of his nature and his related capacity for impressionistic interpretation. The *Short History*'s grace of style and wealth of insight are alike remarkable; chapter 7, which draws on Lloyd's personal experience and memory, stands supreme in his *oeuvre*.

For some time Oxford University Press considered a new edition of the *Short History*, and duly approached me to assist in the task. I have maintained an interest in the island's history throughout my sojourn here without, of course, approaching the depth of Lloyd's pertinent scholarship. Nor do my approaches altogether conform to his. My prose is more matter of fact and uniform; I impose more structures and parameters. One indicator of these habits is that I have persuaded Oxford to add time-span definitions to Lloyd's original chapter titles. The only other substantive change to the original text as now retained is to alter the title of chapter 7 from 'Recognition' to 'Identity'.

However, we have abandoned altogether Lloyd's chapter 8, 'Modernity', covering the years from about 1940 to the time at which he wrote. I found that chapter inappropriate in various ways, most obviously because it treated this long period as a whole whereas I see the time around 1970 as marking as decisive a break as any in post-settlement Tasmanian history. That historic moment witnessed profound crisis for the values which had characterised Western European civilisation during the previous half millennium for its hegemony throughout the world. The usual label for the subsequent era is 'post-modern', and I myself use this (primarily so as to echo Lloyd's 'Modernity'), but another is 'post-colonial'. No wonder its everywhere-radical changes should have had particular impact in Van Diemen's Land/Tasmania, which Lloyd rightly depicted as an archetype colony.

Thus all the post-1940 material comes from my hand. Naturally and gratefully, I used Lloyd's work and cite him by name at various points. One difference between us is that I am more prone than he was to use such direct citation. Readers will find too that I give more space than Lloyd to matters of culture, broadly defined. On the other hand, he was readier than I to arraign forces of arrogance and greed, more rigorous in granting accolades of any kind. Indeed a superficial reading might suggest that I have more sympathy with the subjects of this study than did Lloyd. I do not think that was so. Perhaps the very depth of his feeling for Tasmania sometimes inhibited Lloyd. His remains lie in the earth of his native region, at Penguin's cemetery.

Lloyd's preface thanks for the various editors, colleagues, librarians, and friends who assisted him. May I repeat his praises and repeat the names of those who have given like service to myself: Dennis Daniels, Cathryn Game, Alf Hagger, Tim Jetson, Margot and Sophie Roe, Peter Rose, and Leone and Jeffrey Scrivener.

Michael Roe

Measurements

As this is a historical work, imperial measures have been retained throughout, except for chapters about more recent periods. Equivalent measures and conversion to metric units are given below.

Currency
12d (12 pence) =	1s (1 shilling)	
20s (20 shillings) =	£1 (1 pound) =	$2
21s =	1 guinea	

Weight
	1 pound =	0.453 kilograms
14 pounds =	1 stone	
8 stone =	1 hundredweight	
20 hundredweight =	1 ton =	1.02 tonnes

Length
	1 inch =	25.4 millimetres
12 inches =	1 foot	
3 feet =	1 yard	
22 yards =	1 chain	
10 chains =	1 furlong	
8 furlongs =	1 mile =	1.61 kilometres

Area
4840 square yards =	1 acre =	0.405 hectares
640 acres =	1 square mile	

Capacity
	1 pint =	0.568 litres
8 pints =	1 gallon	
8 gallons =	1 bushel	

Invasion: to 1836

During the last 100 000 years or so, the sun has grown hotter and then cooler, so that the sea rose and fell, and the land masses of the planet have changed shape and position. Sometimes the area of Tasmania has been a peninsula of Australia Proper, sometimes an island. Humans probably were in the area some 40 000 years ago and certainly 20 000 ago were on the Bassian Plain, land now beneath the seas of east and central Bass Strait. Indeed, they were further south, and subsisted in what is now central Tasmania, on the very edge of the glacial regions; perhaps this is the furthest south ever reached by early peoples.

About 12 000 years ago the seas rose again, cutting off such people as lived in the peninsula/island of Tasmania. It may be that these groups had lived in the area for much longer than 12 000 years but their relationship with other Australian peoples is not known. They did not possess the dingo, however, which suggests that the Tasmanian peoples certainly were isolated before that animal became prevalent in the north ... but none of this is known for certain. The culture and development of the people of the island can only be reconstructed from some most preliminary archaeological work and from the fleeting moment in time when the Aborigines came under notice of their European conquerors.

Between 4000 and 6000 persons appear to have supported themselves on the island at the time of European arrival, but the figure is speculative. In the 1830s, G. A. Robinson in the course of his travels recorded every Aboriginal he could find and discovered that he could enumerate no more than about 300. This suggests an even more substantial death rate if estimates of original numbers of Aborigines seriously fail to take into account the impact of introduced diseases.

The island on which the Aborigines were stranded some 12000 years ago was 26000 square miles and situated between 40 and 43.5 degrees south latitude. It was a land of innumerable streams, rivers and mountains with a heavy rainfall on the western side, shading off to the east, brought by the prevailing westerlies that blew, unimpeded, halfway across the southern oceans. The next land to the westward was in the region of Cape Horn. As the mighty glaciers melted and moved, they left enormous numbers of tiny lakes in the central west areas of the mountainous hinterland. From this area of extremely high rainfall derived very powerful rivers, the principal one to become known as the Gordon, draining into a huge arm of the sea—Macquarie Harbour. Snow and ice were to be met with in the highlands even at midsummer.

Few plains existed except isolated areas in the central and eastern parts and, generally speaking, the island was heavily forested. Especially along the littoral of the north-west and north-east were temperate forests of enormous eucalypts. In many places there were about 3500 trees to the acre, on average 50 feet high and 6 feet in diameter. The west and south-west was covered with bush, including rainforests of impressive and fearful size and impenetrability.

The Aboriginal nomads moved over perhaps two-thirds of their island, although there is evidence of their presence in winter in the most remote and inhospitable areas. Why they came into these places is a mystery; perhaps it was on an overland route, the attraction of some food supply, or a source of some material unknown to the modern observer. Perhaps certain groups were driven there by disagreements with their neighbours.

The Aboriginal people formed loose-knit groups, and there is evidence from studies of their languages that perhaps ten distinct languages existed. It appears that certain groups of these people could not understand the language of others, used different personal adornments and adopted different eating and butchering habits and practices.

The basic unit was the family or hearth group, which embodied a husband and wife (the Aborigines appear to have been monogamous), children and perhaps an aged relative or two. This hearth group was subsumed into another larger unit or band which had a collective name and was known by that name to other Aborigines. These bands or clans numbered between seventy and eighty-five, and formed in turn twelve or thirteen larger loose groupings.

2

It would be an error to attach too much significance to the word 'tribe' in this context, though there may well be instructive parallels in the organisation of nomadic peoples elsewhere in the world and especially to the groups of Aborigines on the mainland of Australia. In the island, Group A (whether called 'tribe' or not) could understand or come to grips with the language of its neighbouring Group B, members of which in turn could communicate in a way with Group C—but Group A could not generally understand Group C. The only time that Groups A and C came into communication appears to have been those occasions when the resource of ochre was being mined or, perhaps, when gathering eggs or some such thing. In these circumstances, it may be that groups struck informal bargains, but it is not known whether such groups actually came into physical contact. It is quite possible that customs had emerged whereby certain peoples came to the ochre mines at different times.

There is some evidence of this at what Europeans came to name the 'City of Ochre', a deposit mined at Mount Gog in the north-west. In that vicinity are camp-sites quite close to each other but on different sides of the Mersey River, so that perhaps different organisations kept their distance from each other even when engaged in very similar mining activities.

But as with nearly everything of significance about the Aborigines and their culture, every answer to a question instantly raises many more questions. Quite different artefacts recovered within a few hundred yards of each other, at one mining site, suggest that the different groups of island people may well have deliberately avoided communication with each other. The problem is that when the few Europeans who did so enquired into the life of the Aborigines, the indigenous people were in a state of utter demoralisation and dislocation, so that even careful observers may have noted and recorded conduct that was wildly atypical of the Aborigines when they were undisturbed.

The main groups of island people were the maritime groups who commanded lengthy seaboards and a limited hinterland (the far north-west, south-west and south-east), groups with a shoreline and a hinterland (Oyster Bay, north-east and possibly north) and groups with little or no coastline (Big (Ouse) River, north Midlands and Ben Lomond).

It must be stressed that these general areas relate to a nomadic people who were evidently constantly on the move; the geographic regions should be seen as focal points of a general territory. Yet boundaries were sometimes quite sharply demarcated, frequently being formed by a river or headland or some other natural feature. But even these might or could be crossed from time to time, probably depending on the supply of game and its pursuit. In other words, it is likely that such 'boundaries' were the actual limits of certain fauna and flora, and adopted basically in terms of food supply.

In appearance, the Aboriginal people were dark-skinned with variations from very black to 'red'. Their stature was reported by early observers to be 'average', in late eighteenth-century European terms, and their height was about five feet in the case of women to five feet six inches for men. They had few if any clothes. Women wore a kangaroo skin arranged on the upper body and used it for carrying children and a few pieces of equipment. The men as a rule went quite naked, though both sexes wore strips of skin and necklaces of shell. People above the age of puberty were frequently marked with cicatrices: the skin was cut and then raised in patterned lines by inserting charcoal or something similar in the wound. There is some evidence that this may have been a form of group identification.

The most striking feature of the Aborigines was their scalp hair, which was distinctively tight-curled. It was frequently chopped off short by the women, some of whom had tonsured hairstyles. Men tended to plaster their scalp hair with a mixture of red ochre and grease, so that it resembled a mop or, as one observer noted wryly, the wig of a fashionable late eighteenth-century French lady of quality. Women also adorned themselves with charcoal and ochre, to the extent of using ochre on their pubic hair. Babies were sometimes marked with ochre on their forehead and cheeks.

Mined in several locations in the island, ochre was highly prized, and indeed murder was committed to get it when an exchange or form of sale went wrong. Women carried river stones to use as grinders to render down lumps of the ochre gouged from the mines with a type of chisel, and the grinding stones were frequently changed, probably by the action of fire, to form octagons and similar shapes. Some of the banana-shaped fragments discarded reveal that very narrow yet thick parts of stones were most neatly removed, but it is not clear why this was done nor why so many stones at one site were treated. It appears that the use, and perhaps preparation, of ochre may have been the sole cultural link among all the Aborigines of the island.

The diet of the people was far more various than European observers at first concluded. Nomadic life was governed by availability of food, and there is no evidence that the people suffered from starvation. Observers in the eighteenth century all remarked on the good health and bright appearance of the Aborigines. Yet very little is known of their food-gathering practices in times of normality. However, the men hunted kangaroo and wallaby by cornering these animals and then bashing them to death, or by spearing. They also put down short sharpened spikes on kangaroo tracks and tied grass into loops to impede the animals when they were pursued.

Women dived for shellfish and gathered cockles and the like. Favourite spots were exploited in this way, and some of the women were expert divers and swimmers. A French expedition at Adventure Bay, Bruny Island, in the late eighteenth century came up to a camp-site bestrewn with crayfish shells; the site is exploited to this day for the gathering of the crustacean.

A most interesting feature of the diet of the Aborigines is the fact that they declined to eat scaled fish. There is evidence from archaeological sites, however, that such scaled fish were consumed until about 4000 years ago. It is not clear why such a taboo—if it was one—was applied. On the face of it, the abandonment of a good food supply is astonishing because presumably the Aborigines retained the skill to catch fish, if not by manufacturing hooks then by building fish-traps or 'fisheries' to harvest at high tide the fish that haunted in-shore rocks. It may be that some powerful or influential person died as the result of choking on a fishbone, so that the word went out that all fish were now to be avoided. But this seems very odd if it pertained to all the island and all its widely different groups. On the other hand, there may have been a climatic change that rendered the capture of land food simpler than catching fish … but the technique of fish-traps would not have been lost, because they remained *in situ* once constructed. It may be that only certain areas of the island were affected, but it is a fact that the Aborigines refused with horror offers of fish by maritime explorers.

Food was half-cooked over the open campfire, and there is evidence that the women waited on the men. Children were disciplined by both sexes, and women were secreted from some Europeans who landed prior to formal occupation of the island. A natural curiosity about the sexual characteristics of the (clothed) visitors was evinced by the Aborigines, who were puzzled by the clean-shaven Europeans and possibly concluded that all were female. They were disabused of this when one French sailor was induced to remove his clothes and then and there revealed his readiness for sexual intercourse.

The only liquid generally consumed was water, and shell containers were sometimes left beside streams to facilitate drinking. A limited supply of 'cider' from the cider gum was exploited. It was alcoholic, to a degree. The roots of certain plants were consumed, as were berries, eggs and seals.

The tool-kit of the Aborigines was a light one, as befitted a nomadic people living in a heavily forested land that abounded with food and was nowhere more than about sixty miles in a straight line from the sea (though sometimes hundreds of miles by Aboriginal roads). No metal is known to have been used, and implements were fashioned only from wood, stone and bone. Artefacts found reveal that several varieties of scraper were devised for different purposes, and there is some tentative evidence that pieces of rock flaked off naturally by the action of frost were used as 'natural' scrapers. There is also some indication that certain objects were highly polished and perhaps carried as charms.

No tools were hafted, and there is no evidence that rope or string was manufactured from hair, though sinews from kangaroo tails were employed and a type of grass made into baskets and into ropes to aid climbing trees for birds' eggs or small animals such as possums.

Cooking vessels were not employed, and water was thus not boiled, although containers to hold liquids were constructed from pieces of kelp. These and similar containers such as shells contained so little water that they were almost certainly used only as drinking containers and not for carrying for any serious distance. In the island that would not have been necessary as a rule, such was the rainfall and very large number of streams and lakes fed from the highlands.

Types of canoe-raft, frequently but erroneously termed 'catamarans', were made from bundles of bark or rushes, constructed in a tapered form with the ends lashed together. These craft were propelled apparently with a pole or possibly a spear, and their use was limited to short journeys to nearby offshore islands, in clement weather. Such canoe-rafts were evidently confined to the south and south-east, thus suggesting the dominance of the environment and food supplies: Aborigines employed them to reach islands on which seals lived or, perhaps, where there were known to be very good supplies of shellfish. But as with so many other aspects of the life of the Aborigines prior to the European invasion, there is a great deal of guesswork involved in seeking to grasp their culture.

The overwhelming evidence, from objective observers, is that the people of the island were in a perfect balance and harmony with their environment. They altered it only by firing the bush. To accomplish this relationship with nature, presumably there were forms of birth control practised, but virtually nothing is known of sexual activity except a fairly conventional form of marriage: a man persisted in courting a woman until either he was successful and accepted by her and the hearth group as a partner, or he was driven off, or he wearied of his fancied wife and went away to seek another. There is some evidence from eighteenth-century observers that men beat the women, but it is unclear. Nor is it possible to conclude anything about sexual matters from the manner in which Aboriginal women sometimes attached themselves to Europeans, though it is possible that in some few cases the Europeans treated them better than their own kind did.

It must be supposed that the old and severely injured were abandoned, as is the practice and indeed necessity with other nomadic peoples, though it is interesting that a deformed man was observed by Europeans. He may have been born that way, in which case, why was his life spared? Or was his deformity caused by injuries in adult life?

As a nomadic people, the Aborigines had little in the way of shelters or dwelling places. The characteristic structure was a windbreak, built in the form of a curve from boughs and twigs and placed to obtain shelter from the prevailing winds. The use of hollow tree stumps was also suspected, though not shown absolutely, and on the west coast quite well-constructed shelters, with a roof and possessions and decorations inside, were found. Given the severe climate of that area, such structures might have been anticipated. This may reveal that the Aborigines were not all nomadic all the time, but prepared to see out the winter in the area, perhaps subsisting upon stores. Such dwellings may have been close enough and numerous enough to warrant the name of 'village', but there is no evidence of plants being cultivated or even a primitive agricultural system developed.

The typical Aboriginal moved through the countryside equipped with spears and a fire-stick, with apparent indiscrimination setting alight virtually everything that would burn as he went along ... but this presumably was calculated to revive the bush and thus attract animals by the appearance of fresh and tender shoots. The burnings marked out native tracks all over the island, and thus the environment was modified. After the Aborigines had been killed, an area along the Leven

River in the north-west was found to be producing gum saplings in profusion where none had stood before, and this was attributed to the
removal of the Aborigines.

It is now concluded that nomadic people have comparatively extensive leisure time, but little is known of how the people of the island occupied themselves when not hunting or sleeping. During the time when
Europeans were with them, however, the role of story-teller and dancing appeared substantial. The story-teller spoke of historic wars or love
affairs and of the origin of his people and their environment. The
Aborigines held a belief in spirits and accounted for human existence
by attributing it to beings who dwelt in the heavens and who created
natural features and animals as well as Aborigines. An evil spirit or
force was also thought to be active and to roam among their number
mysteriously and invisibly like the wind, as a sort of bogey-man. Like
Europeans, they also were superstitious, and grew angry with people
who cut hair perhaps or pounded ochre at the wrong time or in the
wrong place, stating that such conduct would cause a storm or lead to
a river coming up, and so on. Yet much of this information is derived
from incidents in which it is possible the Aborigines were concealing
something or, perhaps, having a joke at the expense of the credulous
European.

There is no evidence that the Aborigines dwelt in sweet amity one
with the other. Conflicts arose over women and equipment as elsewhere in the world and, doubtless, over many other events in their
everyday life. Groups fought each other, it was stated, but the fact is that
so little is known that quite contrary conclusions concerning motiva-
tion may be drawn with equal facility.

There is some evidence that herbs and plants were employed as
medicine, as everywhere else; splints were made to straighten limbs
broken in accidents and to facilitate the knitting of the bone. Little is
known of childbirth or mortality at that time, but some evidence exists
relating to mortuary practices. One of the eighteenth-century French
expeditions described and sketched a very elaborate tomb on Maria
Island, but it is not clear whether this was a common form or not.
Did eminent members of a group receive particularly special burial
treatment? Among other peoples this is so, and in view of the descrip-
tions of rather simple cremations during a later period, it may be the
case. But again there is little evidence. What is certain is that how the
Aborigines behaved during the course of their destruction at the hands

of the Europeans may reveal little or nothing or be absolutely misleading about practices during the period prior to European conquest and the turmoil into which the Aborigines were thrown.

Petroglyphs at such places as Mount Cameron West are the only pictorial records of the Aborigines so far discovered, though it seems very unlikely that a people so fond of ochre did not daub something on the walls of overhangs or shallow caves. If carvings of wood were created, they have not survived.

A number of Europeans sought to note vocabularies and some of the French were active in this field prior to the cultural upheaval caused by the British settlement. Yet no European mastered any of the Aboriginal languages and sought to analyse them, though G. A. Robinson in the 1830s certainly recorded thousands of words and boasted he could understand the Aborigines. His field notes do not quite bear this out, but he appears certainly to have had a great ability to communicate with the people he was seeking to placate and capture. How successful he was in understanding them is uncertain, and it may well be that the Aborigines were meeting him more than halfway, because they were very quick at learning English. But to Robinson is owed a great deal, as well as to N. J. B. Plomley, who first enabled Robinson's journals and vocabularies to see the light of day, thus advancing knowledge of the Aborigines by more than 100 per cent at one bound.

When all is said and done, it is likely that the Aborigines resembled their conquerors in many more ways than they differed, and were not greatly different from other nomadic peoples who lived before, during and after their time. Chaffed by Robinson for applying red ochre to their bodies on a special occasion, they snapped back, 'Why do you get dressed up for church?'

By that time in the 1830s, the people whom the Europeans found occupying such a superbly beautiful island, and moving through a landscape into which they had merged in the course of at least 12 000 years, had few enough of their number left who even dimly recalled the period of peace before the nightmare that engulfed and effectively destroyed them and their culture in one generation.

As far as is known, the first European to come to the island was Abel Jans Tasman, an employee of the Dutch East India Company. In 1642 he was sent on a voyage of exploration in search of trading opportunities and in November made a landfall on the coast of a territory he marked on his maps as Van Diemen's Land, after a high officer of the company. A party landed, observed signs of human habitation, but sailed on to circumnavigate the undiscovered continent of Australia without actually sighting it. The Dutch turned their attentions elsewhere.

Expeditions in the eighteenth century touched at Van Diemen's Land and in 1802 Governor King at Port Jackson became nervous about the intentions of a French scientific expedition under Captain Nicolas Baudin. A good public servant, the governor concluded that his masters in the Colonial Office would not thank him for permitting foreigners to gain a foothold in an area that the British had claimed in 1770 and occupied in 1788. He proposed further British settlement to show the flag.

At the same time, reconnaissance of the new territory was being conducted by such as Matthew Flinders, and a fine body of water, thought excellent for a harbour, was found across Bass Strait from Port Dalrymple, and named Port Phillip. King and the Colonial Office moved more or less at the same time to extend British occupation in the new land: the Governor sent Lieutenant John Bowen south to establish a presence at the Derwent and London despatched Captain David Collins to occupy Port Phillip. That was in 1803, and both expeditions employed convicts for their labour force and personnel.

When Collins arrived at Port Phillip he at once found fault with it and, perceiving that the entrance to the harbour was very difficult, decided that this was not the spot for commercial men. Other factors weighed with him, including difficulties of discipline, the hot winds, and want of fresh water. He weighed anchor and early in 1804 arrived at the Derwent, where Lieutenant Bowen had established his tiny enclave at Risdon, on the east bank.

Collins disliked this site too, and quickly moved the entire body of colonists down and across river to Sullivan's Cove, where Hobart Town was established. Shortly after Collins had thus precariously established himself in the south of Van Diemen's Land, King was active again and sent Captain William Paterson to the Tamar, to safeguard Bass Strait and ensure that any French pretensions could not be realised.

During the first years of European settlement, Van Diemen's Land settlers were several times reduced to starvation and only saved by eating native game such as emus and kangaroos, and by the fortuitous arrival of seaborne supplies. Fortunately, wheat was found to thrive in the areas around Richmond and Sorell in the south, and south-west of Launceston, and this enabled the production of all-important bread.

From 1788, Norfolk Island was peopled mainly with convicts, and its inhabitants were subsequently transferred during the first ten years of settlement of Van Diemen's Land. Other settlers were principally twice-convicted prisoners from Port Jackson, with some few convict ships from Britain.

During this period there developed a bandit society. It was composed of men who escaped from such penal discipline as was possible in Van Diemen's Land, and of the inhabitants on the fringes of settlement who enjoyed a life of primitive commerce. These banditti, bandits or bushrangers developed a subculture, perforce roamed and explored the rugged interior of the island and, continually augmented by other discontented souls from the labour gangs, effectively bade fair to threaten central government. Settlers were obliged either to abandon their holdings or to bargain with the bandits. Under Lieut.-Governor Thomas Davey, martial law was declared, but with little effect, because Governor Macquarie in Sydney angrily disapproved of his underling and because the bandits were masters of the hinterland, employing their finely tuned commercial skills.

Michael Howe, an ex-convict, became infamous and took on many of the attributes of the bandit-hero. Impressive as were certain of their exploits—they had entire hamlets at their mercy—the bandits were finally put down when the increase of free settlement became such that they were outnumbered and outgunned by a combination of respectable colonists and the military. The bandits moved readily through the bush at the height of their insolent power but not so freely as Aborigines, the other threat to the establishment of the colonists and their determination to exploit the island.

Because the Aborigines existed in nomadic loosely knit social units, and were constantly on the move, it was possible for the Europeans huddled around the mouth of the Derwent and the confluence of the Esk rivers in the north to have little communication with them. Yet from earliest settlement, deaths occurred when Europeans and the invaded people clashed over food supplies such as kangaroos, and it may be that diseases introduced by the invaders also led to Aboriginal deaths without the knowledge of the British. There was kidnapping of Aboriginal women, especially by sealers in the north, and children were taken, and it would be foolish to suppose that the Aboriginal people meekly fell back without counterattacks against the Europeans as the invaders ventured further inland with ever-increasing boldness.

11

If there was conflict and killing in these early days of settlement, how much more was there when the invaders began to establish themselves, especially after the Napoleonic wars, in the fine pastoral regions that lay between Hobart Town and Launceston. The source of conflict was very clear—both Aborigines and Europeans sought to control the same areas of land. To the Aborigines, the land was their primary resource. They depended on its bounty for subsistence. As a hunter-gatherer people, they had come to utilise and feel part of its entire extent and resources. To the Europeans, the land was essential for business purposes. All immigrants who arrived free came to Van Diemen's Land to better themselves or at least offer their children the prospect of advancement in the colonies; that was what colonies were for. To the newcomer, the Aboriginal, who neglected to till the earth according to biblical injunction, was less than human. He had no skills, it appeared, to teach the European. He went naked, ate brutishly and, in short, was perceived as the perfect savage and without nobility of bearing. The churches did practically nothing. Certainly committees were formed by the concerned colonists, and the administration suffused with the idea that something should be done to save the Aborigines from utter destruction, but little other than agonised hand-wringing was the result.

Conflict with the Aborigines was sporadic but grew in intensity to a peak about 1823–24. Typically the Aborigines sought to intimidate, wound or kill isolated shepherds and settlers advancing their sheep or cattle. A tactic was to fire the roof of the hut and then murder the occupant as he fled. Some such huts on the frontiers were fortified and equipped with loopholes.

The Europeans went on punitive expeditions and shot down Aborigines. Soldiers were equipped to remove this menace to the stockholders of the colony; force of arms told, though it is clear that the Aborigines resisted strongly and engaged in intelligent and coherent tactics to defend themselves. It was of little avail, however, as every fresh ship discharged more free settlers anxious to occupy land under the system of free grants. The Europeans mustered inexhaustible reserves and increasing fire-power; the Aborigines were worn down and had no reserves.

The years of this Black War were highlighted by an effort to capture the Aborigines by forming a line of soldiers and civilians across the island and 'beating' them, as it were, towards Forestier's Peninsula. This episode was much publicised but netted only two captives. Importantly, however, it brought home to the Aborigines the frightening strength of the Europeans and the forces of the army assisting them to clear the land for exploitation.

It was at this point that George Arthur, appointed governor in 1824 to take the penal colony in charge and use the labour force to promote pastoralism and the interests of Britain, approved that a patrol be sent out to bring in the remainder of the Aborigines. G. A. Robinson, a Wesleyan builder, was put in charge. In a series of extraordinarily arduous journeys, Robinson, accompanied by some Aborigines and convict servants, employed his talents to establish communication with almost all the Aboriginal people remaining in the bush and induce them to trust him. The result of this trust was the placing of the remnants of these people finally on Flinders Island, in a sort of concentration camp where most of them perished.

The decimation of the bandits and the Aborigines paved the way for the colonists to occupy all the suitable pastoral land of the island. This they largely accomplished by the mid 1830s, when the system of free land grants, encumbered merely with a nominal rent, had been removed and the sale of land substituted. Having thus occupied Van Diemen's Land, colonists new and old looked out for fresh pastures and, from about 1835, began shipping their stock across Bass Strait to the new lands of the Port Phillip District of New South Wales. John Batman and John Pascoe Fawkner were active in the foundation of Melbourne, but there were many such settlers: James Whyte claimed that he took rams to the area as early as 1833.

In Van Diemen's Land the principal engine of commerce was the commissariat store. It was conducted by the government and purchased such items as meat and wheat at fixed prices in order to victual new settlers and the hordes of convict labourers. The foundation of many a Van Diemen's Land fortune was laid as a result of sales to the commissariat. By the early 1820s, production of meat gave way as a money-making speculation to the production of wool when the British industry promoted colonial wool over that hitherto got from England itself and Spain and Germany. Van Diemen's Land continued to fulfil its colonial purpose: convicts from Britain could be transported cheaply to the colony, thus ridding the metropolitan authority of trouble-makers and at the same time utilising their muscle-power to fuel the wool industry. Van Diemen's Land became interlocked with the economy of the colonising authority. Not only improved fleeces came to make the colony a cog in the imperial machine: whaling also boomed as the island colony filled the role of place of refreshment for British whalers, and as the source of some construction of whaling vessels and equipment.

At the heart of the colonisation of Van Diemen's Land by the British was the deployment of the huge labour force of convicts as virtual slave labour. The overwhelming proportion of prisoners was male, because men were stronger and far more useful than women in an age when muscle-power had not been superseded by machinery. Governor Arthur was in virtual sole charge of the outdoor penitentiary for twelve years to 1836, and brought the system of convict dispersal and management to an astonishing pitch of perfection. Prisoners were landed at an average rate of 2000 a year during this period (including about 300 females), and their exploitation was utilised by two sets of employers.

First, the government typically set convicts to work on extensive programs of bridge-building, road-making and the like. Second, the private colonist enjoyed very cheap labour for his urban concerns or for harvesting and general rural work. Convicts were assigned. This meant that the government, in the form of the Convict Department, recorded requests for labourers and, providing the request came from a man judged to be respectable, his wants were satisfied from the convict arrivals. Labourers accommodated themselves or were housed in private or public barracks.

Discipline was progressively relaxed upon correct behaviour. Most convicts were transported for seven years (though sentences of fourteen and twenty years and life were common) and could be indulged with a ticket-of-leave after a year or so if the master recommended this and the Convict Department approved. This ticket permitted the convict to work on his or her own account on condition that regular reports were made to the police. If the prisoner continued steady, the sentence might be waived and a free or conditional pardon issued. The free pardon, presented only for outstanding public service, restored the convict to the privileges of a British citizen. A conditional pardon also similarly restored the prisoners but on condition they not return to Britain. In this way, some convicts rapidly were rehabilitated and not infrequently became wealthy if not respectable in the eyes of the 'pure merino' settler.

Misconduct earned punishment, which varied from chastisement to execution, and in between was a kaleidoscopic variety of experiences and punitive measures. Female convicts were more difficult to control in terms of punishment. In the early days of settlement they were certainly flogged on the bare back, had their scalp hair shorn off and were subjected to other special punishments. Normally women were lodged in gaol, however, when guilty of misconduct, and the Female Factory at Hobart Town was used as a lying-in hospital.

Female convicts were sexually exploited, though it should be noted that governors such as George Arthur went to considerable lengths to minimise this exploitation by enquiring very closely into the moral character of free settlers who applied for female servants, and seeking to assign female prisoners only to respectable families.

When the Commissioner of Enquiry, J. T. Bigge, recommended to the British Government in the early 1820s that the colonies be organised so as more effectively to exploit the convict labour force poured in, it became necessary to construct places of secondary punishment. The principal one of these was opened in 1821 at Macquarie Harbour, having earlier been promoted by Lieut.-Governor Sorell. There the conditions of labour were as severe as the human frame would stand; the men were employed principally in cutting down the Huon pine logs that grew in such profusion to the water's edge along the Gordon River. Desperate men committed desperate deeds at Sarah Island, the convict station. Some coolly murdered in order to get a 'slant', which was slang for a journey back to Hobart Town for trial and execution, but the actual proportion of convicts who were employed at Macquarie Harbour was small.

In 1830 a new settlement was formed at Port Arthur, where the principal work was timber-felling, timber-milling, and coal-mining. On a tip of land adjacent to the main settlement was established a boys' prison known as Point Puer, an enlightened experiment for its time. Escape from the settlements at Port Arthur was virtually impossible because dogs were tied up across Eaglehawk Neck, the very narrow strip which was sole entry and exit by land to and from the peninsula.

Port Arthur was chosen with care as a place of secondary punishment by virtue of its isolation from the settled areas of Van Diemen's Land and for the prospect of employing convicts fruitfully, while they underwent severe discipline. Certainly it was not a bed of roses, but it came to gain a much worse reputation than it deserved. Depicted as a hell on earth, it was spoken of in the same breath as Macquarie Harbour and Norfolk Island, places where dramatic highlights were also char-acterised as the norm. This was understandable, up to a point, especially when in the 1850s and 1860s men released from Port Arthur com-mitted offences that drew attention to their origin; the evil reputation of the place was further stressed as colonists sought to distance them-selves from their convict past and desperately seek respectability.

Further images were shaped not least by Marcus Clarke's gothic novel *For the Term of His Natural Life*, a work of fiction published first as *His Natural Life* in 1874 and going into many editions. It was lent verisimil-itude by the list of official documentary sources attached to it. The con-duct of Port Arthur as a penal establishment came to be judged by the enlightened standards of penology belonging to the later nineteenth and the twentieth centuries. A 'museum' display enriched by the exhi-bition of leg-irons and other such relics was calculated to send a thrill of horror through the observer and implant a conviction that the bad old days were indeed appalling. Although a sentence to Port Arthur was initially reserved for the dyed-in-the-wool offender and those found guilty of the most grave criminal offences or persistent bad conduct, it should be stressed that the standards of the time were very different from those of a later period and that some inmates of Port Arthur or Point Puer turned out to be the founders of respectable Tasmanian families.

Van Diemen's Land was an extremely violent society, comprising as it did many of the desperate men who had emerged from the social dislocation produced as the Industrial Revolution gathered pace. Not only was bloody flagellation of convicts very common, because it was a cheap and efficient method of punishment that did not lead to the victim being absent from work very long, but so also was execution. Public hangings were conducted at a frequency that rid the colony of malefactors very rapidly in the early years of Arthur's administration. The ritual of executions was ever to be observed, when the doomed vic-tims dressed elaborately in order to be delivered into eternity. The press exhorted its readers to take notice of such events and tremble. The government assisted in brutalisation of the people by rewarding citizens who brought in the head of a bandit. Men on the run from Arthur's convict labour gangs lunged about the colony, their conduct varying from mocking good manners to sudden and ghastly murders. The Wesleyan missionaries imported by the authorities blanched at what they saw and concluded that they could never labour too long in such a barbarous society.

At the centre of Van Diemen's Land was the humourless person of Governor Arthur. He learnt well the skills of colonial administration in British Honduras and was appointed governor of the island colony after listing his main achievements and cultivating patrons in London. Arthur was a proconsul of the first order and the subject of countless attempts at character assassination by the touchy settlers of Van Diemen's Land. The Colonial Office continued to control the development of the colony, and Arthur was ever conscious of his role as chief executive, chief gaoler and guardian of morality. He had been sent to Van Diemen's Land to hold in check the criminality of the Empire and, for his twelve years in office, discharged that function with a skill as amazing as it was comprehensive.

In 1825 Van Diemen's Land was administratively detached from New South Wales and equipped with its own judicial establishments and Legislative Council. During the course of his administration, Arthur led his Council by the nose because he mastered all aspects of administration, because he possessed the power to appoint convict labour, and because he presided over an economic boom. Yet he was loathed by many colonists because he checked them by here withdrawing a name from the Commission of the Peace and there pressing a man to resign.

Despite these onsets by disaffected colonists, who found they could not make a fortune if they offended the evangelical values of Arthur, the governor met the exacting requirements of the Colonial Office. In an age when civil servants expected to advance their interests by diligent embezzlement, Arthur came down hard on the many incompetents with whom he was surrounded as the result of patronage by politically effective gentlemen in England. Treasury officials were revealed to be innumerate, clerks virtually illiterate, customs officers hand-in-glove with the merchants from whom they were expected to extract taxes. Arthur entrapped them by conducting simultaneous audits of related accounts books and treasury chests, intercepted mail to discredit them in Britain, was unremitting in drawing the attention of the Colonial Office to the sexual behaviour of some, and promoted those whom he thought he could trust.

During his regime the press of Van Diemen's Land flourished as if in a hot-house, and despite the governor's determined attempts to control their outpourings by censorship, the newspapers agitated for a legislative assembly and especially for trial by jury. In 1828, Britain enlarged the size of the Legislative Council, and the boon of trial by jury in certain cases came to be vouchsafed, though Arthur feared the worst. He need not have worried unduly because those elements of the colonial population who fancied themselves as legislators and tribunes of the people did not dream of placing any political control in the hands of the great unwashed. The British Government and prominent colonists shared a commonality of interests in seeking to keep effective power in the right hands. The colonists and the British colonising authority drew closer together as the former began to achieve the social status and wealth they so neurotically sought.

Freed of the threat of bandits and Aborigines, the colonists of Van Diemen's Land began to develop a cultural style. At the top, the wealthy and educated promoted schools and subsidised them and their religion, and the state did the same. Holidays celebrated British events such as the King's birthday, St George's Day, and the Christian festivals. Harvest customs were transferred to the antipodes, cricket was played, and there were always horse races and hunting. Pugilists had purses wagered on them as they came up to scratch for round after round, and in the main centres theatrical entertainments flourished. In private, artistic colonists met to discuss their painting and sketches. Lawyers and solicitors abounded because the people were naturally litigious and could afford to take each other to court. Religion remained not much more than a form with many nominal Anglicans, though the Wesleyans perceived the people to be in a fallen state, preached with evangelical fervour and were caught up in religious revivals from time to time. The strength of the Catholic Church was not substantial until Irish convicts came to be transported in large numbers from 1840s, but free people came to the colony in increasing numbers in the 1830s.

By the end of Arthur's administration in 1836, the total population of the colony was 43 000, of whom 24 000 were 'free' (14 000 males and 10 000 females), and 19 000 convicts (17 000 males and 2000 females). About 11 000 free people arrived in the 1830s. Some 75 per cent of the people of Van Diemen's Land were convicts, had been convicts or were of convict ancestry.

2

Imitation: 1836–70

On a spring morning in 1836, Governor George Arthur made his way from Government House down to the wharf, weeping bitterly and supported by Chief Justice Pedder. Usually most undemonstrative, he now revealed his sorrow at departing from the colony over which he had reigned for so long, and made way for a new chief executive of the world's most notorious penal colony. This was Sir John Franklin, the polar hero. Although of undoubted personal courage, the new man was inexperienced in administration of colonies, especially one as turbulent as Van Diemen's Land. He inherited Arthur's smooth-running government and that governor's smooth lieutenants, John Montagu and Matthew Forster, Colonial Secretary and Chief Police Magistrate respectively.

At the beginning, the convict system went on as before. Prisoners continued to dominate expenditure and general business, although the free immigrants and those born within the colony began to reduce the impact of convictism in numerical terms. Yet prisoners remained nearly 40 per cent of the total population in 1840. Franklin's government was soon presented with an enormous administrative problem when, from 1840, all convicts sentenced to transportation in Britain were forwarded to Van Diemen's Land because transportation to New South Wales ceased. This flood coincided unfortunately with economic depression in the early 1840s and at the same time the governor's competence came under attack. His principal difficulties, however, lay in other quarters.

Franklin was accompanied by his energetic wife, Jane, and neither of them cared for the day-to-day business of conducting a penal colony. Rather they sought contact with savants and distinguished travellers who ventured with curiosity to the island colony. The Franklins relished the work involved in promoting eduction and religion and generally behaved as high-minded lord and lady of a reforming manor. The Hobart Town regatta became a regular feature of their patronage, a learned society was formed by their encouragement of science, and the *Tasmanian Journal of Natural Science* was founded. Franklin enjoyed the company of such as Ronald Campbell Gunn, the botanist and public servant whose work was to be of such importance in the acceptance of Darwin's theory of evolution.

The governor was most interested in forwarding primary education and under the guidance of Britain, a Board of Education was established in 1839 to supervise a system of non-denominational schooling. It did not and could not, however, attract the best teachers on the basis of pupils' fees and, in addition, the Church of England raised the most grave objections to a scheme in which the precepts of religious beliefs were not to be an integral part of the school syllabus but an addition, as it were.

In the field of religion, too, state aid was offered from 1838 towards stipends and costs of church building, but again there arose opposition from such as the Church of England on the grounds that if it were admitted that religious truth was attainable by more than one religion, this would lead to the destruction of them all. Less acrimonious was the establishment of the Hutchins School in Hobart Town and a Grammar School at Launceston, and the appointment of the first Anglican bishop in the person of F. R. Nixon was welcomed as an indication of the importance of Van Diemen's Land.

More humble folk began to embrace that peculiarly colonial form of culture that came to be known as 'moral enlightenment'. It was a secular belief with a half-baked ideology that stressed utility, earnestness and abstinence from intoxicating drinks. It frowned upon displays of enthusiasm, embodied a kill-joy mentality and elevated the virtues of the semi-literate. It went great guns in a burgeoning colonial setting where ambitious working people formed the prospectively pretentious. An associated movement was that of Mechanics' Institutes, where the respectable working man might read newspapers and attend improving lectures. It was as if in Van Diemen's Land a fresh form of religious belief was being shaped while the principal churches faltered because they could seldom meet the expectations and needs of a colonial population that lacked a sense of history. In this atmosphere Wesleyanism flourished.

Franklin seldom satisfied the mandarins of Downing Street: he never lived up to the expectations of such as John Montagu, and became the victim of terrorism by rumour, his own bluff incompetence, the malevolence of men who respected strength and authority rather than flexibility and liberalism, and the ill-advised intervention of the governor's wife in official transactions. The Franklins, admirable and cultivated, were the wrong people in the wrong place at the wrong time. The governor vainly looked out for an indication of support from the Colonial Office. He received none and was obliged to retire in 1843. He returned to the sea and disappeared while in search of the northwest passage.

His replacement was Sir John Eardley Eardley-Wilmot, a country gentleman from Warwickshire with an interest in crime. He was offered an opportunity unparalleled in the history of the world to satisfy his curiosity. A new convict system called probation was now in full swing, requiring that prisoners be housed in camps where they should be disciplined and employed with a view to passing through various stages of rehabilitation, and be hired out from depots established for the purpose. Because of the huge numbers transported, the depression of the period and the slackening in demand for convict labour, this system of transportation began to come under heavy criticism. Not surprisingly, the subject of money lay at the heart of this criticism: some colonists objected to paying, through taxes, a portion of the costs of administering gaols and police. Cost-benefit analysis was reinforced by moral considerations as an element of the colonial population began drawing attention to sexual aberrations said to be practised with impunity in the ranks of the convict labour force. Eardley-Wilmot's Legislative Council walked out on him concerning the voting of money for the convict system, and the governor of Van Diemen's Land came under more unfavourable notice from the Colonial Office when he quarrelled with the Bishop of Tasmania, Nixon.

The principal point at issue concerned a conflict between church and state on the question of appointment and control of chaplains to the convict department of government. On other matters also the administration of a British colony entrusted temporarily to Eardley-Wilmot was judged less than satisfactory by his metropolitan masters. W. E. Gladstone, a new Secretary of State, objected that the education of the rising generation was not affected sufficiently by the beliefs of the Church of England, and blamed the governor for this deficiency. More seriously, the

Secretary of State grew alarmed at the meagre reports reaching him concerning what he chose to describe as the moral state of the convicts.

Egged on by James Stephen, principal under-secretary, Gladstone began to be impressed with the lack of commitment exhibited by the governor in this important particular. Bishop Nixon's allies in England lost no opportunity to place the conduct of the governor in an unfavourable light and to spread stealthy rumours of improper conduct at Government House. Preparing to find a reason for dismissing Eardley-Wilmot, the Colonial Office began keeping a record of his shortcomings so that they could muster evidence when the governor, as they began to close in on him, finally received the fatal message. Eardley-Wilmot was said to enjoy the company of young women, and it was further put about that he brought female convicts into Government House for a lewd entertainment. Certainly the governor's wife had not accompanied him to Van Diemen's Land and thus such rumours were permitted to gather strength. Finally, in 1846 Gladstone penned a lethal despatch of official recall and accompanied it with another 'private' document that spoke darkly of rumours associated with the governor of the island colony.

Eardley-Wilmot was incredulous, startled and finally furious at this ignominious end to his gubernatorial career. Mustering such political support as he could, the governor fought back, but Gladstone was shortly removed from the Colonial Office on his way to higher things and avoided having to justify the dismissal. The hapless governor lingered at Van Diemen's Land, awaiting his successor, and died a few days after the arrival of Sir William Denison. The colonists concluded that he had perished of a broken heart and ill-treatment at the hands of Downing Street bureaucrats, and erected a grand mausoleum for the purpose of containing the late governor's mortal remains. At the funeral, Van Diemen's Land clerics behaved with characteristic rivalry when the Catholic and Anglican clergy sought to glide in front of each other in a subtle struggle for precedence in the melancholy procession.

The colonists' daring but confident behaviour reflected the triumph of the successful colonist; by now the gentry had succeeded in forming a coherent class, which appeared to place its impress on the society in a permanent manner. The triumph of the wool industry strengthened their confidence and increased their opulence, and there was constructed in the wool country that stretched between Hobart

Town and Launceston, with spurs to the west and east, a number of colonial mansions that were brilliant examples of the architects' skill. Cool, confident and colonial Georgian, they were epitomised by the country seats of the Archer family—the brothers Thomas, Joseph, William, and Edward, and their father. The homesteads they built on the basis of free land grants, free labour and shrewdness were among the finest in the booming colony. The Archers had a crested family vault in the cemetery of Christ Church, Longford. They also had Panshanger, built by Joseph Archer on a knoll near the Lake River adjoining his brother Thomas' estate. Breathtakingly beautiful, it summed up to perfection the triumph of the gentry of Van Diemen's Land.

At the other extreme of colonial existence were the inarticulate semi-slave labourers, usually with tickets-of-leave, dwelling in slab huts and being paid by the truck system, in kind and not in money. The exploiters rewarded such workers in tea and sugar and made wood and water available to them, which the poor durst not refuse.

A step above these victims of colonialism were such as the Huon settlers. Their only communication with the outside world was by ship to Hobart Town. Mainly labourers, ex-convicts and ticket-of-leave men, they had only a few pounds of capital at the most and aimed to subsist until they could clear enough land to produce some surplus. Such settlers scrubbed the land, felled the small trees and cleared the undergrowth during first years of occupation of the bush. The numerous big trees were ring-barked and left to die. The next stage was logging up, in which bullock teams and hand labour were used to drag logs and branches into heaps for late autumn burning. This continued the second year and with the smaller stumps and roots grubbed out, an effort was made to cultivate a crop, perforce planted between the stumps and standing ring-barked trees. During this stage of extremely hard work, muscle power was clearly king of the economy, but there was some compensation in the first crops from a rich and virgin soil. Most settlers aimed to clear about ten to fifteen acres to support themselves and their families, but in the early stages they were content with a few acres on which to erect a primitive homestead and plant a kitchen garden. The Huon settler's first house was usually a most primitive affair of two slab-walled rooms roofed with sheets of bark held on by logs and stones. The chimney was frequently made of wood lined with mud, the whole surmounted by an old cask that served as a chimney pot.

But not all Van Diemen's Land was as heavily timbered as the Huon when it was being laboriously settled in the era before the great Victorian gold rushes. In other areas the production of wheat remained important. Threshing machines were employed certainly by 1827; they were equipped with a mechanism for cleaning the grain and were commonly hired out. Reapers were in use before 1845, and in that year a Van Diemen's Land variation of the stripper was in operation and reported to reap twenty acres a day with two horses. Most farmers, however, reaped and threshed by hand in the early 1840s, hitting the grain with a flail or treading it out by foot. Advertisements for farm machinery usually mentioned only ploughs, harrows, chains and carts, with an occasional thresher or winnower, in 1842.

When by his death Sir John Eardley Eardley-Wilmot ceased to trouble the Colonial Office and its moralists any longer, the policymakers of Downing Street began to face a mounting barrage of pleas, arguments, abuse and threats from Van Diemen's Land on the subject of transportation of convicts. Sir William Denison arrived to discover that the matter of paying for the costs of police and gaols continued to obsess the local politically effective, some of whom also now objected to the continuation of any transportation.

There came to be formed the Anti-Transportation League, its moral impulse largely derived from northern Nonconformists such as the Reverend John West. Its stern public voice was the Launceston *Examiner*, and Denison found himself beset as he attempted to implement British policy and continue the probation system. With the lifting of the economic depression by the mid 1840s, those who opposed transportation were able to do so on the grounds that it was morally wicked and driving the respectable to Port Phillip. As a great deal of scary evidence was adduced, once again eloquence was shown not necessarily to be the friend of truth. The Colonial Office heard of cannibalism and unnatural practices indulged in upon a scale not dreamt of by the readers of Catullus. The London *Times* took up the cudgels through the person of Robert Lowe, late of New South Wales and dedicated to attacking the British administration. Denison was the subject of intense propaganda by the league, although throughout he retained the confidence of the colony's masters in London.

In 1851, the Legislative Council, though still retaining an official appointed component, was enlarged and liberalised. Those elected, on a very high property qualification, were anti-transportationist to a man, and the legislators began to prepare to take over the government and draw up a constitution to satisfy London. While the members of the Council, aided by executive officers of government and the thoughts of Denison, laboured to produce a written basis for government, gold was found in Victoria. Large-scale emigration set in from Van Diemen's Land to Port Phillip and inflation caused the costs of convict administration to jump sensationally. Transportation of convicts came to an end when the last convict vessel docked at Hobart Town on 26 May 1853, and the colony gave itself up to celebration and marked the end of a chapter by renaming the island Tasmania, to commemorate the discoverer.

Tasmania yet remained a colony in all respects, as did the other provinces of Britain in Australia. The people were fanatically loyal to the Crown and Britain and outdid themselves in patriotism during the Crimean War, donating huge sums of money to the imperial cause and emotionally reacting to the course of events. Side by side with this high loyalty was a great pride in the beauty of the island. Ashamed of its violent, convulsive and most unrespectable past, and conscious of their isolation out on the very edge of the Empire, the people fostered imperial sentiment to interlock with their economic dependence on Britain and cultural unity with it. The green appearance of the colony, in contrast to the summer scorching administered to the mainland colonies, induced the inhabitants of Tasmania to perceive their colonial home as a little England.

Hedge-rows were smiled upon as a reminder of a Merrie England few if any of them had really ever known. The destruction of the native flora and fauna and its replacement by exotics went on apace, a fact that added to the picture of colonists being merely transplanted Britons. The power and strength of the Church of England and the appointment of bishops and governors from England, speaking correctly and not through the colonial nose, reinforced the humble relationship of the colony to the imperial authority. 'Home' was Britain. The literate drew cultural sustenance from the works of Dickens, Thackeray and Borrow, and followed news from 'Home' with nostalgic interest. The Great Exhibition of 1851 was viewed with intense satisfaction. The island took pride in being an antipodean sanatorium and sanctuary for those pillars of the Empire who lived or fought in India, and were obliged to seek rest and recreation leave in the temperate climes of lovely Tasmania before returning to the jewel in the crown. The private school system was slavishly modelled upon that of England, and the public state schools inculcated a British syllabus.

The development of a middle class was checked as the population increase slowed down with the end of transportation and the superior attractions of Victoria, equipped as it was with gold-fields and unlimited opportunities for the resourceful and the unscrupulous, many of whom had received an excellent grounding in Van Diemen's Land.

The triumph of the gentry and of British political forms could not have been more complete when the Constitution Act of 1855 was passed by the British Government. This Act represented the result of no serious struggle for responsible government, because both the metropolitan colonising authority and the gentry were agreed that political power should be transferred merely from one set of rulers to another. The Legislative Council, the House of Assembly and the Crown (in the person of the governor as Her Majesty's representative) constituted the classical trinity of political sovereignty in Tasmania as in the other colonies, with the salaries of the judiciary and civil service guaranteed. Only one or two radical men considered that government should be other than in the hands of the class equipped to govern.

The Legislative Council was retained, with power to block any legislation submitted to it by the House of Assembly. Further, the council was to be elected on a very high property qualification and seat only gentlemen who had independent means. It would be difficult to imagine a more elite body. On the other hand, the illusion of a people's government was fostered by devising a people's House, which had a basic franchise of £10 householders. Even this liberal arrangement debarred many adult males from voting, and the distribution and structure of population made certain that rural districts were able to exert a majority opinion over the urban centres of Hobart Town and Launceston.

Such was the importance of the pattern set in the early proceedings of elections and parliaments in the colony that close attention must be paid to early issues and preoccupations, assumptions and expectations of the people and their representatives, and the events of these first years. Government principally by a chief executive appointed from the Colonial Office and responsible to London was not completely swept away in the mid 1850s, but there was to be no opportunity to cast all blame for colonial misfortunes on the governor and his political masters at home.

There was called into existence in 1855 a Constitution Act, which carefully ensured that there should be government by the propertied class, and on 1 May Her Majesty the Queen assented to legislation that established a parliament for her colony of Tasmania. There was to be an election for the House of Assembly every three years, but members of the Legislative Council retired on a system of rotation, so that it could not be dissolved and was in fact in continuous existence. This provision was to prove a matter of the utmost significance.

Elections for the parliament were spread over a period of three weeks or a month. This permitted defeated candidates to try for election again and was also designed to allow persons who owned property in more than one constituency to vote several times. However, even occasional coincidence of elections did not prevent plural voting. In 1861, for example, a hard-riding James Gibson first thing in the morning recorded his vote at Avoca for the Fingal seat in the House and in the afternoon voted at Deloraine for the electorate there, having travelled across country on horseback. Again, during another election, the *Emu* was chartered to carry up to New Norfolk such of W. S. Sharland's supporters as were resident in Hobart Town.

In 1857 the northern electorates (north of and including Campbell Town) had a total population of about 32000 persons, and the southern ones 49000. By 1870, however, the north had almost overtaken the south in terms of population: 50000 to 53000. In demographic terms the feature of the period was the marked increase of population in the north. Hobart Town's population increased by less than a thousand to 19500 in the period to 1870 whereas Launceston advanced from 8000 to 11000. This palpable change in the centre of population gravity was reflected in continual friction between the interests of Launceston and the capital, complicated by the development of a new regional interest along the north-west and, up to a point, in the north-east. The very marked regional loyalties in the colony were reinforced greatly by the circulation of newspapers: the boundary between north and south was marked in part by the areas where the Launceston *Examiner* and Hobart Town *Mercury* were read, which coincided with business interests. Hobart always had what Launceston and the north regarded as an unfair edge because the capital was the seat of government and the main government departments, and because it possessed a marvellous harbour and facilities for seaborne trade.

Despite the colonists' delight at the prospect of living in a colony with self-government, the first such election in 1856 revealed a remarkable apathy in terms of electioneering, because only fourteen of the thirty seats (nearly all in or near Hobart Town or Launceston) were contested. The seat of Norfolk Plains (Longford) was to have had a second candidate, but at the eleventh hour he walked away across the common and lay concealed in a ditch all day.

Thus was the boon of self-government ushered in—and out, because, in its first eight months' enjoyment of the novelty, the colony had no fewer than four ministries. The first premier was the Launceston member, W. T. N. Champ, with T. D. Chapman as colonial treasurer and Francis Smith as attorney-general. This administration collapsed after four months when, faced with a large deficit in estimated revenue, attributed without evidence to long years of irresponsible rule and extravagant expenditure, it imposed additional customs duties on such items as food and clothing, postage, shipping, tobacco, tea and sugar in an attempt to meet a budget deficiency. In an interesting move, Chapman proceeded to implement the provisions of this before the Legislative Council passed judgment on the bill. At a subsequent conference between the houses, no conclusion was reached on the power of the Council and, thus confirmed and encouraged, that body proceeded for many years to amend bills in season and out.

The triumph of the Council was not generally noticed as upwards of 5000 people attended a meeting of protest at the New Market in Hobart Town against the proposed duties, and noted that the proposed tax was oppressive on the industrial classes, permitted the landed gentry and men of capital to evade a just share of the burden of government, that smuggling and illicit distillation would flourish, and that the principles of free trade were being attacked. Petitions were got up, the one at Hobart Town said to be thirty-eight yards long. The House reassembled after an adjournment and in February 1857 the ministry was defeated.

Champ's administration was succeeded by that of T. G. Gregson, who promptly produced a memorandum. The year's deficit was of the order of £76 000, announced this document, and it went on to adumbrate details of land sales, reduction of salaries and the floating of a credit vote. This was refused by the House, and stirring scenes followed. Gregson had a reputation for turbulence and eccentricity, and possessed a fatal genius for antagonising people. The principal features of his political career were said to be a few speeches on popular topics of the day, two or three discreditable attempts at horse-whipping people (including the nephew of Governor Arthur—but after Arthur had sailed for England), and a duel. Against this ideological background, in the House he indulged in offensive personal vituperation, sought to revive against political opponents the indiscretions of a quarter of a century earlier, and made faces.

The end came for the premier when in March he asked the House to sanction the proposed loan. This was opposed by Chapman whereupon Gregson made a splendidly insulting speech in which he accused Chapman of coming out to Van Diemen's Land as a steward on a ship. There was fearful excitement in the public gallery.

Gregson was succeeded by W. P. Weston, whose administration fell back on retrenchment, land sales and some extra duties on certain imported goods. Then Francis Smith became premier in a reshuffle, and political peace settled over the land.

The number of adult males declined, and there were reductions in import and export figures. The *Daily News*, sole liberal voice in the colonial wilderness, concluded gloomily that there was little chance of the government actually doing anything for the benefit of the industrial classes because the majority of the members of parliament remained largely and deeply concerned with the maintenance of the *status quo*.

The colony exhibited symptoms of collapse. A joint parliamentary committee appointed to enquire into the tariff lapsed for want of a quorum, expansion of the franchise was spoken of as one of the most objectionable features of American republicanism, and had it not been for observations about the chances of gold being found, the governor's speech on the opening of the fifth session of parliament in August 1859 would have been limited to the subjects of the eradication of thistles and the introduction of salmon.

During the period of office of the first parliament of Tasmania, however, there emerged an issue that was to trouble every ministry. This concerned the introduction of railways. The steam, as it were, for this manifestation of the Industrial Revolution came especially from the north of Tasmania and took the form of agitation for a line of rail from Launceston to Deloraine across a level and very fertile countryside. In July 1858 a parliamentary committee looked into the matter, and ten months later a British firm indicated its willingness to lay down forty miles of track. In 1861 the government made a fateful decision when it agreed to bear the cost of survey and plans, provided that the local people raised money for building the line.

But at that point, the House was dissolved and the second of the colony's elections ordered. No startling or new political issues appeared on the horizon, the legislature and government being dominated and dictated to by the Chamber of Commerce. This body was composed exclusively of importers and commission agents, it was said, and it was quite hopeless to expect revision of the tariff because this would involve a collision with those powerful camarillas.

Most of the candidates in 1861 were landed proprietors, merchants and lawyers. There was an element of mild excitement in that five men stood for Hobart Town on a Protection ticket. Fifty-six men offered themselves for re-election, and eleven had a walk-over; fifteen men were newcomers to the House. Apart from the general question of how to raise money, the chief issue was protection for local industry, urged by a section of the press, but the new House of Assembly gave no sign that it would differ in any serious way from the old one. All in all, the election was favourable to the ministry and northern free trade influences. Though Chapman was rejected in Hobart Town, he got in for the down-river constituency of Queenborough and shortly became premier.

The election having been concluded, the Legislative Council now felt the necessity to stir itself by adopting a role that might be termed either public-spirited or intransigent—it refused to accept the next appropriation bill until the colonial treasurer had explained to the Council's satisfaction how he intended to raise the necessary funds. In response, F. M. Innes announced that because he estimated a deficit of £30 000, he proposed a further issue of debentures, together with *ad valorem* duties. The Council, possibly victim of some lapse of attention, passed these measures and then angrily carried a vote of no confidence on the question of the *ad valorem* duties it had so recently approved. When the House disregarded this, the Council characteristically refused to proceed with any business at all and directed the Governor to dismiss the ministry.

The tariff aroused great hostility from the mercantile interests and from sections of the people but, the government persisting, the Council in September 1862 rejected Supply, and Chapman was defeated on the floor of the House. The Legislative Council had struck again although the government would be obliged to decide between *ad valorem* duties and direct taxation—or bankruptcy.

The election of 1862 was about confidence in the ministry and its financial policy, so Chapman's administration was decisively defeated.

When parliament reassembled early in 1863, leadership of the government was vested in James Whyte, member for Pembroke in the Legislative Council, and hailed as leader of a 'liberal' party. The policy of the new men turned out to be further retrenchment, readjustment of taxation and the institution of public works, but a royal commission appointed to enquire into the public service inconveniently found that retrenchment had been carried to its limit by the preceding government. Some other means of increasing revenue without upsetting anyone of importance had therefore to be found. This was difficult, and an attempt to compel local areas to pay for roads and education was hastily withdrawn.

More interest was shown in the approach of the railway era. By early 1862 a survey of railway between Launceston and Deloraine had been conducted by W. T. Doyne, the government surveyor, and it was estimated that £365 000 would be needed to cover costs of building the line. Great enthusiasm in the north was reported, especially among individuals whose land values would be enhanced. One of the most active railway men was Sir Richard Dry, and he stated that £400 000 was the maximum required for a railway. It was proposed to secure this amount by asking the government to authorise the issue of debentures with a guarantee of the interest. Inhabitants of the railway district were to be asked to reguarantee to the government half of that interest, assured by an assessment on their land. In mid 1863 there was recommended the establishment of a board of railway commissioners to usher in the railway age ... but the Legislative Council rejected this and a fresh body was appointed to look into the practicability of a line between Launceston and Hobart Town.

Northern members were furious and blamed W. R. Allison and what the *Examiner* termed his characteristic absurdity. But northern plans went ahead anyway, and a Northern Railway League was inaugurated at a public meeting in September 1863 as the climax to a full day of festivities in Launceston. Most northern members of parliament were in the League, with Dry as chairman and Henry Dowling secretary.

At the same time, however, a main line committee was formed to canvass subscriptions for a railway between Hobart Town and the north; to complicate matters further, a company was established to build a line from Deloraine on to the Mersey; and yet another body, called the Direct Western Railway Company, was said to be promoting a line in order to undermine the league. The enterprise of the north began to be feared, and southern citizens contemplated now with horror the transfer of the capital of Tasmania from the broad and beautiful estuary of the Derwent to the narrow and tortuous mudflats of the Tamar.

As a result of negotiations between Dry and the colonial secretary there finally emerged an agreement by which the government was to authorise the formation of a Launceston–Deloraine railway company and guarantee the issue of railway bonds, with the government to have a lien on the railway plant and revenue, with power to levy a rate on the railway district for any deficiency. Agreement to the whole proposal was reached at a public meeting of the league at which landholders were told they would be polled to determine their willingness to be subjected to a rate if necessary. The *quid pro quo* for parliamentary agreement to this was apparently the passage of a bill authorising the expenditure of £106 000 on public works.

Meanwhile the construction of a line from Deloraine to the Mersey had begun, the company undertaking the work in return for grants of land of one mile depth on either side of the railway. In the south the main line had not advanced beyond the formation of a railway progress association, and in the north a railway poll was conducted, 2238 landholders favouring the measure and only 564 opposing it. The *Examiner* printed a comprehensive account of the day's voting on blue paper, blue being the colour of the league's flag.

In an attempt to promote further public works, and get the colony on the move, the Whyte Government then adopted the recommendations of a select committee on the matter, but the Legislative Council instantly threw out the bill. In these circumstances, the government decided on a bold and desperate venture: in July 1865, the governor informed a horrified gentry that his government had now determined to free the port of Hobart Town, to remove duties from everything except beer, spirits and tobacco, and to substitute a property and income tax of 1s. in the pound (5 per cent) on all incomes over £80 a year. Such a program, concluded the treasurer sunnily, would not only place the revenue of Tasmania on a sure and certain foundation but would also invite trade, commerce, and population and give a healthy stimulus to industry.

It was all too much. What will our friends in England think of us? cried the *Mercury*. Public meetings sprang into life up country to protest, and it was predicted that landholders would sell out rather than pay up. In the House, Meredith's proposal was quickly destroyed, though the final lethal motion opposing his plans was carried by only one vote. In September 1866 the third parliament of Tasmania was dissolved, and members once more went to the country to present electors with a choice between retrenchment (which was no longer possible) and further orthodox taxation (which was also no longer possible). It remained only for the power of prayer to be called up.

The years 1865 and 1866 were very bad ones for Tasmania economically for at only one other time had revenue been lower than it was in 1866; coin held in the banks was never less; the value of exports was lower than in any other year, and imports were only half the value recorded in 1855. On all sides it was agreed that the tax proposal was the issue to be decided at the polls. Even the question of whether or not the government should subsidise the building of the western railway dropped out of sight in relation to the competition of an income tax.

The election in Hobart Town was rowdy, and candidates were handled roughly: W. L. Crowther had no sooner commenced a speech than a man stood up at the bottom of the platform, demanded payment of an account and then threw an egg; Chapman was also the target for a man throwing eggs, which missed, at which Mr Chapman asked if that was an Englishman.

As in Hobart Town, so in Launceston government candidates were defeated at the hands of H. E. Lette, J. Crookes and J. Scott, who were supported by the Railway League, which thus delivered them the seats. Significantly, Charles Meredith, the Treasurer who had promoted the proposed tax, was himself defeated in Glamorgan by his brother John, although anti-government voters going to the electorate were nobbled when some ruffians took the wheels off their dogcart and the nuts off the bolts. Charles Meredith did, however, finally secure a seat for Kingborough.

F. M. Innes spoke solemnly of the natural subordination of one class to another, and enough people believed that the government's proposals would lead only to equality of misery. As the sole candidate for New Norfolk, W. S. Sharland, stated in an injured tone, he disapproved of class legislation such as the direct tax and thought it morally wrong to set gentlemen against poor men.

A ministry led by Sir Richard Dry came into office in November

1866 with Chapman as colonial treasurer and W. L. Dobson as attorney-general. It was supposed to undertake sweeping retrenchment; it withdrew £20000 of grants-in-aid to municipalities, and within a month fell back on the issue of debentures to meet the interest about to fall due on all the other debentures issued by previous administrations.

While the railway issue embittered relations between north and south, the government did succeed in abolishing state aid to religion when a commutation bill was passed. Rights of the clergy were reserved, and debentures of £100000, payable in the colony, were bestowed on the Church of England (£58000), Church of Rome (£23000), Church of Scotland (£8000), Wesleyans (£7000), Free Church of Scotland (£3000) and Jews (£420).

Meanwhile a commission reported on a main line of railway and estimated the cost would be £750 000. To complete a survey and estimate, £6000 was voted by parliament but, as the northerners angrily pointed out, the public and not the local people (as in the case of the Deloraine line) had footed the bill for the survey, and this was inconsistent. Worse was to come because in April 1869 it appeared that the Launceston and Deloraine Company required £50000 more than the earlier estimate to complete the line. This blow to the north did not, however, deter the government from authorising the construction of a main line from Hobart Town to Launceston by a British firm for a total cost of £300000. Captain Audley Coote represented the company and worked out the financial arrangements, after which a railway bill passed through parliament. As that happened, the Western Line was officially opened for traffic in February 1870 two years after His Royal Highness, Alfred, Duke of Edinburgh turned the first sod. The railway age had come to Tasmania.

So also had another indication of the triumph of the colonists, for they now perceived, they thought, the final decline of the Aboriginal people. Late in 1831, the remnants of the original inhabitants of the island were finally removed to Flinders Island from interim settlements at Swan Island and Guncarriage Island. Here the Aborigines were victims of government indifference and confusion of aims. As well, the ravages of pulmonary diseases reduced their numbers so much that by 1837 there were probably not enough left to recover and establish a viable population on their own.

In October 1847, some fourteen men, twenty-two women, five

boys and five girls were transferred to the building of an old convict probation station at Oyster Cove, south of Hobart. Here they sank into drunkenness and immorality, largely out of sight and out of mind, and left without proper medical attention. The last man, William Lanne, died in 1869. His head was removed by Dr Lodewyk Crowther of the Colonial Hospital. A public uproar followed this mutilation in the interests of science, and the whereabouts of the head has never been traced with certainty.

Then on 8 May 1876 the last of the full-blood Aborigines in Tasmania also died when Trugannini succumbed to bronchitis and asthma. Two years after her burial at the Cascades, the Royal Society took possession of the skeleton, but for a century no thorough scientific examination of the remains was made. Ultimately as a result of pressure from people descended from the Aborigines, Trugannini's remains were ritually cremated and her ashes scattered in 1976.

In the opinion of N. J. B. Plomley, the foremost student of the Aborigines, the Aboriginal people failed to survive as a pure-blood group, so to speak, because in the first place they were particularly susceptible to introduced European diseases that could scarcely be cured or even alleviated by the medical procedures of the time. Secondly, there was no realisation that the culture of these people had to be replaced by one that was meaningful to them. Especially useless was the inculcation of forms of Christianity by rote because it failed to come to terms with the spiritual beliefs of the Aborigines. Such crucial elements as the use of ochre for decoration and cultural coherence, the corroborees and language were taken from the Aborigines, and their dignity fatally undermined. Thirdly, there was no understanding that the Aborigines needed to be independent and conduct their own lives. Thus were they destroyed both in person and in terms of their culture—or so the Europeans thought.

3

Consolidation: 1870–91

In the twenty years from 1870 to 1890, the colony of Tasmania enjoyed a revival of fortune. Great changes were made in matters of public and private health, by the settlement of land in the north-west and north-east, and by public works. Railways continued to be laid down, and mineral wealth was discovered and exploited. Tasmania shared in the increased investment made in the Australian colonies generally, and there emerged a form of more coherent, purposeful and active government than had hitherto been the case. Yet the political history of this period as well as earlier and later was frequently centred upon the decisions of the all-powerful elitist Legislative Council, which could and frequently did dictate to the people's House and to the population of the colony what laws or arrangements were to be permitted. An essential element of democratic government is risk and readiness to take a chance, underwritten by the opinion of the ordinary person. To this extent, the timidity and indeed reactionary character of the Legislative Council could not but fail to be fatally damaging to the fabric of Tasmanian society, and its conduct in rejecting and hampering progressive work became so common as to be thought not remarkable.

In 1870 the Launceston and Western Railway was opened to the accompaniment of much display and self-congratulation in the north, but unhappily the times were bad, largely owing to the continued economic depression. It was said that costs of construction had been lavish and that hence the ability of the line to pay its way was reduced ... and not the least of its difficulties was perceived to be the jealousy and spite of southern interests, exemplified in promoting a main line of railway between north and south and throwing obstacles in the way of the earnest and enterprising northerners.

The action of the government in spending public money to promote surveys of a main line infuriated Launceston and environs where residents repeatedly drew attention to the lack of government help they had received and the consequent large part played by expenditure of private capital. It became apparent that the new line had not fulfilled its promise and, in part due to the depressed state of northern agricultural and pastoral interests, was scarcely paying working expenses, let alone making the interest due to the government on the cost of constructions. In these circumstances, it appeared that the government would be obliged to levy a rate, but at the same time, to the continued fury of the north, in August 1871 it had signed a contract for construction of a main line by an English company. By August 1872, the western line was closed, with the government proposing to take over the plant at the same cost per mile as it had contracted for the main line, where construction started by the end of 1872, with 2000 navvies at work, playing their part in a consumer-led recovery.

In 1873 there were indeed signs of a revival in the economy, and the western line began to pick up. The government decided to collect the railway rate due, but there was much murmuring at the government's overall proposal to clear the debt, thought by one party to be too generous and by the other not generous enough. But a rate was to be collected, insisted the government, and passive resistance was predicted. There was indeed resistance, but it was most active because, when distrained goods were to be put up for sale to help meet the railway district's debts, rioting occurred, commencing at Launceston on 4 February 1874.

An effigy was burnt and dragged about the town, and on the following day a large crowd gathered threateningly in front of the Commissariat Store where the seized articles were to be offered for sale. That night the crowd took over and the police panicked, leaving their superintendent alone. He was attacked and injured, but finally the police rallied and dispersed the crowd. Next day attempts to swear in members of the fire brigade as special constables failed, though young gentlemen volunteered. Some 2000 people by now had taken over Launceston and only reluctantly dispersed when the mayor, aldermen and police moved among them exhorting peace.

With this demonstration the agitation subsided, and the greater proportion of the moiety due for 1873 was collected, though the government shrank from collecting the full amount owing. Much bitterness between north and south now existed, and in June 1876 another rail-way difficulty appeared likely to arise when the first instalment of inter-est on the main line's £650000 fell due. A controversy arose between the company and the ministry over whether or not the line had been completed as contracted.

In 1886 there was a threat by the English directors in London to obstruct a £1 million loan sought by Tasmania unless the colony made concessions in respect of matters in dispute. This splendid example of imperial idealism was not publicised by the government and, when discovered, led to a vote of no confidence. This was properly muted, and failed.

A new railway to Scottsdale was opened in 1889 and by then the colony boasted 400 miles of permanent way. There had been none in 1870. The coming of railways to Tasmania was encouraged not only by enterprising northern interests but also increasingly by mineral dis-coveries. Nothing of any importance in this department came to light, however, until in 1871 James 'Philosopher' Smith discovered tin at a place that came to be named Waratah, at Mount Bischoff, inland from the tiny settlement at Emu Bay on the north-west coast. In 1873 a com-pany was formed at Launceston, to exploit what turned out to be the richest tin mine in the world. By 1880 it was producing 4000 tons a year worth some £350000.

As well, some 2000 ounces of gold were recovered in 1870, and ten years later this figure had risen to 51000 ounces, worth more than £200000. Gold was located at Waterhouse in the north-east where the Great Tasmanian mine was promptly salted, although confidence was soon restored when it became clear that real gold was present. The principal quartz reefs there and at Fingal were said to have got into the hands of men whose Victorian experience had made them adept in the art of setting up bubble companies, so that local people were duped by Ballarat speculators.

In addition, deposits of silver were found east of the Penguin Creek on the north-west but did not prove the bonanza desired. In 1872 the Reedy Marsh and Black Boy mines in the Fingal district had gener-ated a township of 650 people. In 1877, the best gold mine in Tasmania was discovered, and alluvial and quartz mining produced some 30 000 ounces of gold in two years. In 1882 the New Golden Gate at Math-inna also began producing gold, and the Tasmanian Iron Company exploited large deposits of iron ore, in the district of Leonardsburgh, near

Beaconsfield, so named in 1879. The presence of chrome caused difficulties in 1877 in the production of iron, and the enterprise never succeeded to any extent.

Most optimism, however, was centred upon the Mount Bischoff workings, and by 1878 the town of Waratah was a sizeable one with cottages and slab huts, but situated in a very rugged country with high rainfall. Communication with the coast was most difficult, and ore was originally removed by pack-horse and sent away for treatment on ships, which came into the Penguin and Leith.

In all these encouraging circumstances, numbers of people coming to Tasmania, temporarily and permanently, increased sharply and had trebled from a low point in the 1860s to 10000 a year by the end of the 1870s. Though emigration continued at a high figure as well, the total population of the colony increased by 14 per cent in the decade of the 1870s with a healthy diminution in the masculinity ratio, so that by 1880 there were 90 females for every 100 males, compared with the amazing figure of 46 in the early 1840s when convict transportation was at its height. In 1876, immigration exceeded emigration for the first time in years, and the overall population increased from 101000 to 115000 in the decade of the 1870s, and then to 145000 in the period to 1890. A substantial part of the increase in population was due to natural increase as the age structure and sex structure of the colonial population shifted to include a higher proportion of persons of marriageable age.

As Mount Bischoff continued to flourish, further attention was paid to the wild and tangled country to the west and south-west of that area. Mount Heemskirk was said to be rich in tin deposits, and claims were taken up there and elsewhere in early 1878. New diggings appeared on the west coast in 1879 and, although most were worked by Victorians who sent their earnings home, mineral wealth alleviated a threatened depression that year: £200000 of gold was exported in 1880 out of total metal export of £362000. By 1881, Waratah had so advanced that it supported a newspaper, and the government imported G. Thureau, a Victorian mining engineer, and appointed him geologist to examine the Heemskirk and Pieman River areas, which considerably impressed that gentleman with their potential. Inspired by visions of wealth and prosperity, the government subsidised a small steamer to run from Hobart to Macquarie Harbour and the Pieman, provided for construction of jetties and conducted surveys to lay a tram track from Trial Harbour to the Mount Heemskirk mines. That was in 1881, after even the Legislative Council approved some money for public works, though it quickly got a hold of itself and reduced by half a vote to help the cutting of tracks in the wilds of western Tasmania.

Exploration was conducted between the Huon and Macquarie Harbour, and the export of gold and tin continued to increase gratifyingly as Mount Heemskirk was further prospected by more than 300 mining companies formed by early 1882, compared to 90 in March the previous year. In 1883, Mount Bischoff paid its fifty-eighth dividend, worth a total of £6000, and in July 1885 the Van Diemen's Land Company, formed in 1825 for wool production but never successful, opened a railway from Emu Bay to Mount Bischoff in an effort to capitalise on freighting the valuable tin ore out of Waratah, the mine having paid nearly £600000 in dividends to 1885.

The period from 1870 to around 1880 was marked by considerable advances in other areas of primary production. Exports rose in value from about £650000 in 1870 to £1500000 in 1890, and though the number of sheep remained stable at about one and a half million, the production of wool increased from 4.2 million pounds to 9 million pounds. This was largely due to the vigorous work of James Whyte in supervising the removal of fluke from Tasmanian flocks by masterminding a dipping program in the period 1869–80, at which time Tasmania was declared clean. Total government revenue went up during the twenty years from £270000 to nearly £760000. Acres in cultivation increased from 330000 to 517000, but acres in crop remained at 157 000 acres.

On the other hand, as acreage in some areas decreased, so it increased in the north-west and in the Huon. There had been a rise in apple production from 120000 bushels to 155000 in the period 1860–80, and this figure was more than doubled in the decade to the 1880s to 370000 bushels, compensating for a decline in the timber trade. In the north-west, tons of potatoes produced went from 36000 in 1870 to 73000 in 1890. The number of trades and manufactories in the colony advanced slightly from 3200 to 3600 during the same period.

Under a section of the Land Settlement Act of 1870, selection was permitted, and during the 1880s a total of nearly 5000 lots was sold, of which 20 per cent was in the county of Devon, on the north-west coast. The main features of this legislation were first, free selection at £1 an acre with one-third added by way of premium for credit;

second, deferred payments extending over a period of fourteen years; and third, disposal of half the purchase money upon construction of roads and bridges. The object was to encourage an industrious class without capital to make homes on heavily timbered agricultural land. There was a right to select a maximum of 320 acres and provide for residence thereon until the land was paid for.

Between 1882 and 1885, in the north-west, 53 000 acres of Crown land was taken up, two steamers began trading to Melbourne, and there was an export trade of £75 000 in 1885, of which £37 000 was in potatoes and £15 000 in timber. Similarly land was being opened in the north-east, especially west of Scottsdale in the early 1880s, but two serious pests had appeared: rabbits spread all over the colony and the codlin moth wreaked havoc on the burgeoning apple industry.

Despite the encouraging signs, political conflict continued when diminished receipts in the early 1870s propelled the various governments of Tasmania towards again proposing direct taxes because of falling receipts from land sales and proposed relief to the railways. When in 1872 J. M. Wilson's government was obliged to foreshadow the imposition of a property and income tax of 2½ per cent (5 per cent on absentees), the government fell and F. M. Innes succeeded to the premiership. He was granted six months' Supply on the understanding that he would not impose a direct tax. The result of this was a deficiency by mid 1873 of more than £100 000 in the budget, which Innes proposed to meet partly by a renewal of debentures and partly by alteration of the customs tariff, together with (he hoped) increased consumption of goods. He also proposed to relieve general revenue and land funds by throwing on local government areas certain charges for education, roads and bridges. This was judged inadequate, and Innes' government was in turn voted out and succeeded by that of Alfred Kennerley in August 1873.

The treasurer in this administration was the merchant P. O. Fysh, and in September he too proposed an income tax of 6d. in the pound (2½ per cent). But sure enough, the Legislative Council rejected the tax bill, with a view to defeat the government. The Council members did not have a very high standard of education. Perhaps they also saw virtue in delay because the economy did indeed appear to be recovering so that perhaps the dreaded income tax would not be necessary after all. Perhaps something would turn up. And so it proved: when parliament next met, direct taxation was not spoken of by the government. Indeed, Kennerley's administration now proposed a very large outlay on public works in the remote districts. Would such a measure meet with the approval of the Council? No. That body threw out the government's measures, and parliament stood prorogued. For the second year running the Council rejected the principal ministerial measures.

The Council continued on its typical course: it rejected a public works bill because the legislation was unaccompanied by property tax proposals, which if they had been put forward would have only increased the Council's opposition.

In March 1878 W. R. Giblin, a new premier, began by taking unprecedented action against the Council. When it passed a bill to re-enact a proviso that the main line of railway could only be purchased by consent of parliament, Giblin thought so little of it that he induced all members of the House to combine and lay the measure aside without a division. But presently Giblin too was defeated in the House when by-elections told against him, and W. L. Crowther formed a government. He also at once fell foul of the Legislative Council, which, in a chamber where only seven men were present, declined to consider the estimates and in December aggressively adjourned itself, after altering a money bill, for months. It then took action so that public servants went without salaries for nine weeks in mid 1879 until an uneasy agreement was concluded between the houses. The Council persisted in its obstructive tactics until it was satisfied that ways and means were provided to bring income up to expenditure. Naturally enough, the Council rejected another income and property tax bill.

In these circumstances, yet another government was destroyed when Giblin's vote of no confidence led to the defeat of Crowther who then sought a dissolution and an election ... but the governor refused him and Giblin was enabled to form a fresh government in October 1879. He at once proposed to revise the tariff and remove anomalies, place a duty on ale and beer, a tax on real property of 9d. in the pound (3¾ per cent), and tax income from dividends, annuities and rents. He further proposed to raise £400000 in England.

The governor's refusal to give Crowther an election was wise, although the Council remained as baleful as ever: in March 1880 it decided, in a move that was practically unconstitutional, to adjourn for three months in opposition to the wishes of the government. By this a debenture bill for £450000 (reduced by £200000 by the

Council) was lost in the consequent prorogation, the Council having earlier rejected public works proposals.

At the same time, Christopher O'Reilly, the new Minister for Lands and Works (a department created by Wilson in 1869) brought forward an important public works scheme involving £163000. There now appeared to have been an erosion of opposition in both houses, with Crowther and Thomas Reibey, member for Westbury and premier 1876–77, having been rejected by their erstwhile followers. A good deal of the credit for continued stability in government must go to Giblin, his political skills undoubtedly aided greatly by increasing prosperity and the work of one Samuel Henry in effecting a sort of coalition. But the Council still showed fight—it rejected £72000 for public works and refused to vote a salary to Henry, who had been appointed to an office under the Land Tax Act. Chapman and Crowther led this opposition in the Council, displaying as it was factionalism of the worst kind.

When parliament met in August 1883, the government renewed its plans to reduce by half the duties on tea and sugar and abolish the duty on machinery. As well, a public works scheme totalling an expenditure of nearly £1 million was also proposed. When the Legislative Council met to consider this most pressing matter, insofar as its abilities would permit, it could not muster a quorum, but finally rejected a bill for destruction of the codlin moth, considerably amended a measure that sought to destroy rabbits, and agreed to consider the proposed huge public works (including railways) proposals that day six months. This led to public outrage, and northern members of the Council received such a very hostile reception when they journeyed home that shortly thereafter the bill was agreed to.

But the Council soon rallied after this setback and splendidly demonstrated its perception of high purpose and sensitivity to colonial welfare by rejecting a bill to prohibit the practice of shooting live pigeons from traps, and introducing business that involved money and was therefore carefully calculated to annoy the House of Assembly.

Then Giblin resigned because of bad health and, on his suggestion, was succeeded by Adye Douglas, with a similar ministry. As a legacy of his widely admired administration, however, Giblin left a successful proposal to give the vote for the Lower House to all ratepayers, instead of only those rated at £7 a year and above, and to allow wage-earners who made £80 or more a year similarly to vote. By 1894, numbers enabled to vote for the Lower House had doubled, as had those permitted to vote for the Council.

The colonists of Tasmania, like their fellow Britons elsewhere in the Australias, as the colonies were sometimes termed, and New Zealand, always attached very great importance to their links with the Old Country, or Home. Especially was this so among the literate, although the inarticulate majority also cheered the Crown in tune with their more consciously loyal elders and betters. The height of imperial loyalty was manifested on the occasion of royal visits such as that by Prince Alfred in 1868. In 1887 it was the Queen's golden jubilee, and in June this was marked by wide-ranging demonstrations and manifestations of patriotism, by a race meeting in the afternoon at Hobart and a general illumination in the evening. The governor reported with quiet pride on the enthusiastic and orderly bearing of the large crowd when he walked incognito through it. On 22 June there was a review of the defence forces, and a huge procession marched to the scene. Addresses were handed to the Crown's representative, and he in turn read out a telegram from the Secretary of State for the Colonies, sending Her Majesty's cordial thanks to the women and girls of Tasmania for their loyal address. Schoolchildren marched through a tent in their thousands, and each was presented with a commemorative medal and jubilee cakes. Fireworks were displayed at night, and there was a grand ball on the evening of the 23rd at Government House, to which more than 900 distinguished guests were invited. Unfortunately it was a very wet night in Hobart and only 550 attended, but it was impossible to overstate the intense loyalty of the people to the person and throne of Queen Victoria. Tribute was paid to the excellent work of the Mayor of Hobart, Mr C. Harbottle, as chairman of the United Jubilee Committee. To mark the festivities, some forty persons sentenced to gaol for minor offences were freed in honour of the occasion. No counter-demonstrations were reported.

Imperialism as it had emerged in Tasmania was very closely linked to military and naval exhibitions of British power. A Flying Squadron anchored in the Derwent in 1868, during the visit of Prince Alfred, and the conduct of its sailors was recorded as admirable, only three of their number deserting. On the other hand, such visits were not always marked by manifestations of harmony and light for the Empire: HMS *Wolverene* was obliged to complain about the particularly virulent form of syphilis contracted by its loyal crew in Hobart Town in 1877. It was with much shame that the local authorities were led to establish a contagious diseases hospital for the incarceration and cure of females apprehended or who admitted themselves for treatment.

Certain of the Tasmanians were also upset when it was decided to bring away all troops from the Australian colonies in 1870, a departure perceived by some with limitless imagination as equivalent to the withdrawal of the Roman legions from Britain. The severing of even such a slight but tangible link with Home exposed faraway Tasmania even more to the cold winds of isolation and hence reinforced the urgency of loyalty to the Mother Country, the Crown and the Protestant succession: in the Franco-Prussian war the Protestants of Tasmania tended to support Prussia and the Catholics to take the part of France. Similarly when the Duke of Genoa visited and appeared at the Government House levee on the occasion of the Queen's birthday in 1873, the Duke and his brother officers were received with much cordiality, but the Catholic clergy as a body kept aloof.

There was a history of tension between Catholics and Protestants in Tasmania; it had been manifested during meetings supporting the Crimean War when Catholic spokesmen were obliged to insist that they were no less loyal to Britain than were the Protestants. Then in 1879 a most interesting example of sectarianism emerged with the visit to Hobart Town of the apostate Catholic Pastor Charles Chiniquy. Such were the passions aroused that the Volunteers were called out in aid of the civil power, a question arose of whether the city council was justified, let alone wise, to let the Town Hall for a meeting that was a sure recipe for religious strife; and much energy was spent on discussing the timing of an appeal from the Catholic bishop to restrain the Catholic element from violence.

Chiniquy had a lurid line in ribald slanders of Catholic women and, although he was clearly unhinged, this did not preclude support from persons who should have known better.

The education of young colonists left a good deal to be desired in the first fifty or sixty years of the settlement of the colony, and it was not till 1869 that the first general examination of teachers was conducted by the Board of Education. Few teachers were systematically trained. Possession of literary talent was thought enough to lead to promotion, but the board now said no to this. As for the schools, many buildings were found to be utterly inadequate and some few even lay in ruin. Many children were aged more than ten before they came to school and then were removed for field labour. Because their attendance was fitful and irregular, many forgot what they had learnt and were a handicap to the children who attended regularly. Indeed, absenteeism was frequently judged as immeasurably worse than no attendance at all, but local school boards appointed under the Education Act of 1869 were understandably most reluctant to use their influence with neighbours in urging regular school attendance.

In short, there was inadequate provision for training teachers, absence of serious local responsibility, the want of power to enforce conditions, and a shortage of funds and inducements to make the absolutely necessary improvements. Perhaps most importantly of all, the teachers were paid pitifully small salaries largely because local school fees went unpaid in far too many cases. In seeking to collect weekly fees, the teacher met with the most miserable shifts and excuses to avoid payment, and especially was he or she financially insecure in the many small schools.

School inspection was minimal because there were so few officials of the board, and in 1875 one such felt it necessary to put in a plea for the assistance of men with an aptitude for bush travelling, unlimited capacity for roughing it, and an ability to swim unfordable rivers in the north of the colony. The reading books of the popular Irish National Schools System were also to be criticised; especially when they really required to be translated into colonial English when such a passage as this appeared to confront little Tasmanians: 'The pearl consists of concentric coats of the same substance as that which forms the mother-of-pearl of the shell; they are produced by the extravasation of a lapidifying fluid, secreted in the organs of the animals, and filtered by its glands.' In 1885 a new Education Act sought to correct some of these many deficiencies, and there followed a year later the establishment of the first technical school in Hobart, followed by another one in Launceston in 1888.

Some of the inhabitants of the colony were not concerned with the education of their children, but all were concerned with their health and its precarious state. The conditions of urban and rural living came under close scrutiny in the 1880s, and a series of reports on the cities of Launceston and Hobart, followed by others on rural centres, revealed the supposed causes of those diseases that struck down colonists. Smallpox was a particular fear, and such colonists as Dr E. S. Hall, an energetic physician and social reformer, never lost an oppor-

tunity to drop a few improving words about vaccination and its benefits. The poverty-stricken among the Tasmanians, however, regarded the
treatment with great wariness, suspecting that it might bring on the
disease, or transmit or originate others, especially those of a loathsome
character. Only outbreaks of smallpox would lead parents to have their
children vaccinated.

Typhoid fever was a killer and, following deaths from that disease in
the mid 1870s, a report was required by the government on the sanitary arrangements in the capital of the colony. It emerged that reliable
data were non-existent but that typhoid, diphtheria and other such
diseases were understood most frequently to arise from the people
breathing gases that emanated from sewage and decomposing animal
and vegetable matter, from consumption of impure drinking water,
and from overcrowding and want of ventilation in dwellings. Other
diseases such as scarlatina were rendered more virulent and propagated
with greater rapidity by the same causes.

Similar conditions existed in Launceston, where deaths had increased
in the early 1870s although the number of inhabitants had not, and
similarly the chief medical officer blamed inadequate drainage and sewerage, with the contents of patent water-closets reported to flow into
open gutters and with no complete and enforced use of earth-closets.

Pig-sties abounded in settled areas of Tasmania, offensive to sight
and injurious to public health, and abattoirs exhibited horrible scenes
of offal disposal. In Hobart the south side of the Cascade Road was a
ditch of sewage filth, putrefying and poisoning the air, but the greatest nuisance and dangers were thought to be the privy cesspits where
human excrement was often kept for years without removal, saturat-
ing the adjacent soil and polluting the air with pestilential emanations,
so that earth-closets at least were required.

By the end of the 1870s, the whole question of public health required
attention, not least the matter of the Hobart Town Rivulet, which
was an abominable open sewer into which faecal matter was discharged
together with soap suds and other putrefactive elements.

No one knew why diseases that had been virtually unknown in
earlier years had quite suddenly made their appearance in the colony,
and Dr Hall remained untiring in drawing attention to their dangers
and origins, as he perceived them. Smallpox prevention was under way
elsewhere, he thundered, such as in Worcester, Massachusetts, and
action was taken in 1883 when, by a Public Health Act for Hobart, it

was laid down that new cesspits were to be constructed, defective ones removed, and all to be filled in by the end of 1886. In addition, an overall drainage plan for Hobart was signalled, and the pail method of collecting nightsoil was pronounced a great step forward in the fight against disease. Throughout the colony a Public Health Act came into force on 1 January 1885. It led to the establishment of local boards of health, which closed down cesspits and, it was reported, banished typhoid from areas where it had hitherto prevailed every autumn.

In the mid 1880s, Alfred Mault, engineering inspector of the board of health, described the situation in Hobart as still deplorable. Sewerage arrangements were generally chaotic, and no plan of them appeared to exist, cesspits were very imperfectly constructed and emptied at uncertain intervals, the gutters of the city were swept at varying inter-vals by Corporation scavengers, sewage lodged in every hollow, and faecal matter was carted to farms at New Town and Sandy Bay and used as manure without being disinfected.

By 1885, in Launceston there were 130 houses connected with the sewers, 70 water-closets substituted for cesspits, 250 premises cleaned and 92 disinfected, 86 notices served for defective privy construction, 186 for defective drainage, 250 for filthy houses, and 25 for filthy sta-bles, cowsheds and piggeries; the yearly visitations of typhoid and diph-theria still occurred. Especially singled out for attention was a ten-acre block on the Inveresk Swamp, which supported a population of 469 souls, about four times the average density of population in Launces-ton. Two-thirds of the cases of fever were traced to the swamps between the railway and the North Esk River, and twenty of them came from a block at the corner of the Esplanade and Invermay Road. One of the problems in Launceston was that a plan of sewerage for the town had been adopted in the 1850s with the result that sewage was discharged straight into the Tamar River. As if that was not bad enough, it was reported in 1886 that cemeteries with one exception were not suitably placed, so that the Scotch cemetery in High Street drained down the steep hill, where a rivulet formed in rainy weather and mingled its waters with those of the overflow from the Lord Street reservoirs, so forming part of the supply to houses in Hampton Vale.

Rural slums were also known: at Brighton a man named Shearman and his wife and seven children, dressed in sacking, occupied one room only, and at Avoca the local policeman's family had the noisome cells between their rooms.

In the late 1870s, 'fever' was also notified at the Furneaux Islands. First settled in the late eighteenth century, these islands came to be the home of descendants of Tasmanian Aborigines, sealers and some ex-convicts. By the mid nineteenth century, there was an established community on Guncarriage, Woody, Tin Kettle, Cape Barren, and Clarke Islands. Mutton birds provided subsistence and a valuable export. Dr E. P. Vines, of Formby on Mersey (Devonport), visited to check the 'fever' and did what he could to encourage cleanliness and fumigation of the houses, in the course of his duties offering interesting comment on the culture of these descendants of the original people of Van Diemen's Land.

Tasmania's origins haunted the island, and promotion of the colony as a 'sanatorium of the south' was calculated to distance the society as far as possible from the horrors and shame of transportation and the destruction of the Aboriginal people. After a lengthy and irritable debate with the imperial authority, the surviving Port Arthur prisoners were transferred to Hobart. A financial arrangement was concluded by which it was possible for the British government to foot the bill for transportation as late as the 1930s, in the hypothetical case of a youthful convict transported in the early 1850s reappearing to claim maintenance in his or her nineties. So close did the convict era approach Tasmania, and indeed from time to time old convicts came under notice right through the century. As late as 1882 the grim imprint of the transportation system appeared when an ex-prisoner of 1852 figured in a murder. It was a pathetic case. The man, employed as a groom and milkman at Campbell Town and dwelling in a kitchen, killed a police constable when a conflict arose over the ex-convict's desire to have a turkey to keep with his pet parrot.

Right to the end of the century, persons in gaol still included those listed as 'free by servitude', and there were many institutions that owed at least some of their objects of charity and cost to the transportation system. In 1870 there were no fewer than 700 absolutely destitute children in Launceston and two Ragged Schools, one at the wharf and the other in Brisbane Street. In most cases relief was given in the form of provisions, but when a standard uniform was issued to the deserving, it provoked a significant cry of 'Tench! Tench!', the convict slang for penitentiary.

But the revival of the economy and a return towards demographic normality generated a spirit of optimism and energy. This was apparent in all areas of Tasmanian public life. In the early 1870s the Tasmanian Public Library was created by act of parliament, with Alfred Kennerley chairman of trustees, and in 1886 another act brought the Tasmanian Museum and Botanical Gardens into existence; there was a huge amount of public interest in the introduction of salmon for sport and commerce; government moved in to decrease the hours at which public houses might be open and to control their general conduct; the administration of Tasmania contributed on a pound-for-pound basis to the various road trusts struggling to provide transport of the utmost importance in the newly settled areas where bad roads were sometimes positively dangerous; an act of 1873 made provision for retreats or houses for treatment of habitual inebriates, and appointed commissions to enquire into prison discipline and lunatic asylums; moves were made that led to the establishment of the university; a government analyst's office was founded so that imported and other goods might be tested scientifically before issue to the public; an inspector of mines was appointed in 1883; a Hobart Tramway Company bill was drafted in 1884 and in 1885 the government sought to control the conditions and hours of work of women and children against strong opposition from such as jam manufacturers and proprietors of woollen mills who considered that ten hours a day for such persons was perfectly reasonable.

An act of 1885 laid down that no women could be employed for more than ten hours a day, or children for eight, except for saleswomen in shops where goods were exposed for sale on Saturday evening, or children employed in jam factories from January to March and in October, who could be employed for nine hours. In addition, the eight-hour day came to prevail by consent and custom (though it never got through parliament) except for agricultural labourers and adult males employed in shops.

Reform and progressive legislation characterised the period. Some colonists strove to raise the age of female consent from twelve years to sixteen and generally reform the law as it related to females; an enquiry recommended that the various friendly societies be controlled so that liabilities for medical and monetary relief in sickness and death could be met; the centralisation of the municipal and territorial police was recommended by a parliamentary committee after evidence of local favouritism and territorial men as ragged in appearance as Falstaff's recruits. In 1885 a conservator of forests was appointed under the State

Forests Act and a beginning made on saw-mill reservations and state reserves in the very important timber industry. Hospitals were opened at Waratah and Latrobe; the government appointed an inspector of fisheries; the Tasmanian Government Railways was formed and in the late 1880s the eminent engineer C. Napier Bell began issuing a series of reports on harbour works to be conducted at such crucial places as Macquarie Harbour.

But a great depression was casting its shadows over all the colonies and, though the mining industry was booming, on 3 August 1891 there was a catastrophe: the Bank of Van Diemen's Land failed.

There had earlier been indications of difficulties or change of direction in the money market, though they were masked in the case of Tasmania, as elsewhere in the Australian colonies, by the boom of the 1880s, which in turn led to the impression that the sky was the limit in terms of investment, profit and development of the colony. Yet prices generally had been dropping in Europe and North America, a phenomenon related to cheaper methods of production and a contraction in the supply of money.

The collapse of investments made by the prominent London bank Barings in its South American economic colonies signalled an end to Australian prosperity in the late nineteenth century. Those who sought to investigate the causes of this and the associated depression found allies and opponents no matter what forms of analysis they used and what conclusions they drew. Baffled observers could fall back only on a stock response commonly and with a touch of desperation termed 'a loss of confidence'. When British supplies of capital were withdrawn from the Australian colonies or sharply reduced, there was a chain reaction. Cautious or timid, wise or unscrupulous, certain speculators removed themselves from the market and put their paper investments and share scrip into hard cash. Lesser men followed suit, rumours of impending collapses gathered strength, and those who had looked up to respectable colonists and institutions for guidance and a nod of approval discovered that their examplars, especially in Melbourne, had been rash or foolish at best and rogues at worst.

The collapse of the Bank of Van Diemen's Land was the first serious bank failure in a miserable decade for Australia as a whole. Not only were the 1890s characterised by the spectacular failure of financial institutions but as well a prolonged drought racked the principal eastern colonies and strikes of unparalleled intensity convulsed them. The common liberal belief that labour and capital had the same interests fell to pieces as class conflict emerged when first the shipping industry and then the pastoral and mining interests were the scene of bitter and protracted disputes.

Established for upwards of seventy years, the Bank of Van Diemen's Land had become a byword for steadiness and reliability in comparison with more rackety money-lenders and, indeed, enjoyed an impressive reputation for probity. Public trust was misplaced. The bank fell victim to greed associated with risky lending and business ventures, reinforced by the bold example offered by Victorian institutions.

When the bank was ultimately wound up by act of parliament, a royal commission had concluded that an alleged £30000 due by other banks was in fact overdraft permission from the London and Westminster Bank, and that another £50000 in coin and bullion put on the balance sheet as an asset existed only in the febrile imagination of the directors. The closure of such an institution came as a bombshell to the public, because no indication had been given to any of the branches of the bank that it was in difficulties.

Such was the impact of the crash that for many years afterwards Tasmanians dated events from 'the year the VDL Bank went broke'.

4

Expansion: 1891–1901

Manifestly the result of duplicity, the collapse of the Bank of Van Diemen's Land was felt particularly on the west coast mining fields in which it had a deep financial interest. Ultimately the assets of the bank were disposed of by a lottery conducted by George Adams, he whose sweepstakes had become immensely popular and been removed from both New South Wales and Queensland by legislation outlawing the enterprise. Impressed by the difficulties thrown in the way of a man without government influence, Adams came to Tasmania. The act of parliament necessary to legalise this novel method of winding up a bank was finally passed in 1893 and, animated with the same spirit, three years later another act helped solve the colony's financial difficulties by presenting Tattersalls with a licence to conduct lotteries. The ostensible aim was to crack down on illegal gambling totes and usher in a government-controlled lottery. These decisions were accompanied by enormous public uproar.

The depression led the government to its traditional method of drastic retrenchment and, although in 1896 the colonial debt was £8 million, revenue improved mainly due to the increase in output of gold, silver and coal and a steady production of tin. The plain man took other steps to make ends meet in hard times, and there was an outbreak of arson for the insurance, an offence that the police found very difficult to detect, though substantial rewards were offered when incendiarism was beyond doubt. In general, however, the mining industry held its own despite the financial crisis and a disastrous fall in the price of silver.

Unemployment alarmed parliament and people, and by 1893, with great strikes signalling the downfall of class cooperation, it was urged that public works be advanced, and this was done all over the colony. Yet casualties continued. In the case of the Hobart Benevolent Society, there was an increase in the number of families on the books from 130 in 1893 to 602 in 1894, and the society was hard-pressed to supply enough relief in the form of soup, blankets and clothing, wood and coal, during the winter. In Launceston, the sister society had its heaviest years in 1893 and 1894, reporting many more cases of real poverty among the respectable class than were normally dealt with as a result of the secretary seeking them out because the families were too ashamed to make personal application for aid. During 1894, 2000 casual cases were relieved, and at the end of that year there were 56 men, 116 women, and 179 children on the Launceston society's permanent roll. In the May following there were 73 men, 142 women, and 280 children, many in the unemployed class, with a total of 974 individuals assisted during the year. The society urged subscribers not to assist beggars, because the money presented to them was promptly spent on drink, but to refer them to 239 Charles Street. It was also suspected that a large number of children were imposing on decent people with spurious tales of want and misery.

The depression also caused trouble in the area of land settlement. Experience of the act of 1870 showed that the yearly payments on 320-acre blocks were too much and the residential clauses were not enforced. Following the relative failure of this legislation to secure *bona fide* settlement, it was repealed by another act of 1890. This rendered it compulsory for selectors 'habitually' to reside on their allotment until the purchase money was paid, and to effect substantial improvements thereon. In 1893, however, it was discovered that 130000 acres were unproductive and seriously in arrears. Selectors were then asked to comply with the conditions of purchase, but with little result because the depression made it impossible for the government to act without causing hardship. Thus another act was passed, which authorised the government to postpone payment of instalments for up to five years on payment of a 5 per cent interest, or an offer of the alternative proposal of transferring instalments paid on the whole to purchase any portion not less than half the area of the block.

This was accounted successful generally, but by the mid 1890s it was claimed that the largest proportion of the best agricultural land remained locked up in sheep and cattle runs, and the question was raised whether such lands should not be bought back by the government because these owners were driving the industrious settler away. Thus closer settlement schemes began. Surveys went forward, especially in the north-west where in such an area as Riana, south of the Penguin, applicants were mostly friends or related to each other and formed a self-contained settlement where they very rapidly improved their holdings, usually less than 50 acres. Some of these settlers presumably came into the area on the basis of legislation providing for purchase during eighteen years at £1 per acre, with one-third added for credit, the maximum selection to be 50 acres, with the government providing costs of survey.

Another remote area further settled was King Island. From 1864 to 1887 it was held under lease and used as a bush run for stock. A surveyor was sent in 1887, and subsequently forty-one selections totalling 6000 acres were applied for and six pastoral leases issued. Settlers principally engaged in pastoral pursuits because stock fattened with marvellous rapidity on the native grasses; there was a fortnightly communication with the mainland during spring and summer. In 1896 about a hundred people lived on the island, and 400 fat cattle had been shipped, chiefly to Launceston. Sheep were also run and low-lying land improved by ploughing and sowing red and white clover, the cattle having suffered when permitted to run free because they fed on poisonous tares. Dairy farming was projected, selections were fenced and houses, roads and a jetty under construction.

The importance for the colony of agriculture was marked by the formation of a Council of Agriculture in 1892. Councillors were drawn from all over the island, a government entymologist appointed, the services of a veterinary surgeon availed of, twenty-eight local boards established and a sturdy *Agricultural Journal* issued. Related to this development was the formation of dairy, butter and cheese cooperatives and factories at Table Cape, Burnie and Launceston with others foreshadowed, and a travelling dairy designed to show producers the latest methods. Producers responded to this initiative as a rule, it was reported, by sending their wives and daughters to be instructed, striking evidence of how labour in the industry was deployed.

At the same time, the fruit export business grew. From the 1890s experiments such as sending fruit in ventilated holds to the English market began to succeed and methods of pruning trees in the shape of a wine-glass improved yields. But dispute arose over the method of control of shipments, with well-grounded fears that the unscrupulous and greedy growers and shippers would ruin a prospectively good market by consigning windfalls and other such fruit unfit for market.

Exports to London averaged around 150 000 bushels in the early 1890s, worth about £50 000, with acreages of orchard from 70 at Frankford to more than a thousand at Glenorchy. Hostile tariffs militated severely against the successful export of jams and fruit to other colonies, though there was a market.

Timber-cutting was also an important industry in the south, although, since first settlement of Van Diemen's Land, timber had been exploited wherever such very valuable and unique species as the Huon pine, King William and pencil pine, as well as the common stringybark variety, could be found. Associated with the felling of trees for building materials was use as railway sleepers, paving blocks, and furniture. A wattle-bark industry existed for tanning, and this began to create anxiety in the 1890s because there was only a lax method of licensing. In addition, such few forestry experts as were disinterested warned strongly against unrestricted hewing down of trees, especially the rare sort. Discussion and action on the forestry front continued to be distinguished by a conflict between those who put immediate gain foremost and those who counselled a comprehensive system of forest management, pioneered by G. S. Perrin in 1886.

Two pests particularly affected agriculturists—rabbits and the codlin moth, with thistles also. Many efforts were made to rid the colony of the former but it proved beyond effective control, largely because there was no effective wide-ranging poison. The pest flourished on both private and Crown land, recognising no boundaries, and because the government land was frequently only thinly occupied, it was almost impossible to police. In addition, the industry of selling rabbit skins became a vested interest and meant that the rabbit was not trapped much in the summer but left until winter when the pelt was of superior quality and worth more. So despite many warnings from those who predicted that the hangman would find work for youths and others who led wild lives trapping rabbits and other animals, the inroads of the creature on pasture and hence on agricultural production became and remained a substantial problem.

More success was ultimately to be achieved in checking the codlin moth, but for a time it too appeared to endanger the entire fruit industry, not a little aided as it was when fruit boards refrained from invoking the full penalties, such as they were, against their own members.

At quite a different level, pleas were made by some colonists for the further destruction of the Tasmanian tiger and the native eaglehawk for their attacks on livestock, but in these cases the animals were scarce enough to be subject of final solutions by local people.

In both rural and urban areas, typhoid continued to be feared for, despite the acceptance of the germ theory of transmission of disease, medical science remained without the medication to check or cure such scourges. The Central Board of Health in Tasmania watched anxiously for signs of typhoid and other dreaded diseases and, at the beginning of the 1890s, rejoiced that deaths from typhoid had been only 49 in 1890 compared with 84 in 1880 and 113 in 1889. One practice that certain colonists had brought with them to Tasmania was thought to contribute to the spread of disease such as diphtheria. This was the custom kept up by Irish settlers of conducting wakes, especially prevalent in certain districts. His Grace the Catholic Archbishop of Hobart was informed of medical men's well-founded fears of the practice of exposing the corpse, and a circular letter was then issued to all Catholic clergy requesting them to do their best to discourage such customs, advice from such a quarter thought to be effectual.

Concern for health was attested by thousands of advertisements in the papers for cure-alls. 'FREE—To all NERVOUS DISABILITY Sufferers, a certain, easy and permanent SELF CURE. Having cured myself after years of suffering, misery and loss of money to quack doctors, I will send full particulars FREE on receipt of an addressed envelope for reply. Address—A Miner, G.P.O. Sydney.' The magic potion supplied by 'A Miner' at £1 1s. an ounce turned out to be Peruvian bark in powdered form, the ordinary retail price being 1s. an ounce.

By 1897 there had been passed an act containing most of the provisions desired by the Central Board of Health: infectious and contagious diseases were better defined and more complete provisions made for their notification; wilful exposure of the body of a person who had died of any infectious disease was made penal; the powers of local boards of health to prevent the spread of infectious disease and to control the milk supply in their districts was extended and the closing of polluted wells rendered easier. The board regretted that the government had made no provision for sanitary inspection of dwellings before occupation, had not permitted the board to approve local appointments, and made no provision for preventing streams being polluted by water-closets.

By 1896 the necessary mapping for the drainage of Hobart had been done and, a report on sewerage recommending discharge into the sea at Macquarie Point having been completed in 1892, the board sought parliamentary approval to conduct the work, inserting into its request the information that 'fever' was most directly attributable to bad drainage.

But typhoid continued to lay low the population in certain areas, and in 1897 there were more cases than ever before, though fewer deaths than in 1891. The disease was particularly rife in mining areas and among hop-pickers where it raged as usual among those who seasonally migrated to the hopfields. Local boards of health were urged to make special measures concerning proper housing for the hop-pickers and especially to prevent the fouling of streams that flowed through or by the hopgrounds.

Some blamed infectious diseases on the disposal of nightsoil by the disgusting pan system, which merely transmitted germs. The Metropolitan Drainage Board in Hobart stated with all the emphasis at its command that typhoid would never be subdued except with a comprehensive drainage system, and produced figures from Munich and Sydney to show how appalling was the situation in Tasmania. As if to drive home the point, in 1898 the surgeon of HMS *Wallaroo* communicated with Hobart to enquire whether it was safe to permit his men ashore. The board that year gloomily noted the highest death rate in Tasmania since 1892, there having been nearly 2400 cases of infectious disease noted, by far the highest ever.

The melancholy bills of mortality revealed 125 deaths from phthisis, 99 from cancer and 53 from flu; there were 802 cases of typhoid reported of which 83 were fatal, measles 912 (45), scarlatina 550 (7) and diphtheria 98 (10). The death rate from measles was the highest since 1881, and half the flu cases were recorded in the largely rural northwest quarter alone. In the new mining settlement at Queenstown there were 24 cases of typhoid in 1899, lending point to the opening of a hospital there. Health authorities concluded that the source of disease was on the Conglomerate Creek (known as the Piggeries) because polluted water was drunk by the reckless or indifferent class of people who dwelt there.

During this period of the 1890s, Hobart continued to decline and Launceston to increase in population and importance. This was in part due to land settlement in the north-west and north-east. During the last twenty years of the century, attention was drawn more and more to settlement in the north-west, where a strong Wesleyan element congregated, and to the Huon Valley, where a high proportion of Catholics took up residence.

Of greater short-term importance in the development of the north was the mineral boom, embodied in the tin-mining industry, especially at Mount Bischoff, mining of coal at Fingal, and gold. New northern railways continued to be opened, frequently against the better judgment of professional railwaymen who correctly perceived that many such lines would never pay their way and were only laid down in response to 'development' without long-range analyses. But these changes in the structure of the colony's economy and pattern of settlement were dwarfed by mineral discoveries of world importance in one of the most inhospitable parts of the island.

This was signalled, up to a point, by the institution of the office of Inspector of Mines. G. Thureau's first official report revealed the wealth so characteristic of the mining industry and the presence of the soulless pirates who always hung about it. For instance, eight men were killed in mines in 1882, including one man who perished in a tin mine, leaving a wife and seven children. They received the sum of £10 in compensation. At that time, some 1500 men were working on auriferous fields and 2500 on the tin fields.

Then in 1885 Thureau reported on something new: at a place called Mount Zeehan (named by Matthew Flinders in 1799 after one of Tasman's ships in 1642) silver-lead deposits had been located. The same year it became known that gold was discovered at the King River and at a place named Mount Lyell, in the same area of the west. Ironically a year later the conservator of forests reported having been at Mount Lyell and its environs after pushing through the bush from Waratah. In describing the pine forests along the Pieman River and especially those of the Gordon, he stressed that these age-old stands of timber must for ever be carefully guarded against devastation by man because under a proper system of forestry management they would yield money in perpetuity.

Then about 200 miners were drawn to a spot named Linda in such desolate country that strong men were reduced to wrecks reaching the area where some copper was found but chiefly gold. That was in 1886.

The most notable discovery was one made by James Crotty, an Irish-born prospector who bought an interest in an outcrop called the Iron

Blow, found to be very rich in gold (and, unbeknown, in copper). By mid 1889, some thirty tons had been sent to New South Wales for treatment, but transport difficulties led to a lull in the working of the deposit.

At the same time further evidence of Tasmania's mineral wealth appeared with the discovery of a silver-bearing ore at Mount Dundas, seven miles north-east of Mount Zeehan, a field that excited very great attention and where some 16000 acres were marked off for lease. By 1890 the new boom town of Zeehan housed a population of 2500, and the mining industry had never presented so hopeful a prospect. The great silver discoveries led to more prospecting and fresh finds; capital poured in for investment in the mines, proposals for railways and harbour works, not to mention bold gas and electricity enterprises, and a government railway line from Strahan to Zeehan opened in 1892.

For a while it appeared that the entire west coast of the colony of Tasmania was composed of precious metals. Incredulous and credulous investors were only partly checked by the crash of the Bank of Van Diemen's Land. Money was squandered, inadequate machinery employed, and management conducted by incompetents. Confidence men swarmed on to the field or remained in the vicinity of the stock exchanges. Capital came from everywhere and immigrants from the stricken colony of Victoria, the economy of which lay in ruins after the dizzy splendours of the 1880s and the construction of Marvellous Melbourne had revealed the mixed blessing of land boomers.

In Mount Lyell and associated mines the colony had a source of dream-like wealth for those shrewd, able, diligent or unscrupulous enough to tap it. Assays of copper, gold and silver led the American Dr Edward Peters, one of the world's most eminent metallurgists, to report that in the past twenty years he had not seen a mining and metallurgical proposition that promised so certainly to be a great and enduring property. Bowes Kelly, the manager of the Mount Lyell Mining and Railway Company, was about to make a fortune (Crotty had already made one and left most of it to finish St Patrick's Cathedral, Melbourne): the immense outcrop of hematite called the Iron Blow, worked for gold until 1890 after being traced up the Linda Valley, was found to have a large mass of pyrites standing in close connection, and it was that which responded so richly to smelting for copper. This lode appeared to descend for ever into the earth and therefore appeared limitless in practical terms; the ore was double the richness of that found at the fabled Rio Tinto mine in Spain. For the year ending 1 July 1894, the value of mineral output in Tasmania was the highest in its history at a total of £707 000, with nearly 3500 people working in the mining industry. A survey of twenty-one miles of railway from Strahan to the mines commenced. By 1895 the Mount Lyell railway, from Teepookana to Queenstown, was approaching completion with rails laid and passengers and freight already being carried, and there was a light steam tramway from Zeehan going some sixteen miles into the Mount Reid country. At Zeehan, a School of Mines had been established by the miners themselves, and had forty-nine students with voluntary lecturers offering the earnest mining student such subjects as mineralogy, chemistry, assaying, mathematics, mine surveying, and mechanical drawing. A mining culture was suddenly established in a wilderness that had known only the nomadic Aborigines for thousands of years. El Dorado appeared in the most inhospitable part of the colony, and investors invested parliament with schemes to supply electric power and railways, and to be cut in on the apparent fortunes awaiting.

Almost ten years to the day after the Iron Blow was discovered, the Mount Lyell Railway was opened in 1896 and the treatment of Mount Lyell ores found to be a brilliant success. Total value of metals and minerals raised approached £1 million, out of which about £200 000 in dividends was paid exclusive of the first dividend of the Mount Lyell Mining and Railway Company. People and principles of sound government were trampled in the rush: the survey 'system' on the west coast silverfields was distinguished by applicants actually being permitted to employ their own surveyors to measure out Crown land. More significantly, the general manager of the Tasmanian Government Railways since March 1886, Frederick Back, counselled his political masters to be wary of overenthusiasm and rashness when it came to mines because, despite confident prediction, the general history of mining revealed that it was erratic and marked by a boom and bust cycle. He opposed sanctioning syndicate railways because they were detrimental to government railways and hence ultimately to all the people. He opposed fly-by-night mining entrepreneurs, some of whom had already distinguished themselves by floating bubble companies and were not above shooting fragments of gold into ore samples. Back repeatedly warned the government against sharing the common dementia and approving too many railways, and drew a parallel with overstocking a farm.

The main problem for the west coast mines was the lack of a suitable port. Macquarie Harbour was superb, but the bar at the entrance prevented any ships but the smallest from entering. Thus it was that in 1897 C. Napier Bell was called to report on the prospect of deepening the entrance through Hell's Gates, adequate for convicts in the 1820s but not for exporting minerals in quantity and importing heavy machinery. The next year Bell concluded a precise report and recommendations for the construction of training walls and breakwaters so that vessels of up to 3000 tons might be admitted—though he could do nothing about the tremendous storms that battered the coast. Citing work done at Galveston in Texas and at the mouth of the Danube, Bell offered an estimate of nearly £200000 to do the work. It was done.

In the financial year 1897–98, there was more legitimate mining activity in the colony than ever before. The amount of revenue was the largest since 1891, and the quantity of gold recovered turned out to be a record. More than 20 per cent of all mineral wealth came out of Mount Lyell, though there was a decrease in silver production when buildings, machinery, and mining plant were consumed in a bushfire during the summer of 1897–98. Some 4500 persons were by then engaged in mining, including a profitable tin mine at Lottah where electric light had been installed and an electric drill, probably the only one in Australia, was in use. The next year the number of miners had increased to more than 6000 as high prices for tin gave an impetus, so that the Tasmanian Dredging Company began active operations at Derby on the Ringarooma River.

At the end of the 1890s, few Tasmanians recognised the economy as having much relationship with that of twenty years earlier, save in the area of wool production and timber perhaps. By 1899, the population of the colony was 183000, compared with 101000 in 1870; imports were worth £1.8 million (£790000) and exports £2.6 million (£650000). The part of minerals in this was: blister copper, which amounted to £738000; tin, £278000; gold, £201000; silver ore, £162000. In other words, more than half the value of exports derived from four minerals.

Equally striking was the distribution of these exports: the city of Launceston exported practically the same amount as Hobart, with Strahan very close behind; similar proportions applied to imports between the two cities.

As Launceston became wealthier so its civic pride increased. Much was made in 1892 of the jubilee year of the foundation of the Mechanics' Institute in March 1842, and attention was freely drawn to the Institute and Public Library, as it was called, where in excess of 18000 volumes, with reading rooms, were available to the public, and other rooms widely used by the industrious. There had been fostered in the north a love of works of art and the wonders of nature, from which now sprang the Queen Victoria Museum and Art Gallery. The first annual report was presented in 1892, the whole splendid institution being opened by the governor in April 1891 in the presence of a large and brilliant assemblage. The subsequent conduct of visitors was noted as of the most exemplary character, as was only to be expected from the proud inhabitants of Launceston and its neighbourhood.

Buoyed up with enthusiasm in what Protestant zeal and enterprise might accomplish in the colony of Tasmania, northerners taking notice of proposals for the Melbourne Centennial Exhibition, promoted in 1885 a Launceston Exhibition also. Following this, and with a view to executing the proposal, the City Council was induced to undertake the erection of a hall in the City Park, to be named after the Queen's late consort, Prince Albert, at a cost of not less than £13000. A Juvenile Industrial Exhibition was considered not ambitious enough, and the scope was enlarged as Sir Edward Braddon, agent-general at the heart of the Empire, forwarded the work and secured exhibitors. Mr Jules Joubert's services were secured as director and then general manager early in 1891, and before it closed in March 1892, the exhibition was seen by no fewer than 262000 people. Children were encouraged to attend when offered nominal rail fares only. Lasting benefit of a moral, economic and ethical kind was thought to have been produced, despite the unfortunate onset of the depression.

In political terms the period of the 1890s was again distinguished by continual and persistent conflict between the two houses of parliament. In August 1892, the government of Fysh was defeated after five years at the helm, and Henry Dobson became premier. As had been the case since the inauguration of self-government in 1856, the differences on the issues of the day were essentially those of whether to balance the budget by imposing taxes and/or raising fresh money by the issue of debentures. As the franchise ensured that members of parliament would more nearly represent all the people, though by no means all, the Legislative Council became more alert to detect any measures that might affect the class they represented, should threatening bills get through the House of Assembly. The conduct of the Council continued to reveal that it was composed of men whose ancestors would have opposed the invention of the wheel. Not that it was alone in offering a shining example of anti-democratic ideology and practice: in 1895, 1553 people had 3853 votes in the House of Assembly by the plural voting system. Of these, 1 had twelve votes, 1 had eleven, 4 had nine, 156 had three and 1204 had two votes. In the Council, 735 voters accounted for 1682 votes; 1 had seven, 3 had six, 98 had three and 590 had two.

Still, it was a sign of the new liberal times that an act of 1891 made arrangements for payment of members of parliament, five years after a similar measure had finally been enacted in Victoria. A fixed sum of £100 a year was permitted for reimbursement in relation to attendance at parliament, but this was reduced to £75 in 1893 as a result of the depression. Members also possessed free railway passes and free travel in their constituencies by mail conveyances, together with postal privileges during sessions.

Dobson's ministry at once set out to increase taxes by imposing liens on income and land, mortgages and probate. The Council opposed all this, and the premier was granted a dissolution of parliament. All ministers were promptly re-elected, the premier and attorney-general without opposition. Sir Edward Braddon, late agent-general, now re-entered parliament and, when Dobson's taxing measures continued to be rejected, the government resigned and Braddon became premier. His government came to office in April 1894.

As the depression continued, the Council consented to pass a Land Tax Bill but in mid 1894 still set its face against other measures that sought to raise a revenue, although financial necessities were all against it finally succeeding.

Drastic retrenchment was all the government could offer as the colonial debt increased, and a serious question arose concerning the connection of the late Treasurer (John Henry) with the Mount Lyell Company and the premier with the Anchor Tin Mine Company. Braddon rode out the storm.

After this diversion, the Council continued to reject proposals for female suffrage but did at last come to a reluctant decision to permit a wider franchise for the House, though it struck out clauses that permitted the representation of minorities under the Hare system of counting votes by a species of proportional representation. However, it was finally agreed in 1896 at the instigation of Andrew Inglis Clark (a liberal who had a likeness of his hero Mazzini in every room) to redraw the boundaries of rural electorates, with one member of parliament each. Hobart was to be consolidated into one division of six members, to be elected by the new Hare system, with Launceston similarly made into a division returning four members, for one year to enable the new arrangements to have a trial. This complicated form of proportional representation was adopted throughout the state in 1907.

When ministers were returned, there were charges of improper conduct in relation to the mining industry, Braddon being accused of company-promoting when in England in 1896. Then Clark resigned from the government, though observers were not sure whether or not he had been made a scapegoat: his views were certainly at variance with those of his colleagues on the extension of railways. Clark became a member of the Opposition.

The economic tide continued to run strongly in Tasmania's favour as timber exports boomed and the production at Mount Lyell increased enormously with the new smelting process. To mark this, members of parliament restored their salaries to £100 a year, with ministers to receive £750, and some public servants who had been retrenched were replaced. Braddon announced his retirement because of ill-health: E. T. Miles, Minister for Lands and Works, and the premier were both pronounced to have been implicated in an improper tender for the Macquarie Harbour breakwater. Miles was forced to resign. The ministry of N. E. Lewis was sworn in, just in time to make arrangements for the colony's contribution to the prosecution of the Boer War.

Tasmania had long been deeply interested in intercolonial trade and reciprocity arrangements, owing to the lengthy period of economic depression and the colony's vulnerability to mainland tariffs. From 1883 it had been an enthusiastic member of the Federal Council, a body formed partly because of French and German presence in the south-west Pacific. Tasmania was particularly concerned, not least for historical reasons, about French transportation of convicts to the area. The Federal Council of recent years had accomplished little, however, except the provision of holidays for the delegates. Indeed, at the fourth meeting in January 1891, only Queensland, Victoria and Tasmania sent representatives.

In such areas as literature and sport, however, there was a growing sense of nationalism and, probably equally important, the realisation that a free trade zone was certainly in the interests of many colonists and business concerns. An Australian Economic Community was called for. The examples of unification in Germany and Italy appeared to illustrate that the formation of nation states was in the logic of history, and differing tariffs became a more significant irritant as the colonies grew and prospered and internal markets for secondary products assumed greater importance. With no executive power or revenue of its own, and no machinery to compel colonies to join, the Federal Council was not a great unifying force, but the impulse for federation gathered strength. It was given a most substantial boost by a report on defence prepared by Major General Sir Bevan Edwards, an imperial officer who did not mince matters. The armed forces of the colonies would do well to combine, he warned. His voice had the impact of authority and opinion emanating from the seat of the Empire in London, and it was heeded. Against this background, and with foreknowledge of Edwards' report, which was shortly to be released, Sir Henry Parkes at Tenterfield made a passionate plea for federation, and all colonies, including New Zealand, were impressed enough to send delegates to an Australasian conference at Melbourne in 1890. Tasmania was represented by Andrew Inglis Clark and B. Stafford Bird.

Clark was particularly important in the federation movement. A lawyer born in Hobart Town in 1848, he became deeply impressed by the American Constitution and republican ideals and was a Tasmanian delegate to the Federal Council from 1888. Then, before the Australian Convention summoned in 1891, he circulated to interested parties his own draft constitution bill, a document that greatly assisted to direct the thoughts of the drafting committee. Bird, the other Tasmanian, was an English-born Methodist clergyman and subsequently farmer, and was interested in finance. From 1894 to 1897 he was Speaker of the House of Assembly and treasurer from 1899 to 1903.

In 1891 a form of written constitution was hammered out, basically the one adopted as the Constitution of the Commonwealth of Australia. The colonies, however, found many difficulties in surrendering part of their independence, and the move to federation was impeded especially by the attitude of New South Wales, where Parkes was defeated in an election. Then in 1893 a conference at Corowa recommended that each of the colonies elect representatives by popular vote to forward the work of federation. Two years later, in Hobart, the premiers approved the Corowa resolutions and recommended that each colony elect ten representatives. The Tasmanians were P. O. Fysh, N. J. Brown, Adye Douglas, William Moore, Sir Edward Braddon, Neil Lewis, John Henry, Charles Grant, Henry Dobson and Matthew Clarke, all except Clarke members of the current government or the most recent one. Andrew Inglis Clark did not stand, and Bird was defeated.

All premiers and certain other colonists joined the elected men and a total of seventy-nine began their deliberations, sitting on and off for twelve months. A great deal of labour was spent on the compromise that would be necessary to prevent the two most populous colonies from utterly dominating the proposed union and to preserve as many colonial rights as was consistent with a wish for federation.

A popular vote on federation was taken on 3 June 1898, though Queensland stood aloof and so did Western Australia, recently catapulted by gold discoveries from a Crown colony to one enjoying self-government. The key colony was New South Wales, which reflected its seniority, economic independence and fear of losing sovereignty by laying down that at least 80000 voters must support a 'Yes' vote for it to be committed to a federation. This figure was not reached when 71595 voted for the federation and 68228 against.

On the other hand, Victoria and South Australia voted in favour of the proposal by majorities of five to one and two to one respectively. In Tasmania there was a huge majority of 11797 to 2716 in favour, nearly 50 per cent of electors on the roll casting a vote. Indeed, the 'Yes' votes amounted to no less than 81 per cent of formal votes. Of the twenty-nine electorates, twenty-five voted in favour of the federation, the four that did not being all in the Midlands or on the east coast. There was also a hefty 30 per cent 'No' vote from Hobart, in marked comparison to the high affirmative opinion of Launceston where no anti-federation meetings at all were reported. It may be that the influence of the *Mercury* was felt when it counselled caution until the financial implications were clarified, and B. S. Bird also voiced a doubt, producing statistics to show that Tasmania would lose financially under the proposed form of union.

The voice of labour as it found expression in the pages of the *Clipper* was similar to that of the *Bulletin* and the *Tocsin*, emphasising what was described as the undemocratic nature of the proposed federation in terms of the powers to be given to the Senate. But it was difficult to sway Tasmanians on the basis of such ideological considerations. It was not so difficult to cast doubt on the financial implications for the future, and it was urged that the contemplated tariff simply would not be adequate to return to the island a sum equal to that surrendered by passing control of customs and excise to a central authority. Even the enthusiastic federalist A. I. Clark was uneasy on the point and declined publicly to support the 'Yes' campaign, choosing to remain silent.

R. M. Johnston, the government statistician, was convinced that the new Tasmanian state would go broke if its income from customs duties and tariffs were removed, predicting that the people would be obliged to depend on federal largesse. It was pointed out that whereas Tasmania derived 44 per cent of its entire government income from duties levied on imports, New South Wales received only 17 per cent from that source, Victoria 31 per cent, South Australia 22 per cent and even Western Australia 38 per cent. In these circumstances it was feared that Tasmania would be forced to obtain from its residents a considerably larger amount by direct taxation than would be the case with other colonies.

As Johnston perceived the matter, the proposed financial arrangements would mean that the smaller states would be compelled to come cap in hand to the Federal Government for handouts, thus being reduced to beggars or poor relations in a federation that they were being told would shower down blessings upon them. He was right, but such fears were confused by a mass of differing tables of figures, and the plain man was rendered uncertain. The Australian Natives' Association and such as the Colonial Treasurer, P. O. Fysh, tried to allay concern by asserting that no one in his right mind should expect perfection in an imperfect world, and he pleaded for people to take the long view and be optimistic. To this note of sweet reason, Fysh added a telling point— if Tasmania refused to accept entry into the federation on the proffered terms of equality with other colonies, then it might be forced to accept less palatable terms later on. Tasmania was too small and insignificant in the Australian context to throw its weight about like New South Wales or demand changes to finance that had been arrived at only after tedious, complicated, and laborious exertions by the delegates and their advisers.

As was clear, the Australian colonies bore no resemblance to the American colonies represented at Philadelphia a century and more previously. There was no sense of Australia being powerfully propelled into nationhood, no sense of outraged urgency or arrogant imperial authority, no democratic ideology being debated, and certainly no sense of nationality sealed with the blood of martyrs. Whereas the American patriots began the document that enshrined their hopes with a ringing cry that all men were created equal and had certain inalienable rights, the Australian colonists began their document with three paragraphs humbly deferring to Great Britain and Queen Victoria.

When fewer than the required number of voters cast a 'Yes' ballot in New South Wales, it appeared that the federal cause had suffered a substantial setback, but this difficulty was quickly overcome. Most importantly, there was an election scheduled in the colony, and the fact that there had been a small overall majority in favour of federation called for political decision. After some consultations, the New South Wales premier Reid found himself able to recommend a new Enabling Act. On 20 June 1899 the crucial support of the voters of New South Wales was secured for federation, and when Western Australia threw in its lot with the other colonies, the final steps in the creation of the Commonwealth of Australia could be taken by the imperial parliament. In Tasmania, opposition to federation this second time round had dwindled to a tiny 791 votes.

As the voting revealed, it was unthinkable that Tasmania could or would stand aside from the federal movement. There were risks indeed, but they were uncertain and the subject of dispute among eminent authorities, whereas the advantages of being part of a larger whole would surely outweigh them. The final opinion of Tasmanians was summed up in the mixture of motive and metaphor expressed by a local orator who said that if the people of the island voted for federation they would establish a great and glorious nation under the bright Southern Cross and meat would be cheaper; that they would survive to see the day when the Australian race dominated the southern seas and at the same time have a market for their potatoes and apples; and that their sons would reap the grand heritage of nationhood.

There was still the prospect of the majority of Australians having the majority of votes in parliamentary elections, but this tyranny of the majority was diminished for Tasmania and the smaller colonies by the arrangements for a Senate which was to give each colony the same number of representatives no matter how huge or tiny it was. Alfred Deakin perceived that such a House would in practice represent not the states but party interests instead. However that would be, now fourteen houses of parliament were called into existence to govern fewer than four million people.

Thus was a price paid for the creation of the Commonwealth of Australia. It was without avail that some protested at the embodiment of essentially anti-democratic sentiments and a state of things designed to perpetuate conflicts and demarcation disputes and inefficiency as the result of conflict between state and federal authorities, with the taxpayer to meet the costs, feather the nests of constitutional lawyers and create a vast and overlapping bureaucracy.

5

Entanglement: 1901–18

Deep loyalty to the Empire in the case of Tasmania continued to flourish and was reinforced by the tiny size of the colony, its distance from the metropolitan authority and its consequent exposed position in the event of war. Periodic invasion scares had for almost a century galvanised the colonists into seeing to their defences, especially those of Hobart.

In June 1897 there came an opportunity to demonstrate fervent patriotism when celebrations of Queen Victoria's diamond jubilee occupied the greater part of a week. The mayor of Hobart presented commemoration medals to 5000 children who sang the national anthem, and in the afternoon gave a free dinner to the poor, an occasion of charity lent depth of purpose by the presence of the governor. At 10 p.m. at the Town Hall a huge crowd sang a hymn of praise at the precise hour of the thanksgiving service conducted in faraway St Paul's. The personal message from Her Majesty and the governor's loyal response was read out from the Town Hall balcony, and there was an outburst of cheers. To mark the great occasions, various charitable schemes were set on foot in deference to the known wishes of the old Queen.

For many years volunteer forces, small in number but enthusiastic, had carried on against government and public indifference, but there now emerged the first serious chance to give the wider world a palpable demonstration of the island colony's eagerness to leap into action should the Empire be threatened. The opportunity arose when war began between the Boer republics in South Africa and Britain in October 1899.

The move to war had been evident for some time, and four days before the outbreak and three days after Western Australia and South

Australia introduced legislation to send contingents, Tasmania also cabled offering colonial infantry. A bill was then passed through both houses of parliament upon the motion of Braddon, authorising the expenditure of £4500 on equipment for eighty men, a fine body of soldiers drawn from all parts of the colony. Commanding them was Captain Cyril Cameron, an experienced imperial soldier who, following the ever-glorious and historic march from Kabul, had been present at the relief of Kandahar under Lord Roberts.

Scenes of both impressive imperial sentiment and local pride were witnessed as the contingent prepared to depart from Tasmania. In Hobart the administrator, in addressing the men, stressed the proof offered of their devotion to Queen and Empire. He emphasised that England had been forced into a quarrel but that the insignificant authors of a turbulent rising could not yelp at the British flag without chastisement. The Queen's message was then read out to the respectful throng: 'Her Majesty the Queen desires to thank the people of Tasmania for their striking manifestation of loyalty and patriotism in their voluntary offer to send troops to cooperate with Her Majesty's Imperial Forces in maintaining her position and the rights of British subjects in South Africa. She wishes the troops God-speed and a safe return.'

Mrs Dodds, wife of the administrator, then presented a silver bugle to Captain Cameron. She said, 'It gives me great pleasure to present to you this silver bugle.' Members of the contingent were then marched to the Temperance Hall where a reception was given by the mayoress, Mrs J. G. Davies, assisted by the mayor (Lieutenant-Colonel C. E. Davies), in uniform, and Miss Davies. Among those present were several relatives of the men, some of whom were moved to tears. The recruits wore khaki uniforms. Mr T. Julian Haywood, the city organist, presided at the piano.

At the later Town Hall banquet toasts were drunk to 'Her Majesty the Queen' and 'the Contingent'. The crowd joined in singing the national anthem and 'Soldiers of the Queen'. Mr A. D. Watchorn rendered 'the Gallants of England' and the chorus from McKenzie's 'Jubilee Ode' was sung by the Philharmonic Society, under the baton of Mr Arundel Orchard. The men left for the barracks to the strains of 'Rule Britannia' and 'Auld Lang Syne'. On the 27th, the recruits left Launceston, the greatest enthusiasm prevailing both there and in Hobart.

Following the disasters of 'Black Week' in South Africa and the unexpected news that the Afrikaner forces were more formidable than had been supposed, a further contingent of forty-five men was organised to leave Tasmania in February 1900, selected from three times that number of volunteers. This contingent was followed by another in early March, a group necessarily quite untrained and undisciplined but capable of riding and shooting well.

Each morning, newspaper offices were surrounded by crowds seeking war news, and telegrams posted outside were eagerly read by all classes. Hobart was decked with flags to mark the British column entering Kimberley and the capture of General Cronje, but those manifestations of delight were completely overshadowed when Ladysmith was relieved. As the result of prior arrangement, the news was announced by firing five guns from the battery between 1 and 2 a.m., at which the population turned out and sang patriotic songs all the rest of the night. Next day there was a stirring demonstration at the Town Hall and a general holiday, with scarcely a person not wearing a tricolour badge or rosette.

The proposal from the mainland colonies to form a regiment of mounted infantry about a thousand strong, from all Australia, was responded to warmly in Tasmania, and fifty men and fifty-five horses embarked for the veldt. In December 1899 a patriotic fund opened and £7000 was collected. The ladies of the colony formed a Union Jack Society (President, Lady Gormanston) to send warm clothing and comforts to the men at the front.

The Boer War was marked by other exciting scenes than the embarkation of soldiers. In March 1900 James Paton stood for parliament, the first aspirant to come forward in the labour interest. He was editor and proprietor of the *Clipper*, judged by the governor as low-class and pro-Boer. Paton got W. A. Holman from New South Wales to lecture on the subject of the war in South Africa, with the newspaperman in the chair. But when Holman began to speak and to cast doubts on the lily-white motives of Britain, he was dragged from the platform by some of the audience and roughly handled while Paton took refuge under a table and then escaped. Paton withdrew from the parliamentary contest.

Although the relief of Mafeking was celebrated with enormous enthusiasm, the role of the Australian forces in Kitchener's campaign against the guerrillas, together with the confusion and shame caused by the execution of 'Breaker' Morant, removed much of the glitter that had marked the war in its early stages. Tasmanians, together with the fellow Australians in the new federation, were obliged to wait for the fulfilment of their lust for recognition as warriors and true-blue sons of the Empire on which the sun never set.

Still, the jam-makers Jones & Company and Moore & Company, of Hobart, secured sales (1.6 million tins) of their product to the British military forces through the enterprise of the agent-general in London, Alfred Dobson. Jam-making and fruit production began to go from strength to strength in the Edwardian era, though, after losing £4000 in one season, Messrs Knight & Company retired from business, and in 1912 W. D. Peacock recorded that Henry Jones himself was so discouraged that he offered to sell his interest in the trade to Peacock for £100, which that gentleman refused.

The growth and confidence of Tasmania was not really tested in the early years of the century, for general prosperity and the work of Braddon in the constitutional conventions led to Tasmania being sheltered from the impact of free trade by the introduction of section 87 ('Braddon's Blot') whereby three-quarters of the revenue from customs and excise was to be returned to the states for ten years.

Education of the young continued to be poor. Fees were paid on an irregular basis, the situation of many teachers was wretched in terms of income and conditions, the curricula were characterised by lack of imagination, and attendance at school was very low. There was an annual enrolment of 23 000 at the state schools, an average attendance of 17 000, and 3000 children of school age did not attend at all—so it was computed in 1899 when many schools were closed by epidemics. Even this was a doubtful figure because some children not attending state schools were claimed by their parents to be attending private schools, a fact that could not be really checked because such schools were not obliged to show inspectors anything except their formal registers. Income of teachers was principally (64 per cent) between £70 and £150, with 21 per cent on salaries between £150 and £300. Female teachers were on substantially lower salaries than men, and no women were in the £150 plus category, though sixty men were.

There also existed the practice of awarding exhibitions, begun in 1860 and continued for thirty-four years. These were tenable at private schools recognised by the Board of Education as 'superior schools', and there existed the belief or assurance that teachers were able and willing to educate exhibitioners up to the Associate of Arts degree. A problem with this system was that most candidates came from a very small minority of schools and that the offer of exhibitions was value-less as a stimulus to improvement in the work of schools generally. There were those educationists who argued that the money would be better spent on free primary education for all instead of free secondary education for the select few.

In 1900 there came the retirement of James Rule who had spend forty-four years as a Tasmanian teacher, inspector and then Director of Education, and forty of those years working unsuccessfully for the abolition of the school fees system. He was enabled to report that in the 1890s the number of schools increased from 240 to 309, gross enrolment from 18000 to 23000, expenditure from public funds from £33000 to £40000, and school fees from £10000 to £11000. Side by side with the colonial schools were 241 private ones, with an enrolment of about 9000 pupils, 4000 in Hobart and 3000 in Launceston.

But the abolition of fees was in the air, though B. Stafford Bird, treasurer in the Lewis ministry, warned that it would cost about £15000 in new taxation. Perhaps it was not worth it: a new inspector of schools in the early 1900s reported sourly that reading was too often taught in such a way that it led to a monotonous sing-song intonation; that history consisted usually of a string of dates and names of sovereigns, whereas a well-told story of a gallant deed or a description of doing of the Empire's great men in the brave old days of old was of infinitely more interest and service to the children than any bald record of events or columns of figures, while the flushed cheeks, kindling eyes, and rapt attention of his listeners would be a very sufficient reward to the teacher of history for his preparation; that in drill the children were well trained in a few cases, but in some instances the movement of the pupils being drilled presented a truly melancholy spectacle; but that in singing, even when little more than a hideous medley of sound was produced, the pupils appeared thoroughly to enjoy it.

By the end of 1900, teachers had their full salaries paid by the Education Department, with school fees collected and paid into the government revenue, and the educational standard of the teachers raised. Most importantly, in 1904 W. L. Neale, of the South Australian Education Department, was appointed to look into the entire system of primary education in the state and, following his report, he was appointed director. Neale's findings and recommendations ushered in reforms in classification of schools and teachers, increase of salaries, teacher training and school inspection, new school buildings and the introduction of a new curriculum and improved methods of teaching.

Then in 1906 an act was passed to register all schools and teachers, and as a result some interesting data were gathered on the private schools, the more disreputable of which were obliged to close their doors. To the astonishment of no one who studied the education of young Tasmanians, it was found that 36 per cent of all children aged between six and fourteen were not on any school roll. This was largely because city schools were perfectly inadequate and the compulsory attendance provided under the legislation was a farce. Strenuous efforts were subsequently made to enforce attendance at school.

The same year a training college was established at Hobart, complete with a scheme of scholarships to encourage those who might otherwise have been unable to advance themselves, and finally free education was achieved in 1908.

The regime of Neale led to a great deal of discontent among teachers, and a series of inquiries was instituted. The upshot of this was a 1909 report, which ventured to suggest that the administration of the department under Neale had been irregular and that Neale's lack of tact in dealing with some of his teachers had greatly irritated certain of their number. Some were convinced that teachers brought from South Australia received favoured treatment. Neale was praised for his high ideals, zeal, and untiring industry in bringing Tasmanian education into the twentieth century, but his services were dispensed with. Such was the fate of a reformer at the hands of his opponents and, it would appear, less than competent administrators.

New regulations, however, were framed, and more power in the way of promoting children from one grade to another was placed in the hands of the teacher and less in the hands of the inspector, who was relieved of the task of mark-giving. In 1911 the Philip Smith Training College for teachers, established through the generosity of a wealthy landholder, was opened in Hobart on the Domain, adjacent to the university, which had taken over the old Hobart High School buildings.

Then in 1913 state high schools were first established at Hobart and Launceston and courses organised for those who wished to go on to university, those who sought to teach, those who wished to take up a commercial career, those who would become tradesmen and those girls who required to be fitted for home duties, according to the custom of the time. Exams were conducted at the end of the second and

fourth year, and entrance to the high school provided for by a quali-
fying exam set by the Education Department, which in 1912 raised the
compulsory school-leaving age from thirteen to fourteen years.

In 1915 arrangements were made for junior and senior bursaries to
be awarded, with special attention paid to children who dwelt in the
country, and at the same time two more high schools, to the inter-
mediate level, were established at Burnie and Devonport. In 1918, a
Technical Education branch took over the conduct of all technical
schools and schools of mines.

When federation was accomplished in 1901, the government of
Tasmania was in the hands of N. E. Lewis's administration, the Braddon ministry having fallen after the shocks of the Strahan Marine Board
scandals. If there was a prevailing political ideology in the new state, it
was not easily to be distinguished from a general 'for the good of the
colony' vagueness, which was invoked when seeking votes in terms
of 'development'. A form of confused liberalism, however, had emerged,
and there was also the beginning of a labour form of liberalism. Tasmanians were well aware of political developments elsewhere, especially in Victoria, but the trade union movement in the island was
small both in numbers and in impact, not least because the west coast
mining boom was geographically utterly isolated from the other main
centres of population in the state; the area of mining population was in
fact as readily accessible by sea from Victoria as from Hobart. Most
importantly, the Legislative Council continued to exist basically unre-
formed, unrepentant, and unyielding to criticism. The fact that it did
not represent the people of the state as a whole was regarded by the
Council as a virtue and as a powerful argument for its supreme political power. Its continued flaunting of control of the legislative process
for the sake of 'interests' remained a permanent problem to every member of the House of Assembly, even if he were elected from constituencies that did not include all adults. This was corrected when, as
one result of federation and its franchise, women received the vote.
The powerful presence of the Council was and continued to be one
of the most important political factors in Tasmania. But there was
another.

This was the rise of the labour movement and the establishment of
a Labor Party. In 1900, James Paton of the *Clipper*, launched in 1893,
had stood in the general interests of labour for the Democratic League
but was obliged to withdraw after the physical attacks on himself and

Holman and accusations by an angry *Mercury* that he was not loyal. This was enough in a period when the theatre put on *British Born* and *Briton or Boer,* when local horses were named 'Bobs', after Lord Roberts, and 'Britisher', and the Tasmanian soldiers at the front identified as 'Tommies'. To support labour in any form was essentially anti-British during the Boer War, with the *Clipper* offering biting sarcasm about the visit of royalty in 1901. For the people of a free democracy there was a galling nameless insult in the gaze of a typical British aristocrat, perceived the paper, and in the splendour of that gaze Hobart snobs, it was observed, grovelled happily all the week.

The election of the colourful King O'Malley to federal parliament for an electorate dominated by west coast miners revealed that much might be done by labour forces, though the level of commitment to 'Labour' by miners was marginal and the coherence of O'Malley that of a shrewd showman. He was a master of publicity stunts and said to have held the largest meeting ever seen in the important silver town of Zeehan in 1901. He allegedly sued a Launceston clergyman when an earthquake, prayed for to teach sinners in the congregation a lesson, actually eventuated, and was also said to have put up the Earth for sale. He variously offered to run the Australian Capital Territory, a ministry of insurance, the Commonwealth Bank (with or without pay) until it was properly started, Australia's defences in preference to importing British officers, and the British Empire. He also observed that parliament was the only institution in the country operated by unskilled labour and stated that all the powers-that-be in Tasmania were corrupt. This sort of thing went down very well in some quarters, and O'Malley naturally attracted supporters.

Following the federal elections, the interests of labour received a certain amount of stimulation, especially on the west coast. A Political Labour League was formed, and when Lewis's ministry was defeated after it too tried to introduce income tax, three Labor candidates were successful. These were J. J. Long (Lyell), G. M. Burns (Queenstown) and W. Lamerton (Zeehan). Crosby Gilmore (Waratah) supported Labor but not the Labor pledge. As one result, the Mount Lyell Company sacked Long for daring to be political to the point of winning a seat in parliament, and did not look favourably on other Labor men.

An important factor in arousing the voters to a consciousness of the labour interest was the *Clipper,* taken over by W. A. Woods after Paton was ruined by libel cases, and dedicated to the political education of

Tasmanians, especially in relation to the land monopolies said to sustain sinister reactionary forces. The 1903 election could not be regarded as a triumph for Labor. The association between the Labor members and the trade union movement, such as it was, remained equivocal and uncertain, and the election was in fact a great victory for W. B. Propsting, who became premier in April. He had offered a liberal program, which, as elsewhere in Australia, included many of the points advocated by Labor, such as old-age pensions, land value taxation, and compulsory purchase by the government of certain large properties for closer settlement.

The cry was often heard that Tasmania could never advance until such old estates, thought frequently to have been granted to magnates in the convict era, were purchased and 'developed'. The *Clipper* especially said this, giving space to the ideas of A. J. Ogilvy who tirelessly argued for land taxes and land resumption but to no avail while the Legislative Council remained *in situ*. In parliament, when Woods moved for the Council's abolition, only the Labor men supported him, the Liberals shrinking from taking such a radical step.

Propsting's administration survived barely twelve months because he was at once confronted with an antagonistic Council, which regarded him and his program as wicked, evil, and immoral. Defeated, he was succeeded by J. W. Evans, Propsting himself securing a seat in the Council and then, to cap it all, becoming a minister in Evans's government. As the *Daily Post* commented brightly, when the faithful clubbed together to send Propsting as a missionary to the Legislative Council to convert and reform, it would have been wiser had they simply clubbed Propsting. It is difficult to imagine a more telling example of the political scene among non-Labor groups in the state.

Subsequently the Liberals and Labor tended to run in double harness, as at the federal level, but Labor's task of educating the people to vote for it went forward at snail's pace; in 1905, Labor supporters were estimated at 2000 only and trade unionists at merely 1500. In these circumstances, the work of the controversial and radical Anglican bishop J. E. Mercer and the ex-Presbyterian cleric John Palamountain became important as did the visits of mainland Labor men such as J. C. Watson, W. G. Spence, and Frank Anstey, who conducted consciousness-raising sessions.

In 1906, seven Labor men were successful in a House of thirty-five and began to trouble such supporters of caution as the *Mercury*. The extraordinary conduct of Propsting did great harm to the Liberal cause, and the workers began to consider that support for Labor was quite possibly in their interests. Leader of the party was John Earle, whose power base on the west coast was broader than that of the more intellectual Woods, about whom there clung an odour of scandal: he was not Tasmanian-born, he had travelled a lot, he had changed his name, and he was suspected of embezzlement. In addition, Earle was supported by a coterie of able men centred on L. F. Giblin. Their influence may have been decisive. Others thought it fatal to the development of an intellectually adventurous Labor ideology. The *Clipper* was most important in Tasmania: it was the only paper to foster a working-class sense of identity, to try to reach out to the small farmers, and to urge women to vote Labor. At a time when the *Mercury* omitted or misreported Labor news, the *Clipper* gave information on the franchise, reminded people to enrol, raised funds, and so on.

In 1909, J. A. Lyons was first elected to state parliament for the House, after being a teacher irritated by the administration of Neale's Education Department, and was one of twelve Labor men in a House of thirty members (reduced from thirty-five), elected under the Hare–Clarke system and composed of five six-member electorates. Labor had won two out of six seats in every electorate except Darwin, which included the west coast, where it won four.

Among those prominent in the onslaught on Neale had been N. K. Ewing, a very able and ambitious lawyer who represented the teachers, and his political objects were temporarily satisfied when his election to the House in 1909 led to the defeat of the Evans government at the hands of an alliance between Labor and a Liberal League—but when Earle became Labor premier, his opponents realised what they had done and brought him down, so that Lewis was reinstated and Labor cast back from whence it had so impertinently arisen.

Woods and David Balchen commenced to form the Workers' Political League in 1907, while Woods remained editor of the *Clipper*, and the party continued to gain strength in Tasmania as it did on the mainland and to represent a wider cross-section of the people. The admirably cheeky *Clipper*, sustaining a lethal blow by losing a libel action, was replaced in 1910 by the *Daily Post* as the voice of labour; the latter secured the services of Edmund Dwyer-Gray, member of a distinguished Irish literary family associated with the Dublin *Freeman's Journal* and Parnell. Under Dwyer-Gray, the *Daily Post* perceived socialism as the peak of human progress, Tasmania having only reached a stage somewhere between feudalism and wage slavery. Dwyer-Gray regarded the Legislative Council not so much as a lion in the path of progress as a stuffed donkey. This body, said the *Daily Post* bravely, regarded Tasmania's colonial constitution as if it were a revelation brought down from Mount Wellington by a modern Moses.

But the socialist objective of Labor was not adopted in Tasmania, partly as a result of the pragmatism of the Australian Workers' Union, partly because Tasmanian workers had been cowed, defeated, and knocked about for so long at the hands of their strong opponents, because industrial trade unionism lacked the cutting edge of ideology it received elsewhere, and partly because intellectual Labor men such as Giblin and W. E. Shoobridge were really more liberal than anything else.

The federal election of 1910 put Labor into office at the national level and was a huge encouragement to the movement in Tasmania. It was only a question of time, exulted supporters, before Tasmania had a viable Labor government. This was aided by the establishment of wages boards in 1910 and, the same year, a carters' and drivers' strike that paralysed Hobart, when the men struck work for £2 instead of £1.10s. for a 56-hour week.

Under the Hare–Clark system of voting, in 1912 Labor secured fourteen of the thirty seats in the House of Assembly. Labor publicists maintained that every kind of lie had been told about Labor and thousands of pounds spent by the anti-Labor forces to keep the party out of office.

Labor's accession to power in the House finally came in 1914 in a curious way and was largely the result of potatoes. One J. T. H. Whitsitt defected from the Solomon Government because he was not satisfied that enough had been done to induce mainland states, fearing the Irish blight, to accept Tasmanian potatoes; in 1911 nearly all crops of the old Redskin variety were destroyed and replaced by the blight-resistant Brownell for export to New South Wales. At the same time as the eccentric Irishman Whitsitt stood by the potato, a by-election in Denison was won by Labor and it secured office, although the governor did his level best to place conditions on the appointment of Earle as premier and was subsequently rebuked by London.

Thus Labor, with Woods as Speaker, depended on Whitsitt and, of course, had no representative in the Legislative Council, the members of which could thereby claim that when they annihilated Labor bills they were dutifully reflecting the equivocal claim the party had to the House of Assembly.

The new government was not in power and gravely hindered in office. Nevertheless, it managed some quite important reforms. Earle, earlier denounced as pro-Boer and blacklisted by some mine managers, soon followed the path of Hughes and Holman and was drawn further by the tentacles of respectability and responsibility to the Right. It was a measure of this that the *Mercury* likened his policy speech in July 1914 to that of a Liberal, an unassailable argument that Earle had parted company with Labor ideology as it has been perceived by such as the *Clipper* and *Daily Post*. Earle struck a note frequently to be heard from Labor in Tasmania: he spoke heavily of 'justice' for all sections of the community, without considering that some sections might already have their share and more.

W. H. Lee became Liberal leader in 1915, and during that year and 1916 the question of conscription for the war became ever hotter with the conduct of the Prime Minister, W. M. Hughes, in England and, probably most importantly of all, the catastrophic losses sustained by the AIF at Fromelles and on the Somme during that dreadful (northern) summer when the Australian infantry was chopped to pieces in the onsets launched by Haig and resisted to the last foot by the German army. Some 27 000 Australian soldiers were lost on three miles of ridge east of Amiens in about ten weeks, the ground was literally soaked with the blood of sons of the Empire, and Australia began to bleed to death. So it was that a struggle beyond imagination was to lead to the destruction of the Labor Party in Australia. When W. M. Hughes agreed to ask the people whether or not they wanted conscription for overseas service, he virtually single-handedly tore down the party he had done so much to construct, revealing the strength of his attachment to the Empire and the weakness of his association with those in the Labor Party who had grave reservations about Hughes and his cronies.

But meanwhile, in the first year of the war in Europe, the party did well enough in Tasmania. All that could be done was done to succour the mining industry, which had been so dependent on German markets; Ewing, leader of the Liberals at the time, undertook to offer all reasonable support to the government in the crisis. The Legislative Council, however, reacted sharply when Labor sought to take action against war profiteers and threw out no fewer than seven bills passed by the House. Then Labor failed to make headway in by-elections, and the Council took a savage axe to a Lyons budget when the treasurer attempted to redistribute wealth along the lines pioneered by Lloyd George in England. Earle upset many when he refused to grant preference for trade union members on the grounds that it was sectional, and the labour movement began to split, as elsewhere in Australia, on the subject of Labor policy versus the defeat of Germany—as if the one could not be accomplished without the other. A proposed truce with the Liberals came to nothing, and in the election of 1916 the Liberals won narrowly because Labor had been unable to deliver and had been seen to shilly-shally.

One of the most significant things done during the first year of the war was the government's takeover of the production of hydro-electricity. In 1891 the sudden prospect of substantial mining development on the west coast, especially that related to the silver discoveries at Mount Zeehan, induced John Coates & Company of Melbourne to look into the construction of gas and electric works, and at the same time, by the Australasian Rights Purchase Bill, electric works were foreshadowed on and near the Henty River, on the west coast. The Australasian Rights Purchase Association was then taken over by the Tasmanian Water Power Electric Company in 1892, which in turn let a contract for a track to be cut from Zeehan to the Pieman, but it took too long and there was a dispute.

In 1895 it was proposed to erect works at a spot near the junction of the Pieman and Heemskirk rivers, to generate electricity to supply light and power to Zeehan, the falls for motive power being 150 feet high. But it was predicted that there would be difficulties in the summer unless storage reservoirs were built, and so the scheme was abandoned, though a fine waterpower was obtainable there. The same year, a Hobart Gas Company Electric Light Bill was canvassed, with interested part̶i̶e̶s̶ ̶c̶i̶t̶i̶ng examples from North America and Europe.

The great attraction for persons interested in supplying electric power was Zeehan, where in 1896 there was recorded a proposal to erect steam works to supply electricity, the people becoming irritated by being forced to use kerosene. More than that, the cost of firewood for the boilers at the Silver Queen mine nearly doubled to supply the power needed for light, pumps and the town, which had at least nineteen hotels, it was asserted, of which Clarke's boasted sixty or seventy rooms. Meanwhile electricity was being harnessed at the Lottah tin mines, near the Blue Tier, in the north-east, but the original Zeehan scheme came to nothing at that time.

In these circumstances, a Zeehan Electric Light and Power Bill (1898) was canvassed with P. J. E. Fowler, a newspaper proprietor, the leading light as it were. There was by then an electric plant at the Silver Queen mine, and Fowler proposed to generate electricity by steam and was strongly supported by A. Morrisby, chairman of the town board. He drew attention to the dark and hazardous state of the streets and the danger of kerosene causing fires, so that insurance rates ran as high as £5 per £100, with 600 cases of kerosene consumed every month. By 1900 the Zeehan Electric Light and Power Company had a lease for its site and commenced construction of a station building, and soon Zeehan became the first town outside Launceston and Hobart to have electricity.

In 1895 the energetic northern city characteristically took the initiative and became the first city in the Southern Hemisphere to be connected with the new electric light: Launceston City Council harnessed the waters of the South Esk in December 1895 and generated 600 horsepower at the Duck Reach power station, with arc lamps studding the principal streets. In 1911 the Hydro-Electric and Metallurgical Company at the Great Lake started works to generate power at Waddamana for the treatment of ores by electrolytic methods, and three years later these assets were bought by the state when a bill was passed in August 1914. Thus came into being the Hydro-Electric Department, which by 1916 had installed generators at Waddamana to create power for domestic lighting and trams in Hobart. After nearly five years, then, the Great Lake power scheme came into operation, with Mount Lyell ready to take its 20000 horsepower within eighteen months.

At the same time as these technological changes were ushering Tasmania into the twentieth century, however, the system of alliances constructed in Europe and the nationalistic ambitions of parts of the Austro-Hungarian Empire proved a fatal combination. When Germany invaded Belgium in an attempt to neutralise or defeat France, Britain was drawn into the continental conflict, and the arrival of Armageddon was signalled on 4 August 1914 when war was declared.

The outbreak of the Great War was greeted in Tasmania, as elsewhere in Australia, with protestations of loyalty to Britain and the Empire, as had been the case with the outbreak of the Boer War. But in the Edwardian period a considerable amount of material was produced to make Germans offensive to true-blue Britons; the Kaiser had upset Britain by his attitude to the Boer conflict and generally Germany was recognised as an economic rival to the British Empire. Thus people with names that might be of German origin were at once persecuted, and Tasmania no less than anywhere else offered abundant evidence for a study of the pathology of racism. This was made worse by the distress in the mines and outcries from people who earned a living trapping wallabies, rabbits and so on because one of their markets had been Leipzig, now cut off.

In 1916 the question was decided of whether the hotels should close at 6 p.m. or 10 p.m. (the government had already reduced closing time from 11.30 p.m. to 10 p.m.), the drink question to be resolved by conducting a plebiscite (mistakenly termed a 'referendum'). The case for moderation, if not prohibition, was immeasurably strengthened by the sobering news that His Majesty the King had let it be known he would abstain from alcoholic liquor, except for medicinal purposes, for the duration of the war. The conflict was obviously serious and the point was underlined further, were that possible, when the staff of the University of Melbourne also stated they would abstain.

The Tasmanians voted for 6 o'clock closing, the liquor trade finding it very difficult to muster a good argument against the King. This vote was conducted at the same time as the state election in which Labor was defeated, and it was a measure of the political differences perceived between Labor under Earle and the Liberals that some paid more attention to the liquor question than to the election.

A month later the first Anzac Day was commemorated in Tasmania with enormous emotion, as elsewhere in Australia and in London. Imperial feeling and Australian patriotic sentiment existing easily within it reached the heights. Australia had been blooded. Australia had been tried and not found wanting. All the world looked up to the effortless mighty endeavour and contempt for all odds displayed by the Anzac soldiers at the Dardanelles. Further to mark the day, men of the newly raised and all-Tasmanian 40th battalion marched to a reception as emotional as that offered to the 12th—which had covered itself with glory at Gallipoli, and included many Tasmanians in its ranks.

When Hughes decided to put the case for conscription to the people at a plebiscite in 1916, being unable to get legislation through the Labor-dominated Senate, he set fire to a fuse that blew the Labor Party to smithereens. In Tasmania, Earle had first of all opposed conscription but, after conferring with Hughes in Melbourne, he changed his mind. This *volte-face* had the effect of confirming the trade union movement's worst suspicions about their leader and his attachment to the ideals of the party. Earle's actions also had the effect of bringing the industrial and parliamentary wings of the movement together when it appeared a split was possible.

Conscription meetings were marked with violence, frequently caused by men in uniform attacking anti-conscriptionists. Censorship prevented full reports from being published, though the *Daily Post* was one of the few, if not the only, daily in the nation to hammer the conscriptionists. Such purveyors of news as the *Mercury* filled the role of dutiful propaganda sheets for those who wanted conscription and opposed Labor.

Frank Anstey made guest appearances and created great uproar when he continued to allege that Hughes had made a deal to import foreign labour if conscription was approved. Hughes himself attracted huge crowds for his memorable performances, simplifying the case to one in which all who dared to vote against conscription were traitors or worse. The highly emotional state of the people was exacerbated by the constant casualty lists from France and the suggestion from such as the *Mercury* that German money was being used to help the anti-conscriptionists. Not least, no Irish Catholic leader strongly opposed conscription in Tasmania, and indeed the eloquent and flamboyant Father T. J. O'Donnell very actively supported it. When a bomb was exploded at a conscription meeting at Beaconsfield in October, it was stated that clearly only an anti-conscriptionist would detonate such a fiendish device, though, curiously enough, no one was ever charged with any offence.

In Tasmania as elsewhere the Germans were portrayed in cartoons as unspeakable savages; every useful prejudice was called up and, despite Hughes's numerous tactical blunders, such as enrolling men for home service, loyal Tasmania revealed the depth of its feelings by voting strongly in favour of conscription—49 493 to 37 833. The conscription vote included the strongly Labor west coast, but here the popular hero King O'Malley had remained silent on the issue and Earle, the local boy made good, favoured it, revealing the extent of patriotism in the mining community. It was of great significance, in terms of attitudes to the war, however, that the largely rural electorate of Franklin came closest to voting 'No'. This lends great strength to the argument that country people feared further labour shortages if conscription were introduced. But the vote was such that indeed the fruitful question is: why did so many vote in favour of conscription?

Joseph Lyons became state parliamentary leader of Labor when Earle resigned and shortly confronted the problems of a general election when Hughes's Labor defectors plus the Liberals combined to inflict a crushing defeat on Labor in 1917; the party so recently in office in Tasmania won no seats in any of the Tasmanian electorates for the House of Representatives and no seats in the Senate. Even the crafty King O'Malley was defeated, but his opponent did drop dead only five days afterwards; he was succeeded by W. G. Spence, the great trade union organiser of yesteryear, though the Tasmanians were loath to vote for an absentee and ex-Labor man. Successive by-elections confirmed the triumph of the anti-Labor forces in 1917, and the crushing of the General Strike that same year by hunger and employment of 'loyalists' brought Labor to the lowest ebb ever in its short history in the island state.

The situation in Russia and the slaughter on the Western Front in 1917 induced Hughes to try again for conscription, but he lost allies by suddenly closing the electoral rolls as if afraid to permit the people to enrol, disfranchising people of German origin and changing polling day from a Saturday to a Thursday for the first time ever. People became more suspicious of Hughes' authoritarian proclivites. The 'No' vote in Tasmania was directed by a youthful Labor man named Robert Cosgrove and much made of the treatment dished out to conscientious objectors in New Zealand, where conscription had been adopted. Tasmanians rather tended to look to New Zealand, as fellow islanders, as fellow high-loyalists, and as a people who could teach Tasmanians a few tricks about farming.

The campaign this time was marked by the *Mercury's* tirade against Catholics, helped along by the Easter Rising of 1916 and encouraged by the suspicion of isolated Protestant Tasmanians of a religious group that worshipped in a foreign language and therefore could not possibly be true-blue despite the sudden enlistment in the AIF of Father O'Donnell, after an emotional speaking campaign in favour of conscription. The mood was changing though: now increasing numbers of returned soldiers actually went on to the platform to denounce conscription. Women became more active in the campaign, and when the day of voting came on 20 December, Tasmania voted 38 881 in favour and 38502 against. This was amazing, for some 10000 people who voted in 1916 had not voted in 1917 at all, revealing reservations about Hughes, and a majority of more than 10000 shrunk to 379. There were those observers who saw the hand of the *Daily Post* and Dwyer-Gray in this result, for the arguments from that quarter had been dignified and reasonable throughout, in marked contrast to the eldritch screeches of other newspapers. Again the central and south rural areas of the state tended to vote against conscription more than some would have judged from their political flavour. The west coast swung back towards the 'No' position.

The war appeared likely to go on forever. By the end of 1917, Tasmania had enlisted 14205 men. New sectarianism emerged as patriots sought for a scapegoat, and a Loyalty League was formed to root out undesirables, first in Launceston. It flourished along the north-west coast where there was a very high percentage of Methodists, perhaps the highest in Australia. They were especially distrustful of Catholics perhaps because Wesley's undemonstrative religious services, as they had developed by the early twentieth century, found Roman ritual particularly offensive and unpalatable. More than that, however, it was the loyalty of distant and vulnerable Tasmania to the Empire that sharpened the sense of threat, real or imagined, from the Catholics, the age-old enemy of Protestant England—and Catholic was identified with Ireland, that springboard from which the Old Country's enemies on continental Europe had ever sought to launch themselves on Protestant England. Every schoolchild in Tasmania knew the stirring story of Good Queen Elizabeth, Sir Francis Drake and the defeat of Catholic Spain.

With the ending of the war, anti-German feeling burst out again even in victory—especially in victory—with the demand for punitive indemnities from Germany, held to be the true cause of all the misery and the deaths of so many Tasmanian boys. There was a fight in the lobby of parliament between H. J. Payne and G. C. Becker, the former sneering at the latter as 'Herr' Becker. Tasmanians of German origin suffered silently and continued to do so all their lives.

The survivors and heroes of the glorious AIF began to arrive home to hysterical welcomes from the people and very slow administration by the Repatriation Department (which should properly have been named the Rehabilitation Department). Unemployment increased, and the Returned Soldiers' and Sailors' Imperial League of Australia, knowing the physical and moral strength it mustered, left no doubt it would fight for soldiers' rights of employment. By October 1919 it had 7000 members, some of whom terrorised Labor speakers to such an extent that Launceston City Council refused permission for open-air political meetings. Loyalty to England and the Empire was never so high and implacable opposition never so great towards anyone who thought the war not right and spoke in favour of anything un-British. In this paranoid atmosphere the Loyalty League flourished as it extended its perception of the threat of Catholicism and Sin Fein to the threat of everything and anything thought currently or at some time in the future to threaten the Anglo-Saxon Protestant ideal.

In 1919 Labor was defeated shatteringly and appeared to be down for the count because, in seeking to win back its erstwhile supporters, the party stranded itself between Left and Right and appeared nothing to everybody. In these dark days of defeat, Labor's first premier John Earle found it within his saddened soul to liken his former party mates to whipped curs howling in the night. The Great War had accomplished some terrible things.

One thing the Great War did was to create an elite of returned men in the society, their quality of heroism emphasised every Anzac Day, their superior manliness and status exemplified by soldier preference in employment. But for most people the immediate effect of the war was the most obvious one: about 13000 sons of the state embarked for the war and nearly 2500 were killed. The losses the people were called upon to bear were never to be forgotten. On many a plain living-room wall there had appeared the strange dignity of still photographs of men in uniform who, it was stated in writing, had fought for God, King, and country—and who did not come back to the plains and bush, the paddocks and the streets of their beloved island. Men who had never handled anything but an axe had learnt to handle a rifle and did not return. Those who did survive were frequently never the same men again: some became drunkards, some became steady and swore the Great War was the best thing that ever happened to them; some knocked their wives about and committed terrible crimes; some returned to their employment as if nothing had happened to them and thought little of medals and glowing testimonials in Bean's *Official History of Australia in the Great War;* some who had gone into the Somme at the age of sixteen and seen and done things they could not begin to imagine, returned to a shiftless life and, like so many others, migrated interstate and joined the 6th Division in 1939.

On King Island there had been a population of 1000 people, and 63 men enlisted and 8 were killed; from Ulverstone's total population of 2000, 243 men joined the AIF and 55 were killed; at the nearby township of Penguin, 107 men enlisted from a population of 1120 and 26 did not return; from the mining centre of Queenstown, 300 men enlisted from a total population of 3700 and 55 were killed. Somewhere between a third and half of all eligible men in Tasmania enlisted in the AIF.

Far from home had the heroes been slain. The gratification of a family funeral, so important in that era, was denied their next of kin so that Anzac Day became a time of annual mass obsequies to compensate, the service conducted at the closed grave of the local war memorial. Perhaps there was a sinking feeling that the boys of Tasmania perished and fought for less than worthy objects ... but that was an unthinkable thought, and the Anzac legend and tradition was firmly fixed in place as a sort of defence mechanism. No relatives had gazed on the face of the fallen, as had the kings and clan chiefs of their distant forebears so that those responsible might ponder on their conduct in causing such death and pain. Few if any Tasmanian next of kin would ever manage the journey to the other side of the world to see the grave of the soldier. There remained in the memory of many grieving Tasmanians only the sounds of the distant marching, only the shouts of a vanished army.

6

Distress: 1918–39

When the Earle Labor Government was defeated in 1916, Walter Lee became premier. As elsewhere in Australia, the Labor Party was disheartened by what appeared to be the collapse of reason among the working classes of the world who had not paused to join the rival armies in what some Labor men believed to be a trade conflict in which the working class would fight, bleed and die for the increasing profits of arms manufacturers and others who would do well out of the war. In Tasmania the party was also downcast thanks to the upheaval of the 1916 conscription plebiscite and the Australia-wide destruction it had wrought among Labor supporters, not least being the apostasy of Earle.

In 1919 Lee's Nationalists, as they were now christened, won the state election, the same year as the men of the AIF began returning and the island was smitten by the Spanish influenza pandemic. Fortunately it struck the island late in the winter when people's resistance was improving; the dispersed character of the population of Tasmania also evidently made the spread of the infection more difficult for the deadly virus. Many efforts were made to prevent the flu, including sealing off the island insofar as was possible and greatly inconveniencing tourists, imposing quarantine, and using cotton masks, which were about as useful as using barbed-wire fences to keep out mosquitoes. Medical science did not know what to do about the flu, and the disease created great alarm in Tasmania as elsewhere in Australia.

The government was concerned about the outbreak and deaths and signs of panic: the face of the victim was apt to become discoloured, and the horrifying ghost of Black Death walked again among the more credulous. An emergency committee was appointed, and all Hobart divided into thirteen districts, each supervised by a clergyman who visited every dwelling to report on the needs of those suffering from the flu. But this led to an unexpected finding because the visitors seeking to succour the victims of the pandemic found evidence of living conditions so appalling as to be unbelievable.

So alarmed was the Rev. H. E. Hobday that he persuaded a reporter from the *Mercury* to accompany him on his rounds, and there was published a series of articles that shocked the respectable. 'In Darkest Hobart' was the title of the stories, printed in September 1919. Therein were described hovels worse than any in the East End of London where rents were high and ceilings low, families large and rooms small, the floors eaten by rats and walls swarming with bugs. Several of these disgraceful dwellings were discovered to be owned by those described delicately as 'public men'. Such a place in Argyle Street consisted of one room divided into three, with no fireplace except in the tiny kitchen. In the centre 'room' a married couple and their five children were all recovering from three weeks' illness caused by the flu. The investigators found widespread unemployment and undernourishment beneath their very noses.

In parliament the radical David Dicker, who had been persecuted during the war because two visiting actresses said they heard him say something that might prejudice recruiting, observed that wealthy men in Hobart were now taking action to clean up sources of ill-health because they were afraid they too might fall victim to the flu. Certainly a homes bill to make provision for the construction of houses and advances of loans for approved building was passed as investigators stressed the necessity for reform, but as the crisis subsided few fundamental changes were made.

The return of the first members of the AIF to be discharged led to what became known as the soldier settlement scheme. Early in 1916 a national meeting in Melbourne decided with enthusiasm that returned heroes should be settled on the land, a step in line with pre-war concern about closer settlement and reduction of large estates. In November the Lee Government introduced such legislation. Some members of parliament who knew the difficulties of farming and whose judgment was not clouded by feverish patriotism were doubtful about such a plan, but pride in the AIF, continued recruiting drives that necessarily elevated the volunteer soldier as a hero, and the premier's natural impatience all combined to encourage the idea. An impulse as least as ancient as Alexander's and Caesar's settlement of their demobilised warriors on the land emerged in the form of a statement that any Tasmanian who returned from the front line would be given free a piece of the precious island he had been fighting to defend from the Kaiser's ambition. The fantasy of the sturdy yeoman, and the idyll of the good life to be enjoyed only in communion with nature and her bounty, was flourishing like the green bay tree.

The basic ideology of the scheme was not the only thing wrong. Selection of applications was defective as well as the allocation of blocks and finance. Incredibly for a state in which the agricultural land had been made fruitful only by incredible toil and hardship, the Lee administration arranged no preliminary training program for the potential farmer. This became part of the impossible duties of the inspectors attached to the Closer Settlement Board who travelled tremendous distances each year seeking to help the hapless soldier-settler.

In the first year after peace, the board calculated that perhaps half the new men were making good progress but that nearly one in five was making none at all. The board solemnly declared, against all the evidence of practical observers, that want of knowledge, thrift, and perseverance was the trouble. There were other problems. Some men were rendered unfit for farming as the result of physical or mental war wounds. Some soldier-settlers reacted to the peaceful environment of their home island by seeking sudden and violent change and then equally as impulsively craved complete rest. In 1926 it was stated that too many men drank, destroyed their properties and were dishonest, and that they had indeed been advised by members of parliament not to pay their instalments.

To meet its undertaking, the government also purchased going concerns, and this of course led to increased prices all round and raised rents. The result was that repayments could not always be met, and the board continued to receive heart-breaking, angry, or bitter and bewildered letters from ex-soldiers begging to have their repayments decreased or waived until they got a start.

Land was also subdivided along the earlier lines of close settlement but on no clear economic principle: the average size of the farms in the Richmond district was a little over forty acres and, in the Oatlands and Penguin areas, down to twenty-five acres. Some such properties, if carefully and skilfully managed, could be made to pay, but bad seasons and low prices, together with increased freight costs, told against even the best or most fortunate soldier-settler.

By the mid 1920s the rural idyll had, yet again in the history of Australia, been revealed to be rubbish in the majority of cases. Ten years after the end of the war in Europe, only about 800 of 2000 soldier-settlers survived on their farms in Tasmania. Undercapitalisation, the depredations of rabbits, the ruin of the Irish blight in potato-growing areas, and the lack of skill on the part of the ex-soldiers, all put paid to the dream of many a settler.

In June 1926 the government in time-honoured style appointed a royal commission to investigate the disaster; the board and various interested parties contrived to keep the sad facts a secret, though experienced farmers who lived near soldier-settlers were only too aware of their problems. It was the crowning irony of the entire farcical business that the commissioner appointed knew little of farming. Such was one result of the men of the state answering the call to defend the British Empire and its values as they appeared in Tasmania.

In 1922 the Lee Nationalist Government won the state election again, but there was turmoil in parliament. Post-war prosperity was not evident in Tasmania. A newly formed Country Party emerged and the Labor Party revived with men such as J. Lyons and, above all, A. G. Ogilvie making themselves prominent, as the harassed Lee administration appeared unable to meet the expectations of the people after the war to end all war. Still, wages boards had been reconstituted in 1920 but the Nationalist Party declined as it became clear that the finances of the state were not in good order. Workers' Educational Association work was suspended, and even school dental clinics closed in 1923 as economy measures. As the Nationalists became more dissatisfied with their leadership, so did Labor under Lyons become more confident and strike a note of authority. A group of turbulent government members voted with Lyons, the Lee Government collapsed, there was a brief interlude under the leadership of J. B. Hayes, and then, in October 1923, Lyons became premier. A vote of no confidence in the new government was lost when no fewer than seven Nationalists and their allies voted for Labor.

Labor may have been in office in the House of Assembly, but it was certainly not in power because it was confronted with the Legislative Council, a body that continued to oppose progressive legislation in season and out.

In 1922 and 1923 it had emasculated Lee's financial policy in its desire for greater economy; its opposition to what it termed 'labour legislation' assisted the Nationalists to their demise in 1923. The advent of a Labor administration naturally offended the Council and confirmed its unswerving opposition to parliamentary democracy based on one value, one vote. Clearly here was an unequivocal sign that the pretensions of the people required to be crushed and their daring conduct reduced to its natural deference and timidity. The Council's ideological position translated in practical terms to a belief that financial difficulties could be resolved by sacking public servants and, where that was impossible, reducing their salaries.

In the three years following Labor's victory, proposed legislation rejected by the Council included a Workers' Compensation Act Amendment Bill, an Occupational Diseases Bill, a State Arbitration Court Bill, a Fair Rents Bill and a Rating Reform Bill. Even when employers and employees agreed on moderate and useful legislation, the Council destroyed it. It is a remarkable fact that even the *Mercury* began to grow uneasy when the Council insulted the intelligence of the House of Assembly by rejecting the Arbitration Bill: was it possible that the Council might actually cause irresistible pressure for its reform or abolition?

In 1924 it appeared that the Council had gone too far when it amended a money bill, which the Assembly claimed was equivalent to delaying the voting of Supply and thus endangered the ordinary service of government to the public. But what were the legal powers of the Council? No one really knew. The chief executive of the day was the Administrator, Sir Herbert Nicholls, a new governor being awaited. Nicholls agreed to sign the bill as it left the Assembly and, at Lyon's request, simply disregarded the Council. That body of course was most put out and upset, representing as it thought the best interests of the state. In these circumstances, the government sought the advice of London whereas the Secretary of State advised the Administrator to ask the law officers of the government what they thought. These officers advised Nicholls to keep on signing. He did, and an instructive encounter shaped itself.

Even the people had a say because, following the government's persistence in ignoring the Council, a state election was held and won by Labor. This was a most inconvenient result for the Council, and consultations between it and the House commenced. As a result of meetings between J. Lyons, A. G. Ogilvie and R. Cosgrove (for the government), and F. B. Edwards, T. Shields and C. Eady (for the Council), a decision was reached that embodied agreement that the Council had the power to reject money bills. An impression of the people's sovereignty was conveyed by a further agreement that the Council could only suggest amendments for certain other financial proposals, which, however, were to be on an annual basis.

If anything could be concluded from these transactions, it was that the Council emerged with its powers virtually unimpaired. Credit or otherwise for this was attributed to F. B. Edwards and H. B. White, the latter the parliamentary draftsman. It is interesting that Labor's policy was in fact abolition of the Council.

Prior to his succession to power, Lyons had made numerous powerful attacks on the evils of capitalism and the prospects of war and misery said to be carried within it, but during his premiership little more than lip-service was paid to such ideology. It is highly significant that his wife (later to become Dame Enid Lyons) induced this Labor premier to cancel his subscription to the *Australian Worker* because the official Labor publication, she judged, was too biased, intolerant and bitter.

Other factors watered down Lyons' radicalism, not least of which was his increasing preoccupation with Tasmania's economic difficulties under federation. It was a crowning irony that the customs union sought for so long by Tasmania should turn out to be judged by the people as an absolute curse. During Lyons's term of office, and before, publicists unwearyingly drew attention to the high taxes paid in Tasmania and to the adverse effects of the Navigation Act, the provisions of which were brought into operation in March 1920.

This was a constant source of complaint in Tasmania because it was held to lead to increased freight charges and leave the island more and more at the mercy of the shipping lines. The principal complaint was that ship-owners, under the act, were obliged to pay wages and maintain conditions that led to high charges, avoidable if wholesome competition were permitted. It was said that the tourist trade suffered as well and that overseas vessels could not carry interstate passengers unless the ships complied with the provisions of the act.

Worst of all, a series of maritime strikes dislocated shipping services and left Tasmania without the important tourist trade in summer. In successive seasons there was a coal strike, the Spanish flu, and a seaman's strike. It was all too much. The *Mercury* summed up the feelings of many Tasmanians, especially those in the south (including the jam magnate Sir Henry Jones) when it condemned the Navigation Act, the arbitration system, and Australia's tariff policy as a triple-headed vampire that sucked Tasmania white.

Since the Tasmanian Grant Act of 1912, disability payments had been made by the Commonwealth to a total of £500000 over ten years. That arrangement expired in 1921 but was continued till some permanent scheme could be devised, and this turned out to be the Tasmanian Sinking Fund Agreement of 1928. A royal commission found that Tasmania's difficulties would not be materially decreased by sweeping away the Navigation Act. Amendments to it did permit the carriage of passengers between Tasmania and the mainland, but the overseas shipping companies did not take advantage of this. The expected benefits from federation were proving to be an empty dream, and Tasmania discovered that companies did not invest as an act of social policy.

In 1925 a Tasmanian Rights League was formed, to represent all localities and political opinions, in response to what was perceived as the failure of the Bruce–Page Federal Government to recognise Tasmania's claims. It sought a federal ferry service with ships manned by employees of the federal authority. The *Mercury* agitated for secession; Launceston wanted ships run by non-union labour.

Beset with difficulties as he was, Lyons stressed more and more the non-party conduct of government; he spoke of the interests of all Tasmanians; he disarmed the Opposition by his patent sincerity and willingness to run what was really an informal coalition ministry; he came to see militant industrial action as unpalatable, and perceived the strike weapon solely as action by one part of the community against another. Lyons appointed Sir James O'Grady, a former British Trades Union Congress president as governor of the state. This underlined the premier's patriotism and classless attitude at a time when similar views were held by the powerful RSSILA; no one was as loyal to the Crown and Empire as J. A. Lyons (Catholic and anti-conscriptionist); the Duke of York nowhere received a more loyal welcome than in Tasmania when he came to open the federal parliament at Canberra in 1927.

Yet in 1928, at the state election, Lyons was still automatically opposed by the Tasmanian press, which decided that all the good he was said to have done was really due to the Nationalist Opposition, led by J. C. McPhee. Confronted with this perfidy, the premier thanked the press for playing the game. In many ways Lyons succeeded, where S. M.

Bruce failed, in de-politicising politics in the period after the Great War. He did it by neglecting to pursue Labor policies even when the finances of Tasmania, thanks to federal subventions in large part, had become less shaky, and when he had an elected majority in the House of Assembly. No doubt the existence of the Council would have prevented much or indeed any progressive legislation from being passed without considerable difficulty, but Lyons failed to reveal to the people how the Council treated the people's representatives. Even moderate Labor supporters found the Premier's conduct increasingly hard to swallow.

Worse than that was the Lyons Government's reduction of land and income tax, against ALP policy, in such a way that the middle and small landholder was seen to be shabbily treated. The final difficulty of Lyons's position was revealed when this legislation was attacked by the Nationalists on behalf of the small property owners and working classes. Lyons would have made—perhaps indeed was—an excellent Nationalist. He resisted the Hobart Trades Hall Council in an attempt before election to obtain from all Labor candidates an undertaking that there would not be any deviation from Labor policy and that there should be legislation passed in accordance with that policy. The THC was especially unhappy at the Lyons Government's refusal to put up a bill giving preference to trade unionists and establishing a 44-hour week.

Lyons was defeated in 1928 when representation fell in the south. The worsening economic plight of the state, with the approach of the Depression, was one reason; J. C. McPhee's capable leadership of the Nationalists was another. There was also Lyons's failure since 1927 to have a southern representative in his ministry, there was a scandal concerning Ogilvie and his legal firm's connections with a trust fund, there was a fear indeed that the active Ogilvie himself would succeed Lyons, and there was the failure of Lyons to re-admit G. W. Mahoney to the party after he stood as an Independent Labor candidate.

At this defeat, perhaps the premier had begun to realise that he had been too easy-going and trusting and all things to all men. The outgoing leader of the ALP expressed sorrow and disappointment that his political opponents had not played the game when they boasted that the Opposition should take any credit going. Lyons had pleased many Tasmanians but disappointed the generation that perceived in the triumph of Lenin and the Bolsheviks a harbinger of social justice and prosperity for all, and that indeed the meek would inherit the earth.

J. C. McPhee succeeded Lyons in June 1928 on the eve of the Great Depression. He became interested in public affairs as a result of his activities in the Australian Natives' Association and the temperance movement. His administration was confronted with the intractable problems of the Depression and unemployment, and obliged to preside over a period when the Premiers' Plan adopted conventional economic wisdom and reduced public expenditure until something should turn up. Record floods in 1929 added to the increasing misery of the people when Launceston and the north in general suffered from an extraordinary rainfall.

Such was the onslaught of the Depression that the people affected were scarcely able to consider the source of it, though to many who had been out of work in the 1920s anyway, the Depression represented little in the way of change. In 1928, unemployment among reporting trade unions was about 11 per cent but leapt to 27 per cent in 1931 and 26 per cent in 1932, before dropping slowly to 7–8 per cent in the two years before the war of 1939–45.

What was to be done about the huge number of unemployed? With a distinct prospect of turbulent spirits asking questions about the causes of social upheaval and hardships in the land of the working man's paradise, the McPhee Government sought to integrate unemployment relief policies and the rural sector. This was partly because the constraints of wages boards and arbitration awards would thus be avoided and primary production increased with the aid of the Department of Agriculture. With some caution, Ogilvie (now heading Labor) agreed to cooperate in this great emergency, though suspicious that the plan would be used by some to grease the fat sow, as he put it.

Subsidies were offered to property owners in this business-led recovery scheme, leading to criticism that interest-free loans were going the way of the rich and that women were employing their husbands. In 1932, Lyons as Prime Minister (having transferred from state to federal politics and from Labor to anti-Labor) now became more involved in relief schemes when state and federal authorities contributed to a fund whereby the municipalities were enabled to borrow at low interest, the scheme to be administered by the state unemployment councils. In addition money was granted in the form of unemployment allowances to prospectors, with aid for experimental rock-drilling and boring operations in the industry.

McPhee's government survived the election of 1931, a measure of the Opposition's policy because Ogilvie established links with J. T. Lang, the fiery premier of New South Wales. It did not go down well in loyal and patriotic Tasmania when the leader of the state Labor Party declared that the breakdown of the monetary system was the cause of unemployment. Ogilvie also did not gain votes by drawing attention to the pitiful exhibition of Lyons and the state premiers down on their knees begging the Commonwealth Bank Board and its chairman, Sir Robert Gibson, for some tokens with which to trade. Ogilvie continued to condemn the policy recommended by Sir Otto Niemeyer, the visiting agent of the British banks, because, said Ogilvie, those people who continued to draw interest were increasing purchasing power at the expense of the workers.

Echoing Lang, the Labor Party in Tasmania sought postponement of the payment of overseas interest till the government and the British bond-holders agreed to an equitable reduction in interest and a just scheme for the liquidation of capital liabilities. Advising the Federal Government was ironically enough a son of Tasmania—L. F. Giblin, gallant officer in the 40th Battalion, a member of the Tasmanian Labor Party and one who had shared a study at Cambridge with J. M. Keynes. This experience did not notably make him a Keynesian.

Probably the major undertaking or private project in Tasmania for the relief of unemployment was the YMCA occupational scheme. Established first in Hobart in the second half of 1931, and then at Launceston and on the north-west coast, it sought to train boys aged between fourteen and twenty for agricultural work and for employment in industrial trades and clerical pursuits. One of the impulses was a fear of demoralisation and anarchy among the unemployed and the danger of the future adults of the state becoming wasters. In this scheme, farms, or 'colonies', were purchased by the government to train youths in forestry and agriculture. Farmers stood ready to accept boys, despite Labor protests that it was an example of sweating and a disgrace that these boys were to be paid only 5s. a week to work for farmers for nothing.

In addition, a Toc H mothers' and girls' club was set up to train girls for service and to make clothes for distribution to the unemployed. Girls' classes were established and, to avoid compromising morals, lounges for the unmarried were opened each evening, where there was community singing, games, and talks of an uplifting character.

Church of England men's societies also conducted an unemployment scheme in Hobart to find odd jobs. Here the *Mercury* and wireless station 7ZL publicised the idea to purchase small plots of land whereon the unemployed might grow vegetables ... but there was a problem in this because such Christian charity led to competition with other gardeners. Rotarians also made an effort to help their fellow Tasmanians in a 'spend for unemployment' campaign on a state-wide basis, in the belief that expansion of private credit was the most appropriate measure to revive the economy.

Returned soldiers were also active, demanding a reasonable share of preference in distribution of relief work. Lee refused and informed the RSSILA that his chief concern was provision for the most necessitous cases as they arose. There emerged an Anzac Relief Association, its exertions lent point by the most strong objections to the idea of repudiation of overseas debts, as suggested by such as J. T. Lang. RSSILA spokesmen contrasted the traitorous proposal of repudiation with the honour, self-respect and reputation of the Empire and themselves as guardians and custodians of the memories of the Great War. That was in August 1932, and the RSSILA introduced a civil patrol movement, supported by voluntary public subscriptions and supervised by the police, to provide householders with such services as protection of their homes. Some saw this as an excellent precaution to safe-guard the property of the people when repudiationists stalked the land, others saw it as the preliminary move to establishment of a fascist New Guard.

But the typical response to the Depression in Tasmania was the self-help scheme. Such a one was conducted by the young men of St Andrew's Church, Launceston. Here were made toy aeroplanes, wheelbarrows, hobby horses and folding chairs. The community assisted by donating cases and other such raw materials.

There were always trouble-makers, however, complained the do-gooders, and considerable disquiet arose when communists gained influential positions in the Unemployed Workers' Movement. Particularly was this so in Launceston, and it drew a predictable reaction from the city council and ex-servicemen. In Hobart, however, moderates such as G. W. Mahoney gained control of the UWM, and at Glenorchy they were openly antagonistic to communists. At the Beaconsfield Forestry Reserve, however, a government announcement that wages would be reduced from 12s. to 10s. a day led to a disturbing series of incidents, involving the UWM threatening to intimidate scab workers. There was a demonstration in Launceston, but the UWM was compelled to back down.

The UWM was also very suspicious of the government's establishment of 'concentration' camps of single men, which it was feared would be conducted by the military and used to break strikes. There were confrontations, moreover, between members of the UWM and returned soldiers. On Anzac Day 1931 in Launceston the display of red flags infuriated the loyalists, who burnt them, together with a large calico notice outside a house, stating that the occupant had served in the war 1915–18 with the result that he now had no work, no home and no rent. Loyalists publicly threatened decisive action against those judged less than true to God, King and country, and of a low standard of morality. For its part, the Launceston city council cracked down on those it considered were disloyal, despite objections to the ban raised by three of its alderman, the ALP, the WEA, and the Freedom of Speech League. The anti-British tone of the radicals and communists—or, rather, their conviction that there were higher and more worthy objects than mindless adulation of the Empire—was particularly offensive in loyal Tasmania.

When a reinvigorated Labor Party won office in 1934, and no fewer than thirteen new members were elected, the worst of the Depression was over, but the distribution of relief remained one of the principal duties of government. The confusion of private schemes, charities, and government responsibility led to a most rigorous examination of persons seeking relief. In 1934, for instance, applicants could be refused if they possessed a player piano, wireless set, motor, or cart and horse. Persons seeking relief were obliged to register at the Public Works Department in Hobart or Launceston or at local council chambers, where wardens obtained a police report on the applicant and then decided on the amount of aid to be offered. Orders for provisions depended upon the number of dependants and whether the person was in the town or country. The basic rate was 7s. 6d. worth of rations a week, and recipients of the dole were permitted, in addition to sustenance, to earn the value of their rent plus up to 10s. a week for a worker with four or more children. Single unemployed women not living in their parents' home were generally ignored, though some sustenance was paid in winter. The need for constant reapplication, stern control, a harsh administration and the social disgrace of applying for relief meant that dole seekers had frequently exhausted all their resources before making application.

With the coming to office of the ALP in 1934, new government enterprises began to absorb a number of the unemployed, in the form of works for the Hydro-Electric Commission, established by a statute of 1929, the Public Works Department, Forestry Department and so on. On taking office, Labor increased sustenance and work for dole rates by 20 per cent in the cities and 30 per cent in the country when it took money from the consolidated revenue of the preceding government.

The solution to unemployment in Tasmania lay largely in the hands of the Federal Government, and certainly the Lyons administration in Canberra did allocate some funds for public works and mining. Municipalities came to handle the matter locally, with state and federal funds. Thus is was that the road to the top of Mount Wellington ('Ogilvie's scar') was completed, but some local government authorities were slow to use the facility of money offered. Launceston council was one such, and Kingborough council refused with great hilarity a request for a first-aid kit for the men employed on local government relief works. One councillor said that the next thing would be a request for armchairs, and another representative observed that the men were not likely to work hard enough to have an accident. Thus was the Depression lightened and enlivened for some by local government wit.

The principal social problem was in the cities, because farmers tended to employ relatives in unpaid but sustaining work, and the relatively small number of people affected made the problem less difficult for government. The Hobart Relief Canteen feared, as did many, the results of the Depression, because it perceived people with their spirits broken to such an extent that it would be difficult for them ever again to regain former courage and outlook, modest as they might have been. Medical men reported that the standard of health was more a social problem than a medical one: insufficient clothing and underfeeding made the people a prey to disease, and observers continued to worry about what would become of the rising generation, starved and dispirited as some of it now was. An official school nurse reported that one in eight of the children she supervised was suffering from some degree of malnutrition. At Wellington Square school, Launceston, hot milk was distributed daily to more than 170 undernourished children. The Salvation Army soup kitchen in Hobart in the winter of 1938 supplied soup and bread each day to 150 families, including 1500 children; in June 1939, some 200 persons a day were still being succoured in this way.

Though the government did take responsibility for some sustenance, it was reluctant to accept any for housing and clothing. This was a field where charity could do its age-old work, but the government was obliged to provide boots when men began arriving for work on the Mount Wellington road wearing dancing shoes, sandshoes and slippers, discovering the truth, if they did not already know it, of the adage 'cold as charity'.

The administration of A. G. Ogilvie, which took office in 1934 and extended the duration of parliament to five years, became associated in the people's minds with the gradual emergence of the state from the miseries of the Depression. Ogilvie was a lawyer who joined the Labor Party and became a member of parliament in 1919. In 1923 he became attorney-general in the Lyons Government, was made a King's Counsel in 1925 (the youngest in the Empire) and gained a great reputation for vigorous debate and, unfortunately for him, for shrewdness verging on sharpness ... but he remained in power until his sudden death in 1939 at the age of forty-seven, after he had won a great victory at the polls with a most able team of ministers including Robert Cosgrove, T. G. D'Alton, E. Dwyer-Gray, J. F. Gaha, T. H. Davies, and E. J. Ogilvie.

The Labor Government increased the construction program of the Hydro-Electric Commission and built a new power station at Tarraleah, giving at once a general hope for new industry and immediate hope and income for the victims of the Depression. Newsprint was also promoted as an industry well suited for an island with Tasmania's timber resources. In 1937, Australian newspaper proprietors amalgamated with Sir Keith Murdoch's Derwent Valley Company Pty Ltd, to form Australian Newsprint Mills Ltd, and in 1937 Ogilvie made available a large concession at the headwaters of the River Derwent, in difficult mountain country. At about the same time at Boyer, near New Norfolk, was established a newsprint mill. With L. R. S. Benjamin as general manager, it became the first enterprise in the world to produce newsprint from hardwood. At Burnie, similar concessions were granted to Associated Pulp and Paper Mills and hydro power made available.

In the early part of the century, a Department of Public Health was established in Tasmania, under Dr J. S. C. Elkington who led the fight against smallpox and exhorted local authorities to look to the health of the community. His greatest work was in recording the health of children, and books he wrote on it became models of their kind. By 1911

Elkington and his department had reduced infant mortality from 111 per 1000 to 76. Under successive managements, by 1917 the child welfare scheme had accomplished a further decrease to 21 deaths per 1000 births. Investigation of goitre was commenced in 1921, and Ogilvie's government brought in free medical services to rural areas and did a great deal in the improvement of health. New hospitals were built at Hobart and Launceston, the former ironically enough continuing on the site on the banks of that Hobart Town Rivulet which had served as an open sewer and source of disease since Governor Collins's camp in 1804.

From being backward in education, Tasmania, from the time of Neale's reforms and his new education in 1905, became very experimental in this field. In the 1920s it achieved three notable firsts when, in the area of infant education, Miss Amy Rowntree launched the first pre-school centres, when a correspondence school was started by R. Solomon in 1919 to help children in isolated areas, and when H. Parker launched Australia's first Department of Educational Psychology section.

During Ogilvie's regime, he began considering the use of wireless for state school education as early as 1925 and a year later proposed swimming instruction. More experiments went forward with the establishment of two area schools at Sheffield and Hagley, to the great interest of educationists elsewhere, to meet the needs of pupils in districts where primary production was dominant.

At the same time the principal private schools continued to attract pupils, the extension and strengthening of the Catholic schools especially demanding enormous work and sacrifice in the face of the money spent on the state system. St Virgil's College, Hobart, was established in 1911 by the Order of Christian Brothers, St Patrick's in Launceston was also founded by that Order, and the Deloraine Convent started in 1895. St Mary's College, Hobart, was started in 1895 by the Presentation Order of Sisters. An unusual school was the Society of Friends' School in Hobart, established in 1887 in relationship with a long-standing connection of the colony and state with the Society of Friends. In the north, Scotch College was founded in 1900 and, privately owned, officially recognised by the Presbyterian Churches in 1925. Methodist Ladies' College, Launceston, was established in 1886 and St Michael's Collegiate School, Hobart, ten years later. Fahan School for Girls at Sandy Bay came into existence in 1935.

Thus, with the addition of the earlier schools such as Hutchins and Launceston Grammar, Tasmania had a wide variety of schools by the 1930s. Yet for various reasons, the state high schools continued to be held in very high regard by parents, partly due to a succession of resourceful and energetic ministers and directors of education, and because governments came to place public money into the schools that the children of the people were obliged by law to attend. This was also one area where the constraints of travel actually militated in Tasmania's favour. In comparison with other states, the overwhelming majority of the children did not have far to go to school though the terrain might be difficult, and hence the state saved, relatively, on costs of school transport.

As elsewhere in Australia, the 1920s was the age of the 'flapper' and of a new attitude to women. In 1922 two women stood for parliament, and a Tasmanian Women's Non-party Political League was formed. The object was to put forward female candidates, to obtain full civil rights for women, to improve conditions in education and public health, to obtain a firmer consideration of social questions and immediately to bring the Mental Deficiency Act into force. The same year Miss B. M. Reed became the first female dentist in Tasmania, her surgery at Latrobe; in 1923 Launceston's first women's club was formed; and by 1924 there were female Justices of the Peace.

The movies also caught on in Tasmania as elsewhere, the state getting a bonus in terms of its dual identities as historic and scenic by the appearance of *For the Term of His Natural Life* on the one hand and *Jewelled Nights* on the other, the first a lavish film based on Marcus Clarke's famous work, the second a romance adapted from Marie Bjelke-Petersen's novel set in the bush of the north-west coast.

But modernity could be taken too far. In 1926 Ulverstone council forbade the dancing of the Charleston within the municipality and was asked by ministers of religion to close down an open-air *palais de danse* in the interests of morality. Tasmanian Bright Young Things were checked.

As the government railways continued to lose money, in 1932 the Lyell Highway finally gave the capital of Tasmania a direct road link with the west coast, though there still remained mining fields that were accessible only by rail, so that local school teachers were warned of the approach of department inspectors by a prearranged series of whistle blasts from the engine driver. The automobile became very popular as elsewhere, leading to construction of new and better roads and expansion of settlement. The Tasmanian Autocar Club was formed by 1911, with a daily motor service running between Burnie and Launceston by 1923. In 1926, to help deal with speeding motorists, all Tasmanian traffic police were trained to estimate speeds, and experiments revealed they were correct about 75 per cent of the time.

From its European settlement, Tasmania depended utterly on sea transport and hence it was not surprising that entrepreneurs should arise in this field very early. The most important in the period between the wars was the Holyman family. In 1919 died William Holyman, father of Thomas Henry, William and James, who became very active in a shipping business, centred at Launceston after moving from Devonport in 1899. By 1931 there were no fewer than nine Holyman steamers plying Australian coastal waters, and the company began buying up Bass Strait islands.

Air transport began in Tasmania in 1919 when Lieutenant Arthur Long, of the Australian Flying Corps, flew copies of the *Mercury* from Hobart to Launceston and Deloraine, the first commercial flight in Australia. In December of that year he also made a flight from Stanley to Torquay, Victoria, the first Bass Strait crossing. Upon his return from the Great War, Victor Holyman established a branch of the Australian Aero Club at Launceston in 1928, and four years later persuaded his family to buy a plane and begin an aerial service between Launceston and Flinders Island. Holyman then joined forces with L. M. Johnson, also on the Flinders Island run, to form Tasmanian Aerial Services Pty Ltd, the necessity for travelling to Bass Strait islands being one of the main impulses that led the Tasmanians to be early aviators.

In 1933 there was completed the first journey to Melbourne via Flinders Island, made by Holyman and Johnson in three and a half hours. When Johnson retired, his interest was purchased by the Holymans, and Holyman Airways Pty Ltd was created. As a result of a contract with the Federal Government, a thrice-weekly air service to Melbourne began in October 1934, but was followed by two fatal crashes in two years. Ten passengers and Vic Holyman were killed in one of these. Victor's brother Ian, however, kept the company intact, and in 1936 it amalgamated with Adelaide Airways to form Australian National Airways Pty Ltd, which then branched out to cover all Australia by 1942, and ultimately was absorbed into Ansett Transport Industries Ltd.

Great hopes were held out for the development of Tasmania by the establishment of hydro-electric enterprises and the linking of all centres to this source of energy. Following the takeover in 1916 of a private company experiencing difficulties, two 5000 horse-power turbo-generators were installed at Waddamana to generate power for domestic lighting and trams in Hobart, and three years later a construction program began for the installation of additional plant at Waddamana. In 1923 Miena Dam at the Great Lake was completed to supply additional power to the Electrolytic Zinc Company, and the next year another such dam was constructed at the south end of the lake, blocking the inflow into the River Shannon. Storage capacity was further increased and ultimately the flow directed on to the Waddamana turbines where 63 000 horsepower was generated. Sub-stations reduced the current to a point where general distribution could be accomplished. Rural areas began to receive the boon of electric power and modernisation that enabled not only light and electrically driven pumps and other machinery to be installed but also electric kitchens, with all their advantages of cleanliness and refrigerated storage of such items as milk. By 1927 a line of electricity had been opened from the Great Lake to Sheffield, Devonport, Ulverstone and Penguin.

The Electrolytic Zinc Company was established during the Great War at Hobart and was headed by H. W. Gepp who, with W. L. Baillieu, set the company on its feet. In a project comparable in scale to the establishment of the Newcastle steel industry, Gepp overcame metallurgical difficulties and in the foundation years designed a plant that came to produce very high quality zinc of 99.95 per cent purity, together with the important by-product, superphosphate. In 1919, the government announced that it would spend £2 million on hydro-electricity, and among the beneficiaries was a new enterprise, also at Hobart. This was Cadbury Brothers' confectionery enterprise at Claremont and in 1920 it obtained an option over 246 acres for a factory. An estate was to be laid out in accordance with modern town planning principles, along the lines of Bournville in England, and a year later W. Pascall, an English director, arrived to inspect progress.

Other industries started at this time included Kelsall & Kemp Ltd of Rochdale, which opened woollen works in Launceston in 1923; a year later Patons & Baldwins secured 200 acres also at Launceston for a spinning mill.

Those same dairying districts that provided the confectioners

Cadbury-Fry-Pascall with milk frequently also produced potatoes for export to New South Wales. In 1933, as part of the increasingly active intervention of the government, potato seed improvement work began at the Tewkesbury potato research station, south of Burnie, to promote the industry. It was in such areas that victims of the Depression were encouraged to learn agricultural skills.

Water and timber were always abundant in Tasmania, and a Forestry Department was formed in 1919 but for some time received little money. Then in the 1930s the government was informed that past neglect, greed and lack of forestry management had left the state with only fifteen years' supply of timber, and brought action that would at the same time, it was thought, lead to reafforestation, forest management, and production of paper pulp.

Associated with Tasmania's natural appearance was the subject of conservation of its resources and exploitation of its environment for the purposes of tourism. In the 1930s little was thought of a serious conflict between these two, but in fact the ground was being laid for a clash of very wide interest. The scenic character of the state and the prospect of tourism had long been realised in Tasmania and the benefit to be derived from visitors acknowledged by the issue in 1899–1900 of Australia's only colonial pictorial postage stamps and by advantages offered to mainland residents during the summer.

In 1885, some 300 acres in the vicinity of Russell Falls were proclaimed a reserve through the efforts of L. M. Shoobridge, and in 1893 the Tasmanian Tourist Association was formed. Members included J. W. Beattie and the government botanist L. Rodway, who was also in the Royal Society, the Field Naturalists' Club, and a National Park Association. Beattie and Spurling of Launceston began photographic work in the 1880s and promoted the scenic beauty of the colony by such means as lantern lectures.

The idea of national parks was forwarded as a result of publicity given the creation of the Yellowstone National Park in the United States, and in 1904 wilderness and the Tasmanian mind came together when the Tourist Association proposed that Crown land at Schouten Island and Freycinet Peninsula be reserved for native flora and fauna. There was a favourable response by the government, and in addition a reserve was formed on part of Mount Wellington as well. Then W. G. Crooke took up the idea of creating a national park in the Russell Falls locality and at Mount Field. A National Parks Association came into existence under which 27 000 acres of reserve were set aside in the Cradle Mountain–Lake St Clair region at the beginning of the Great War. In 1915 also the National Parks Association succeeded in inducing the government to pass the Scenery Preservation Act. The park was officially opened in October 1917. In the meantime, the Tourist Association had got into financial difficulties, and in 1914 a Government Tourist Bureau, under E. T. Emmett, was created.

In the north, Gustav Weindorfer, an Austrian, and his Australian wife fell in love with the Cradle Mountain area and there constructed a chalet, opened in 1912. In the early 1920s the north-west coast newspaper the *Advocate* suggested the creation of a government reserve and, when a northern branch of the Royal Society was established in 1921, it became active in supporting Weindorfer, but he became greatly discouraged and hurt by racist persecution during the Great War. In 1922 an area was proclaimed under the Scenery Preservation Act and a reserve of 158 000 acres gazetted. In 1925, 42 000 acres near the national park were reserved as state forest, the largest area to that date.

Fauna had for long been under attack in the island, though an Animal and Birds Protection Act was passed in 1919; this was strengthened in 1928 after a number of hunting seasons dangerously reduced certain species. By 1930 there were two official bodies specifically orientated to conservationist or protectionist objects: the Fauna (Animals and Birds Protection) Board and the Scenery Preservation Board. With the death of Weindorfer in 1932, a group of his friends bought his land and the Waldheim Chalet to forestall timber interests. By 1940 the Scenery Preservation Board had proclaimed about 470 000 acres of scenic reserve and the Fauna Board about 800 000 acres of fauna reserves, and the next year some 23 600 acres of Frenchman's Cap had also been proclaimed as a scenic reserve.

The administration of A. G. Ogilvie was marked by that premier's response to the Depression and to the necessity for Tasmania to be 'developed'—by which was meant the establishment of numerous labour-intensive secondary industries. It was this that led the government to advance the interests of the Hydro-Electric Commission more and more in the quest for industry. It appeared to Tasmanians of the time that, given their abundant supply of waterpower, there was no limit. Simplistic popular thinking perceived that the supply of rain and therefore water was endless and clean, compared with the smoke and grime associated with coal. Few if any considered that the spoliation of the countryside was other than minimal and a small price to pay for development and employment of the people. Could not Tasmania become a second Switzerland?

Behind this thinking lay a constant comparison—to Tasmania's disadvantage—with Victoria and New South Wales, whither so many young Tasmanians went. In the 1920s it was commonly thought that the state was victim of a brain drain. Certainly the population was increasing but slowly, from 191000 (1911), 214000 (1921), 223000 (1931) to 242000 (1941). The birth rate was the highest in Australia but the state did not retain the Australia-wide proportion of the middle years and younger age groups. Emigration still often exceeded immigration. This was so in census year 1911 by 4000 people and in 1941 by 6000, with a virtual balance between the two in 1921 and 1931.

Tasmania sought to share in S. M. Bruce's 'men, money and markets' slogan, and in the island state immigration from Britain was handled as part of the Department of Agriculture in 1921. However, in the first four years of the operation of the notorious Navigation Act there was an annual loss of 3500 people from the state, and the natural increase of 1923–24 failed to overtake this deficit. The 1920s were bad years for Tasmania: the birth rate in 1926 was the lowest since 1850 and the marriage rate the lowest since 1918.

In the period between the wars Tasmanians maintained a great pride in their state but did not reap the benefits they had been led to believe would flow from federation of the colonies. That federation was truly the creation of a free-trade zone, and an island with Tasmania's disadvantages was bound to feel the draught. Not least were Tasmanians at once angered and proud by the constant passage of young sportsmen, and especially footballers, from their clubs to the top of the tree in the Victorian Football League. In the sporting world so important to so many Australians, Tasmania held its own perhaps only in the area of tree-felling and sports associated with the timber industry. The idea that the state was 'sleepy hollow' became something of a fixation and led Tasmanians probably to overemphasise the attractions of Melbourne and Sydney and to overvalue the importance of development and industrialisation, although the work of the Hydro-Electric Commission in bringing the comforts of modernity to the ordinary Tasmanian could not be criticised by people who had known only wood-stoves and kerosene lamps.

As much as the Ogilvie administration accomplished in the Depression, it also shared in the difficulties of its predecessors at the hands of the Legislative Council. Many and varied were the things accomplished in the emergency years of the 1930s, but not among their number was checking the wide powers of the Council. In 1937, Ogilvie came into serious collision with that body when certain of its number objected to some of the premier's statements and rhetoric, jumping to the conclusion that Ogilvie was about to lay Tasmania in ruins—as if it were not in that state already—by his 'socialistic' measures. Thus the Council, convinced the state was in the grip of a madman, reduced an item in a Finance Bill involving an extension of 'socialism' in the mild form of government medical services being offered to the people in rural areas. At this, Ogilvie promptly introduced a bill to settle the hash of the Council once and for all, the Council arguing that the matter in dispute formed no part of essential services to the people but was merely an extension of them. Ogilvie appeared determined to destroy the Council's power to frustrate the wishes of the people's house and observed that he would abolish the Council as soon as he could ... but he did not. Conferences commenced, Ogilvie assessed the feeling of the state and concluded it was conservative and, the question of the Finance Bill resolved, the matter was taken no further. Presently the death of Ogilvie and the outbreak of the war led to the whole matter being shelved.

7

Identity: c. 1940

On the eve of the Second World War, Tasmania's population was approximately 244 000, of whom 123 000 were males and 121 000 females. They were distributed generally into the regions of the south (106 000), north (74 000), north-west (54 000), and west (10 000). The population of the City of Hobart stood at about 57 000 and that of the City of Launceston at 38 000, but between a quarter and a third of those numbers could be added to take account of surrounding local government areas which were integrated into the two principal and oldest settlements in the state.

By the late 1930s and early 1940s, the main regions were fairly clearly recognised by their industrial and rural economies, their centres of focus (Hobart, Launceston, Devonport and Burnie, and Queenstown), and their commercial radio stations and daily newspapers: the *Mercury* in the south, the *Examiner* in the north, and the *Advocate* in the north-west, with the last devoting special space to the affairs of the mining-dominated west coast. These three main newspapers were principally owned by different interests (the Davies family, the Rolfe family and the Harris family respectively), which in turn also owned a number of radio stations. Other regional papers were published from time to time.

Such was the terrain of the rugged state and the limited strength of radio signals transmitted that people in the north and north-west could not readily hear southern radio stations, nor Hobart hear programs emanating from outside its region. Radio station 7QT Queenstown catered for the west coast and 7DY Derby for the north-east. All commercial stations tended to broadcast similar material in terms of ubiquitous serials and radio plays and talent quests, and were linked to the local newspapers for news broadcasts. Brass-band music was popular.

In the north-west and to a lesser extent in the north, however, Bass Strait was little impediment to clear reception from Melbourne. This orientated the areas more to the capital of Victoria than to the capital of Tasmania, reinforcing cultural and commercial links that had been present since the settlers of Van Diemen's Land began colonising the Port Phillip District of New South Wales in the 1830s. Indeed, the Victorian Methodist circuit included Tasmania, and that religion was especially strong in the north generally. The Australian Broadcasting Commission catered for a minority audience from transmitters in Hobart and Launceston as well as directly from Melbourne. Its mass influence was slight, though its cultural impact may have been substantial in some quarters, not least being the development of the children's Argonauts' Club in the early 1940s, and it influenced the outlook of some Tasmanian young people in a most important way by encouraging literary and artistic talent.

The newspapers and commercial radio stations, however, remained of great significance in regional terms. The price of apples (south) or potatoes and stock (north-west and north) could be principal headlines until the war came. The papers took themselves very seriously in editorial comment, continuing the nineteenth-century practice of the editor offering virtual sermons on the events of the day and their significance for the region. It might not have been a Tasmanian paper that began a leading article in late 1917 with 'As we have so frequently warned the Czar ...' but it could well have been. Periodicals such as the *Weekly Times, New Idea* and *Women's Weekly* revealed to Tasmanians the wider world of interests relating to the man on the land and to women. Newspapers all had women's pages, offering the mixture of social gossip and sturdy common sense so characteristic of Australian women's journals. The *Listener In* from Melbourne was widely read and filled its pages with Victorian wireless programs, with comment on them and the radio stars of the day.

Display and classified newspaper advertisements reflected regional business and interests, offering the wares of local shops and stores, and answers to correspondents in rural areas were coloured more than a little by hints of local dramas and events, values and interests. A reader who sought to know whether old-age pensioners could legally back horses received the reply, 'Yes, and goats too'. Seasonal requests for fruit pickers or potato diggers reflected regional economies. Notices from time to time warned traders to be wary of accepting credit from certain people where marital relationships were evidently under strain, pleaded for the return of (winning) Tatts tickets unaccountably lost or allegedly purloined, and threatened or hinted at the infliction of 'bootlace uppercuts' to enemies whose identity was gleefully recognised by readers in the know.

As elsewhere, numerous readers perused newspapers backwards, beginning with racing and football news and next moving on to items related to their districts. In country areas, newspapers and mail were delivered late each day by mail cars or buses that threw out private mail bags as they went past.

The radio stations and newspapers in winter gave considerable space to football, the prospects for the season and predictions for the games, with eccentric experts such as 'Stab Kick' laying down the law. Regionalism was enormously strengthened by the presence of three main football organisations: the Tasmanian Football League (south), the Northern Tasmanian Football Association and the North-West Football Union, and there were smaller competitions elsewhere, such as on the west coast. In this region games were played on gravel surfaces because no suitable soil existed on the few naturally flat areas. Local municipalities frequently had their own teams, which were supported keenly, thus making it very difficult to alter the boundaries of local government areas.

Radio readers of teams were known to inject comments about players such as 'I hope he hasn't forgotten that load of wood he promised me for next week', a task made difficult in some areas when teams might consist of Smith (8), Brown (7), and a few players with other surnames. No public implications were drawn from such facts, but in some areas the suggestion of inbreeding was clear, and certainly there was a common image on the mainland of Tasmanians having developed hillbilly proclivities. Some isolated parts of rural Tasmania were at once close-knit and deprived, and relationships close to incestuous were hinted at.

As elsewhere in Australia, religion was not seen as a powerful factor in everyday life. The pressures of colonial emergencies and hardship meant that the principal religions did not exert obvious power, although the Catholic Church tended to retain its adherents more than most if church attendance is a criterion. Fringe religions such as the Christian Brethren and Gospel Hall flourished in the north-west, and Seventh Day

Adventism attracted a few. This had unexpected results in some areas. There men accustomed to lend and pool farming machinery and labour found that their neighbours were unwilling to be available on Saturday but perfectly ready to lend a hand on Sunday, so that rural economies were threatened.

The antagonism and marked bigotry of some Protestants to Catholics strained social relationships, especially in places where clerics were sure and certain of their theological ground. The Irish origin of most Catholics had always led some Protestants to suspect them, and the views of Catholics on such matters as drinking and gambling were frowned upon by such as the Methodists, who held strong opinions on the sacred character to the Sabbath, the intrinsic sinfulness of drink, and of what was said all too readily to flow from it.

Everywhere in the state, but especially in rural areas, the churches were of significance principally for marriages and deaths. Forty per cent of all marriages were conducted in the Church of England, 15 per cent in Catholic and 16 per cent in Methodist churches, and 7 per cent in the Presbyterian Church. Civil marriages and minor denominations accounted for about 10 per cent each. The clergy sighed when very nominal adherents sought a church wedding as a matter of right.

Weddings were occasions of great social importance, and the local significance (real or imagined) of the family and its outlook and income were revealed by the number of guests and the style of wedding breakfast. This could on occasion be taken to extremes, and it was not unknown for rival in-laws to beggar themselves seeking to outdo the other in the variety and value of wedding presents.

Honeymoons interstate, especially to Melbourne, could sometimes be afforded, but more often the newlyweds travelled to Hobart or Launceston or toured the state by rail or motor coach. In the rural areas the return of the couple to their home—sometimes the parents' home—was frequently marked by an occasion known as a tin-kettling. Its origins in antiquity, this custom was very widespread in Tasmania and practised on the Victorian goldfields in the 1850s. It tended to be predominantly male in its image and practice. A captain was appointed by general understanding and a date set for the occasion. Men and youths from all over the district gathered near the victims' house around nightfall and then proceeded to tin-kettle the couple out of their new domesticity by creating as much noise as possible. Men spent days beforehand loading shotgun cartridges, which were to be fired off into the night sky, thereby risking and sometimes causing horses in stables to take fright and break out, to the fury of the owner and great delight of the tin-kettlers; men blacked their faces; it was known for old wagon wheels to have their hubs filled with gunpowder before being rolled down into the houses or detonated under verandahs with fearful results. When the man of the house emerged, it was the custom to invite his tormentors in.

The date of the tin-kettling was usually an open secret, and the female friends and relatives of the bride provided food while the husband supplied liquor. Sometimes the tin-kettling festival was held out of doors in or near a barn, and fires were lit for warmth and cheerfulness as the keg was broached, Cascade beer in the south, Boags in the north. One celebrator with a wooden leg got drunk, fell in a fire and set his leg alight. The fire was put out by throwing buckets of water over him. Sooner or later the groom attempted a short speech of welcome to his friends, and the captain also spoke. Dancing and telling of stories marked the occasion, the music usually that of a piano, squeezebox, violin or mouth-organ. In some cases the violin accompanied an exhibition of old jigs or 'steps'. Recitations were offered by those bold enough to think they could hold an audience. Not every newly-wed couple was offered a tin-kettling, but normally the occasion was an enjoyable one and basically marked the respect in which the host and his wife and their families were held.

By the late 1930s in Tasmania, few women had babies at home. The small size of the state and the social services work accomplished by the government ensured that maternity hospitals were readily available, though this did not preclude the mother-to-be undertaking arduous journeys by horse and cart to the nearest maternity hospital. Relatively affluent neighbours lent cars on occasion, but more frequently mothers who lived in the country areas went to stay with relatives in a town when the birth of their baby was imminent.

Children in Tasmania were likely to be spoiled at home in their very early years, but in the rural districts there still existed a good deal of exploitation of child labour during and after school days. The primary schools continued to be conducted in a very authoritarian manner, and some young women still took up teaching through the 'monitor' system. Good teachers could always encourage promising children to go on to further education after they had turned fourteen, but many parents were indifferent or hostile to learning and sought to have their offspring enter the workforce as soon as possible; in some areas the local doctor was the only university-educated man who came into contact with the people, and his encouragement of likely children was sometimes of crucial importance because he was listened to with respect, especially if he had successfully cured someone.

Entertainment was generally similar in Tasmania to that of other parts of Australia. Anzac Day was marked with great solemnity. Preceding this public holiday, schoolchildren were assembled to hear a returned man of the Great War spell out the values embodied in the word *Anzac*, and the names on the school honour roll might be read out, reminding children of the men who had fought. The Anzac Day services at local war memorials became sharpened in their significance as the war clouds gathered over Europe and a martial spirit was engendered. Empire Day was also celebrated, though its solemn message of imperial unity was not so marked as that of Anzac Day, in part because in some areas it became associated with the presentation of apples and sweets to schoolchildren. Sunday school picnics and church anniversaries were also important occasions for many children. Forms of children's racing were mandatory at the picnics, frequently conducted at some picnic resort, and the award of book prizes at anniversaries enabled the transmission of the improving Christian message.

Tasmanians were as obsessed with films as anyone else. The term *talkies* persisted in some areas well into the 1940s and the glamour of Hollywood lent colour to the lives of picture-goers. The contrast between Hollywood's image of the world and the poor of the Derwent Valley was incredible, especially in the Depression, but all film-goers made a point of dressing well to go to the pictures. Everyone stood for the national anthem, and films adjudged good were applauded as if the actors and actresses were on the live stage and could take a bow.

Among the popular sports, football, horse-racing and cricket stood pre-eminent, though many more attended football matches or watched contests on the turf than attended cricket fixtures. Cricket was very widely played and taken most seriously but was not a prominent spectator sport. Tasmania was not formally in interstate cricket competition, but its footballers were constantly sought by the big Victorian teams, who employed talent-spotters.

There were distinct regional variations in some other sporting occasions. In Hobart and the south, the Hobart regatta was marked out as it had been since the days of Governor Franklin. It was the occasion for picnics and relaxation as well as a venue attracting the sideshows that travelled around Australia. The event was also customarily marked by the arrival in port of a warship; its ratings added the desired naval flavour to the entire occasion. The Hobart Agricultural Show was also a holiday, enabling farmers and graziers to offer their stock in competition, though the agriculturally richer north had the best exhibition of Tasmanian sheep and cattle at Launceston each spring. Newspapers pooled reporters and resources to offer readers an exhaustive list of winners and place-getters and details of exhibits. All Tasmanian centres of importance had such shows and stock sales that drew buyers from all over the continent from time to time, especially to purchase Midland sheep, which continued to produce the best fine wool on the market.

Another form of entertainment was the Boxing Day and New Year carnivals, which came to be associated especially with the north and north-west. Here was a series of occasions highlighted by bicycle races and pedestrian events. The Burnie Gift and Burnie Wheel Race enabled Tasmanian athletes to compete with Australia's best and, on occasion, visitors from abroad. Such holidays were a great day's outing in which thousands of people had picnics and gaped at or were induced to part with money to sideshows, ranging from throwing a penny on to a circle to boxing matches and freak shows. Harry Paulsen's troupe of pugilists and wrestlers dominated, and courageous, foolhardy or impecunious locals tried their skill, cunning and brute force against the visitors, who sometimes included a faded star of the ring.

Tossing the sheaf was also popular at sports meetings, local men vying with each other to see who could toss a sheaf or a bag of hay the highest over a bar as it was pulled higher between two poles. Men also competed in 'stepping the chain' to see who most closely went an exact twenty-two yards as measured by the officials. Ploughing matches were also conducted, men using a favourite pair of horses to display their skills in ploughing straight and neatly.

Women's part in holidays tended to be confined to exhibitions of cakes and goods made at home, though some rode horses in show-jumping contests. Hunt clubs were confined largely to the Midlands, where the landscape permitted this recreation. Lesser mortals hunted rabbits with dogs and guns and possums with lights, and some kept ferrets, which they released into rabbit burrows with nets set to catch the rabbits as they hurtled out to escape the ferrets. Capture of rabbits for their skins was a pastime and a business for those who went into it in a big way. Rabbit skins were particularly sought in the winter, when the climate led to the production of thick pelts and high prices, and traps might be set by the hundred. Poisoning was resorted to, and the use of some, such as strychnine smeared on pieces of apple, led to the loss of animals other than rabbits.

Wood-chopping was the sport that reflected Tasmania more than anything else. From early in the century and before, areas in the forest country of the Huon district and the north were able to offer employment to men who became extremely skilful with the axe. Informal competition rapidly became formalised, and champions emerged—Tasmanian axemen in the AIF competed in France and Belgium with lumber men from Canada, bushmen from New Zealand and their fellow Australian diggers who had worked in such timber areas as Gippsland.

In the Tasmanian form of competition, blocks of wood of particular measured thickness were nailed to permanent fixtures, and there was intense competition as the contestants were counted down by voice to their handicap, the champions still standing nonchalantly by their blocks even as those first away were turning to begin the second side. Skill and timing as well as physical strength and fitness were all-important as the great chips flew and the crowd cheered on their favourite axemen.

As well there were tree-felling contests in which the axemen competed to mount trees by deftly inserting 'shoes' and, when at the top, chop through the block there affixed. These contests were remarkable and dangerous exhibitions of a skill in which Tasmanians took great pride, where men literally put the final edge on their axe blades with razor strops, where a man would sometimes show off by raising his axe in one hand and, slowly bending his elbow, bring it down to the tip of his nose, and where the axemen draw gasps from onlookers by descending from the 'trees' with incredible speed and ease. Local axemen's organisations publicised competitions in tiny centres as 'world championships', and indeed they possibly were, given the extent of the timber industry and the skill of Tasmania's axemen. Champion tree-fellers became folk heroes. Certain families were especially well known, and their skills and iron nerve admired by all.

As elsewhere in Australia, death was the occasion for manifestation of local solidarity and solemnity. Irish-Tasmanians sometimes marked this by the conduct of wakes, where the body of the deceased was laid out in an open coffin and grieving relatives kept watch. Occasionally the mourning took on its ancient and traditional forms, with keening and outbursts of sorrow and the corpse addressed as if it still lived and could respond. There was no limit to the number who might attend a funeral, and hence respect for the deceased was measured by the number of people who came to the funeral if not the church service, itself normally a harrowing occasion. At the end of the 1930s, a funeral could bring an entire rural district of Tasmania to a halt. The carriers of the coffin were carefully chosen to represent family and friends and the chief mourners always specifically named in reports of the obsequies. Men uncovered their heads when the hearse made its solemn way to the graveyard. Relatives and acquaintances came from afar, not an easy thing when so many Tasmanians had connections on the mainland who were only enabled to attend a funeral at some considerable cost in time and money, for all were obliged to come by boat.

Those who attended such melancholy events were brought closer to their Tasmanian origins and their community by the sight of earlier gravestones and epitaphs, some of which most likely bore the same surname as the deceased. Epitaphs could be moving. At St Luke's, Richmond, a man who died in 1838 had inscribed for him:

This world is a pleac full of crooked streets
death is the market plaes weer all men meets
if life was marchendyse as men could by
he wuld live and soon must dey

Notices of deaths and funerals were commonly given in newspapers, and on local radio stations they were invariably preceded by the playing of solemn music, which alerted the listener to bad news. Floral tributes were frequently the production of certain female members of families who perceived one of their most important roles in the making of wreaths. Usually constructed from the English flowers that flourished so well in Tasmanian gardens, these tributes were sometimes of quite exquisite design and pattern, a folk art. Trade unions and benevolent institutions such as the Oddfellows, Druids, Rechabites and church organisations went to great trouble to mark the death of a member by offering a wreath and making sure they had official representatives at the funeral, as an indication of respect for the departed.

As at weddings and funerals, the role of women in this society as a whole was fairly clearly demarcated, and though it was not unknown for women to work at harvest time alongside men, this was unusual because in rural areas work at most levels was still overwhelmingly based on the necessity of great physical strength. This factor, reinforced by social assumptions, meant that women were largely excluded. Girls were expected to become wives and mothers and housewives, or perhaps go into teaching or clerical work, or some of the new secondary industries in Hobart and Launceston that called for female labour. A certain number of girls always went nursing. The artistic learnt the piano or violin perhaps or were taught singing, but the opportunities for advancement were extremely limited in such spheres. Common hobbies among girls were collecting and pressing flowers, sketching and painting, or crochet work and knitting, which would lead to dressmaking, at least on a part-time basis. The gathering of clothes and objects for a glory box was taken for granted as something a young woman should do.

Most people still burnt wood in their domestic fires, despite the spread of electricity and use of gas in Hobart and Launceston, and the production of cooked food was regarded as a special female skill and indeed duty. A great deal of bread and jam was consumed by Tasmanians, but basic diet was dominated by meat and cooked vegetables, followed by a pudding for the main meals. Dental health was bad, and many people took it as a matter of course that they would wear false teeth. In urban areas where wood was purchased, theft of fuel sometimes occurred. One preventative was to let it be known that shotgun cartridges were carefully placed in auger holes in certain pieces of wood and concealed therein, so that the thief would experience unexpected action around the fire one night.

The principal and most valuable farm animal in Tasmania, at a time when tractors were still comparatively rare, was the Clydesdale draught horse. Stallions 'stood' at various places and their services were advertised; sometimes they were travelled to sire foals on good mares. The loss of a horse was catastrophic, and for men who depended so utterly on horsepower for their livelihood the decline of a favourite was a tragedy, such was the association between man and horse. There existed private and government veterinarians, but often farmers had inherited their own remedies and treatment, ranging from folk cures, which had sometimes a basis in science, to deep common sense and empathy with their animals. Some men were renowned for their skill in treating certain animals as others were for repairing certain types of machinery, such as the binder, and could be sent for from afar. To call in the vet, however, was to indicate that the animal was practically given up for dead or suffering from a condition that baffled the entire district.

The crucial importance of the horse led to the production of chaff and the giving over of areas of land to run horses and grow grass to feed them upon. Chaff was cut and grain threshed by itinerant chaff-cutters and threshing-machines or 'drums', in the 1930s brought to the site of the oaten hay stacks by traction engines, the route of which could be traced on the roads by the crushed blue metal that they created in their ponderous path. Machine owners employed casual labour around a core gang, and the men camped near the machine, sleeping in the open or under whatever cover they could find. The work was hard, hot and dusty. Workers were supplied by the women of the property with breakfast, morning lunch, dinner, afternoon lunch and tea. All main meals centred upon large quantities of meat and tea, the men critically comparing the fare with that supplied by other owners locally or per-haps on the mainland where some men might have been shearing or droving or getting whatever employment they could. Tasmanian men who had travelled the mainland told tales of heat, distances and drought that were at once exotic and entrancing to the locals.

The supply of tea was kept up to the men in buckets all day long, and careful tally was kept of the number of bags of chaff or grain pro-duced. Payment was by cheque to the machine owner, though some-times disagreements arose about whether the farmer should pay the feeder. This was the important individual who had the job of feeding sheaves into the machine at the proper rate so that it ran at maximum capacity and was not underfed or so overfed that a temporary jam could occur.

The growth of speedier transport was by 1939 beginning to break down the regional distinctions within the state, with their local cultures, but telephone books listing subscribers under tiny districts reflected the fact that few people sought to communicate with those they did not know. Apart from those who emigrated to the mainland, people scarcely ventured out of their region, and a journey from the Huon to Hobart—perhaps a day trip by boat—or from Derby to Launceston could be a great event, long the subject of story. In many areas the only journey people made, except perhaps on the occasion of a death or some extraordinary reason, was to a weekly stock sale, though peo-ple might holiday with relatives in town or country.

In rural Tasmania, the other main impulse to move was probably to a clearing out sale, where a property was sold and the occupants decided to auction off unwanted equipment, furniture, goods and sundries. Here the auctioneer came into his own, a man equipped with knowledge of the area derived from long experience, a sharp sense of humour and the knack of shrewdly summing up what was worth pushing for sale, what was not. Like storekeepers he knew who was worth money and who was not, and whom to trust. Settlement of accounts was normally on a seasonal basis.

The physical dangers that Tasmanians knew varied from region to region, and though the usual forms of infant and childhood diseases struck everywhere, they probably were more severe in crowded urban areas than in the country. Patent medicines continued to be widely taken, typically against forms of pulmonary diseases and 'female complaints'. There existed a stubborn belief in self-help, characteristic of colonials and people who still regarded admission to hospital as ominous in the extreme, even if they could afford it or were insured against illness. In city and country, old wives' tales and remedies abounded. People wore bags of camphor around their necks; scalding hot poultices were applied; copper bracelets were held to be effective against rheumatism; onions were rubbed on the soles of the feet against whooping cough; the water in which the brooklime was boiled was thought to be a general cure-all. Deaths and injuries caused by falling trees were not uncommon in some districts and of course could not be guarded against as disease, and, it appeared, neither could the affliction of infantile paralysis, which struck Tasmania in 1937.

People everywhere had vegetable and flower gardens and fruit trees. Most fruit could be made into forms of wine, and vegetables were occasionally turned into alcoholic beverages by those who had inherited the recipes. Bees were kept in some regions, and 'bee trees' sometimes yielded honey in the bush. Some Tasmanians manufactured a potent honey mead, but little illegal moonshine was made. Some still manufactured their own candles, killed and scalded pigs, and slaughtered sheep and cattle. Bread was made at home, and so commonly were boilings of jam, put into bottles with the tops cracked off neatly by application of a hot hoop of iron.

In the way of clothing, little was home-made in terms of the main over-garments, though a Tasmanian 'bluey'—a short thick overcoat— was favoured in some areas such as the west coast. Tasmanians except those of the more educated classes dressed in a way that could be described as old-fashioned. Women were not chic and smoked only if they did not care about being thought respectable, thought it was smart in some circles. Mrs (later Dame) Enid Lyons recorded her Tasmanian astonishment and shock at seeing Mrs Ada Holman, wife of the New South Wales premier, smoking cigarettes, with Mrs Holman's initials on them.

Nearly all men wore a hat, especially for best. Tailor-made cigarettes were not yet in fashion generally. Men used cut-throat razors, though some still wore beards. Boots, not shoes, were frequently worn and were kept in excellent order. Combination underwear was common among men and youths, the flannel undershirt was usual, and collar studs still in favour for attaching shirts when the owner got dressed up or sought to cut a figure.

Women's dress and advertisements reflected a conventional female role centred upon a 'smart' turn-out and beauty aids. Charmosan Face Powder, for example, at 2s 6d. for a big double box, was claimed to give instant youthful charm to the skin no matter how plain it might be, concealing and subduing faults and signs of age and staying on for hours. Subtle, chic and modern, it was said to take years from the looks of the beneficiary.

A svelte appearance was regarded as highly desirable, based on the ubiquitous corset, Berlei brand claiming to have achieved a major breakthrough in the 1920s by discovering that every woman belonged to one of five figure types. Corsets were offered for sale at 7s. 11d. Floral frocks could be purchased for 5s. in the summer of 1939, and an OS navy floral frock with white lace front, collar and long sleeves for 35s. Ladies' bloomers cost 1s. 6d. a pair, blouses 2s. 11d., tweed tops 1s. 3d., and princess slips, lace-trimmed with brassiere tops, were 2s. 11d.

Accessories such as hats, gloves and handbags were regarded as essential wear for most occasions, and gloves could be bought for 11½d. a pair. Sewing machines were owned by most women, and many advertisements suggested that a good deal of wearing apparel be made up at home, with rayon and cotton weave in vogue at 1s. 11d. a yard. One-piece bathing suits were the fashion, and shorts had become popular, especially for beach wear.

On the whole, there were few serious signs of women's 'liberation' if the popular press is any indication, though it was thought quite proper to encourage girls and young women to ride bicycles, which could be bought for £1 down and 5s. a week. Birth-control devices had been generally available at least since the 1890s, and on the eve of the war of 1939–45, advertisements on the women's page discreetly offered such items as Kareen, 'recommended by the medical profession', and 'medical goods'.

On the darker side of Tasmanian life in 1939, sinister murders were known to be committed, sometimes with entire districts closing ranks if it was thought necessary, so that even police might not pursue their enquiries very extensively. The people were generally suspicious of the police, and a man on the run might receive much sympathy. Most families in the rural areas owned firearms, and many districts knew who among their number was a crack shot and whether or not a man might use a rifle or shotgun seriously. Rape and murder were known, as was the destruction of the body by placing it in a stump or hollow tree and setting fire to it. Disputes might be held off or defused when it became known that certain families were quite capable of killing, so that interlopers removed themselves. Most quarrels, however, were settled privately, though animosities might smoulder for years in the form of feuds and pay-backs. Formal fights occurred. It would become known that a fight had been arranged, and friends of the opposed parties, together with curious onlookers who were careful not to take sides, would gather on a Sunday morning to see the two rivals square up and either fight to a finish or be persuaded after a few hits that honour was satisfied.

The isolation of Tasmania led in 1931 to a secessionist move in the south through the *Dominion* monthly magazine, but it got no further than other such impulses in states and areas of Australia that attributed their troubles to the Federal Government and its alleged disregard of local interests. Yet Tasmanians continued to feel different from other Australians and were certainly seen to be so, as are all islanders. A visit to Melbourne, and adventures there, would be the subject of anecdotes to impressed listeners for years. The constant emigration of local people and the insignificant immigration reinforced this sense of apartness and particular identity. A slightly defensive pride in coming from Tassie was emphasised.

There was an implicit continuity with the past that sometimes took explicit form. In 1951, 'A Call to the People', signed by high church dignitaries and the chief justices of the states, urged everyone to look to moral revival and to go forward together in the face of communist triumphs abroad and perceived unrest at home. In the form of a leaflet, the Call was posted up on railway stations and the like. In Tasmania, across the uplifting passage that called 'on all our people to remember all whose labours opened this land to the uses of mankind ...', and ending with 'Fear God, Honour the King', some wag wrote,

> They hitched us to their ploughs, my boys
> to plough Van Diemen's Land.

This provocative quotation of part of a convict ballad recalling the violent origins of the state and society was unusual, however, although the countryside was thick with buildings that reminded people of their origins. Not least was the remains of the Port Arthur settlement, but its partial destruction in bushfires at the turn of the century was not greeted with sorrow. There were those who wished the place had been entirely consumed with flames, so that what was seen as a very recent and disreputable past might have its shame put out of sight as well as out of mind. Tasmanians did not wish to be reminded of their history and indeed took active steps in some cases to remove incriminating evidence from old documentary convict records. The rising generation was not encouraged in family history or genealogical research for fear of what might be discovered. A convict ancestor was nothing to be proud of or easily accepted. On the contrary, he or she was the subject of shame and a figure in a past over which it was desirable to draw a veil. Disinformation about family origins was common, but there was a great pride in respectable origins. The death in 1889 of one Robert Thorne was big news: he was born at Hobart Town in 1808 and was claimed to be the oldest native-born resident, with a brother who had been born at Port Phillip in 1803, his father a sergeant of Marines.

Five years later, in 1894, origins of a different kind were evoked: in the House of Assembly, George Crosby Gilmore, member for George Town and a lawyer, took it that he was accused by Allan McDonald, representative of North Launceston and an ironmonger, of being a transported convict and felt so incensed that he punched his accuser. This was said to be the first fracas of the kind for twenty-five years.

Did this sort of thing confirm among Tasmanians the belief that they were indeed different from other Australians? Perhaps; it certainly helped. Those other Australians perceived Tasmanians sometimes with slight amusement as country cousins suspicious of the big city, people who took the precaution of sewing up their pockets or purchased money belts when venturing to Melbourne for fear of pickpockets, who were convinced that they would be taken down on the mainland, and who emerged from backblock areas where all kinds of curious customs prevailed.

But there was also conveyed, at the same time, an image of Tasmania as a little Merrie England, a picture cultivated and promoted by and for middle-class holiday-makers from the mainland, such as Martin Boyd. His was a picture of a more positive kind, one of fishing for blackback and of the 'apple isle', where there was a temperate climate and a relaxed lifestyle. But Tasmania was not seen as the place where one sought employment, except perhaps in certain specialised technical fields associated with hydro-electric engineering or the mining industry.

On the eve of the war that began in 1939, then, Tasmanians generally had developed a number of regional differences, economies and outlooks, highlighted by the spectacular difference between the life of a Queenstown miner and that of a grazier in the Midlands, close though they were as the crow flies. The big division was between town and country, but Tasmanians were rendered essentially one subgroup of Australians by the presence of Bass Strait. Some perceived that even a form of dialect or dialects had developed, though this assertion might be doubted if tested by any serious linguistic analysis. Yet there were odd expressions and words that identified people of Tasmanian origin.

The most common was the use of *tissues* for cigarette papers and the form *num 'un* for a strange fellow. Other expressions are of obvious derivation, such as 'the other side' for the mainland of Australia and 'down on the front', an expression used by people in the hinterland for those dwelling on the sea coast. As well, various British dialect words were probably ossified in the island. Few folk tales from Home appear to have survived, though some Irish-Tasmanians still told stories about 'the little people', and it is curious to note that, in one area of the north-west, people on one side of a river performed dances with different steps from people on the other side, though the tunes were the same; and that in another area, the identical small bird was variously termed a chat, a nun, a bullfinch by people from closely adjacent districts.

Weeds and native grasses also had quite different names in different regions and districts, a fact that led to considerable confusion and misunderstanding.

Other expressions and terms included *slewed* (become lost or confused); *trinkling* (running water); *setter* (a hard case); *throw off* (to criticise); *jag* (a small load drawn by horses); *nointer, rooshun* (Russian?); or *radical* (a mischievous child); *shook* (stolen); *planted* (hidden); and *cronk* (out of sorts or ill). *Creek* was commonly pronounced 'crik' and *sat* as 'sate' or 'sut'. Some or indeed all of these might well have been common in other parts of Australia, as might have been the calls used to horses or bullocks in directing them, or numerous other calls used to attract animals. There were such exclamations of amazement as 'Hell and Tommy White', the common use of *durst* for dare, a horse being so weak it 'couldn't pull the hat off your head', 'to run in the red steer' (to start a fire), 'to ride a razor bareback to London'; sayings such as 'go day come day, God send Sunday' and 'there's been many a good day's work wasted waiting for it to rain', and 'to rain pitchforks'. Other expressions are clearly based on songs, such as difficulties being referred to as 'a rocky road to Dublin'. Among children, counting chants and skipping songs existed in many variants, and among adults there were numerous parlour games that appear, however, to be wholly inherited from Britain.

There was an extensive lore on snakes, of which Tasmania had in fact only three varieties, though they enjoyed numerous local names. Reptiles to be met with in Tasmania were all venomous, their bite ranging from venomous to extremely venomous indeed, depending on the type of snake, its size, and the amount of poison it had the opportunity to inject into the victim. Some made odd sharp barking noises and could be extremely aggressive. The presence of a snake could be deduced from the strange piping notes of some birds, an unforgettable and hair-raising sound. Snake stories were of infinite variety, and everyone could tell of numerous encounters and the strange conduct of the snake. Some held that the hoop snake definitely existed and had been witnessed bowling down hill with its head in its mouth upon unsuspecting travellers, people swore that they had seen snakes swallow their young, other tales recounted that a person once bitten would always be attacked again because the snake knew, that milk would entice a snake from beneath or in a house, that a snake could have its attention taken by a hat thrown down near it, that some snakes would attack a man on horseback, and that the bite of the 'goanna' (blue-tongue lizard) reappeared every twelve months in the form of sores.

Tasmanians were always perceived to be different, from the days when the Derwenter shearers were singled out by their style of clothing—tall hats and kangaroo knapsacks or 'Derwent drums'—when they went over the Strait during the period before the gold rushes. On the diggings, a few years later, inhabitants of Tasmania came to be distrusted and feared as the Vandiemonians, all labelled as convicts and ex-convicts, and up to all kinds of tricks and dishonesty, but showing particular satisfaction in contemplating their past and expressing loyalty to their island.

At a later period it was commonly stated, on the other hand, that Tasmanians were different because they were so friendly to visitors. This was probably true because the isolation and, when on their home ground, their apparently relaxed view of the world, gave them no reason to be antagonistic to other people who visited the state, providing those visitors did not criticise. It was based on a confidence that, however, was superficial. Edginess was another dimension always present. It was essentially based on Tasmania's history as it was commonly understood and the state's Cinderella relationship with the rest of Australia, but the Tasmanians did not take refuge in their past.

Hobart and Launceston and some of the older townships such as Ross, Campbell Town, Oatlands, Richmond and Sorell were obviously centred upon their historic buildings, but the provincial settlements had never been much more than outposts, service centres for the surrounding pastoral areas and garrison towns when units of the British army occupied the colony. It was literally only a matter of minutes before one could be out of these centres and into the real Tasmania of mountains and hills, streams and rivers and extremely rugged country. If there was a bush or provincial image about the stereotype Tasmanian in 1939, it was partly because he or she reflected only too well the lack of urban modernity and the want of style, and the all-pervading bush.

Yet there also existed in the island state a very wealthy class that wielded power through the Legislative Council especially and was far from being unsophisticated. These people were the gentry who had occupied some of the best pastoral land in the world from the very early nineteenth century and had been the confident masters and mistresses of a virtual slave labour force of convict workers. Educated, cosmopolitan, and cultured in comparison with their fellow Tasmanians, they and their descendants enjoyed economic independence and a sense of security verging on arrogance that enabled them to travel widely, to educate their children among their social peers, and to insist on forms of address, deference and conduct that were the striking opposite of the usual Tasmanian egalitarianism. Though their power declined as parliamentary democracy was ushered in, the experience and survivals from the past meant that still their interests were ensured representation and notice at all levels and substantial power through the institutions of the state, in the form of legislative and private organisations such as clubs and informal networks. But people of the wider world as they were, the gentry still stressed their loyalty to the island and remained first and foremost Tasmanians, which was only to be expected, considering how well they had done.

Federal members of parliament also stressed their common Tasmanianism over and above the interests of party from time to time. Differences based on ideology could be submerged in order to promote Tasmania's interests. No mainland members of federal parliament took so much trouble to represent their state and make a point of being reported at home.

But over and above this sense of difference and attachment to the island state, the people continued as in the past to identify very strongly with the British Empire and the Old Country. In the last resort, and especially as Britain edged nearer to war, all the Australian states thought they would depend on Britain and its might, and the Royal Navy especially, for defence against the King's enemies. Had not Tasmanian schoolchildren for years gazed at maps of the world that had satisfyingly large areas coloured red?

But Tasmania was especially conscious of its vulnerability. It could always be cut off as no other state could be; the industrial upheavals and shipping strikes of the 1920s had forcibly brought this home. It reinforced its historic loyalty as nothing else could have, similarly to the case of New Zealand, where there prevailed a similar sense of Anglo-Saxon origin and isolation that fostered imperial feelings. There strongly persisted a sentimental and economic attachment to Home—not least strengthened by the apple market—which reached a point where Burnie could seriously be advertised as 'the Liverpool of Tasmania'. And above all perhaps this was immeasurably strengthened by the numerical dominance of the Church of England and the presence of

English-born governors whose style was admired, and who offered a comforting link with safety and respectability. This was particularly important when it is realised that a youthful convict who arrived in 1853 was still alive in 1939. So close to its unrespectable origins was Tasmania on the eve of the Second World War.

8

Modern ease: 1940–67

A. G. Ogilvie perceived the world's crisis in the late 1930s. His European travels, which included a meeting with Mussolini, led him to condemn the Axis powers. Ogilvie excelled among Australian politicians in readiness to accept Jewish refugees, and urged such defence preparedness as would make the nation's skies 'black with aeroplanes'. In J. A. Lyons (who died in April 1939, mourned by many, always scorned by some) Tasmania had offered a prime minister appropriate for post-depression recovery; had Ogilvie lived, he might have led Australia at war. Yet the Premier's martial ardour was as rare among Tasmanians as in the wider world. Early in 1938, when Ogilvie invoked black skies, a student of the University of Tasmania affirmed that 'to take up arms for a cause, and especially such a cause as freedom, is to destroy by one's own hand what one seeks to save'. Few would have spoken thus, but many would have echoed the thought.

When war came the response was vigorous enough, if often disappointing authority and super-patriots. Some 29000 men and 2000 women joined the forces; around 300 of them won gallantry awards. Deaths numbered 725 soldiers, 290 airmen, and 145 sailors. Political pressure secured re-creation of the Australian army's 40th Battalion as comprising recruits mainly from Tasmania. It went to Timor in mid December 1941 on a mission of hopeless defence. Survivors spent years as prisoners-of-war in a vast range of camps. Probably it was one of them whom Ross Parkin—a splendid depictor of prisoner experience—met in Burma:

> 'Cossy' had survived a childhood of being passed from one rough foster-parentage to another. That's how 'Cossy' grew up into a hard-working citizen: small, sturdy, hunch-shouldered and good-natured; and with a sense

of humour born of being on the receiving end of life all the time. Drover, station-hand, butcher; a man with a national pride in his Australia.

Bernard (Barney) Roberts and John Bowden are Tasmanian autobiographers who tell effectively of the war. They suffered less than 'Cossy' yet gave prime years of their lives, away from beloved homes.

Lloyd Robson remembered children like himself becoming 'aware of war through movie films, the emotion of teachers when a son was killed or posted missing, and above all by the obvious feeling with which Anzac Day was marked by adults'. Civilian men undertook various forms of defence precaution; women served with Red Cross and by fund-raising. The Japanese thrust of summer 1941–42 honed feeling: 'The impossible has happened,' said Hobart's *Mercury* of Singapore's fall; 'British prestige lies humbled in the dust.' On 1 March 1942 at least one Japanese plane flew over southern Tasmania, threatening a raid, but the raid never came.

Enough American troops went to Tasmania to echo their Australiawide stir. An Australian Air Force base outside Launceston brought less exotic newcomers. One was Geoffrey Dutton, whose account of off-duty hours supports the view that the war opened erotic liberation. A new era now promised in more tangible ways. Out of the world's convulsion came an ease that promised to smooth Tasmania's old asperities.

Political history, if never halcyon, yet gave some backing to this picture of ease. Labor continued in office throughout the period. Following Ogilvie's death Edmund Dwyer-Gray was Premier until December 1939, and then continued as Treasurer while Robert Cosgrove took leadership. Born in 1884 to small farmers outside Hobart, 'Cossy' (his nickname too) was Catholic by religion and a grocer by trade. 'He did business shrewdly but also pleasantly,' W. A. Townsley has remarked; 'he quickly recognised a bargain . . . and knew how to clinch it.' On that foundation Cosgrove built much. During the royal visit of 1954, Townsley further comments, Cosgrove and his wife Gertrude seemed to become 'part of the permanent institutions of the state', and the point has more general bearing.

Yet crises always lurked. The new Premier won the elections of 1941 well, but in 1946 his majority fell to one. Late in 1947 charges broke of his having accepted bribes from road transport interests.

Cosgrove stood down (and Edward Brooker became Premier) while inquiries proceeded. They found him not guilty, but a taint persisted. In 1948 the Legislative Council forced another election. Cosgrove won it, and those in 1950, 1955, and 1956. Through these years he lacked a clear majority in the House of Assembly; guile and fortune kept him in control. Within his own parliamentary ranks Cosgrove had some critics. Chief of these from 1946 was R. J. D. Turnbull, a medico from Launceston, ambitious and radical in a way, popular with both the general community and trade union dissidents.

Cosgrove also had to meet those forces, arising from the early Cold War, that wracked the ALP throughout mainland Australia. Tasmania had its Soviet-sympathetic Leftists, notably William Morrow, who nurtured a power base in the Australian Railways Union and won a Senate seat for Labor in 1946. Losing endorsement in 1953, Morrow formed a breakaway group, yet some of his kind of radicalism persisted within the ALP. Bigger unions regularly berated Labor ministers. The Communist Party kept a modest presence.

Anti-Communism found its loudest voice in J. R. Orchard, an ex-schoolmaster and current Launceston businessman who had long spells in parliament between 1948 and 1966. The Legislative Council used Cold War rhetoric when forcing the election in 1948. Tasmanians returned a (narrow) 'Yes' vote in the 1951 referendum, which vainly sought Commonwealth power to ban the Communist Party. Guilford Young, Archbishop of Hobart from 1954, showed hostility to the federal ALP and was ready to foster Catholic assertiveness. The Tasmanian Cabinet, and Labor parliamentarians generally, were now less Catholic than before 1940, but not much. Cosgrove's ultimate values were close to those fellow churchmen who broke with H. V. Evatt in the mid 1950s and formed the Democratic Labor Party, but he never joined that move himself. Rather, through feint and compromise, he kept his government in office and his party almost intact.

The national split had some echo. George Cole, ALP Senator from 1949, shifted to the DLP and held his seat under that banner until 1964. Democratic Labor fought many other polls, if to little effect. Into this situation burst the Hursey case. Frank and Dennis Hursey, waterside workers, refused to pay a union levy in aid of the ALP. That union, locally and nationally, was under Leftist, including Communist, leadership. The Hurseys were Catholic and inclined to the DLP. Through early 1958 Hobart's waterfront saw Hurseys, unions, stevedoring authorities, and the police engage in not-quite-violent con-frontation. The state's Supreme Court found for the Hurseys, but on appeal the federal High Court declared political levies valid. The late 1950s also marked the arrival in Hobart of Brian Harradine, to become a force in union and party politics. His opponents within the ALP long accused Harradine of subversively upholding counter-forces, in Catholic Action style.

The Cold War frosted university affairs, notably in 1958–59 when conservatives blocked appointment of G. F. E. Rudé, a brilliant histo-rian and a Communist. A wider pertinent issue was the current chap-ter in the old struggle for state aid to Church schools. Archbishop Young extolled this cause, which tangled with ideology, class, and Commonwealth–state relations. In the past many conservatives had baulked at subsidising Rome, but now that changed, and in the later 1960s the state aid cause triumphed throughout Australia. In part it was a Pyrrhic victory, marking both politicians' readiness to use religion for their purposes and the ebbing of religious passions. Yet in Young, and in J. P. McAuley, who became the university's Professor of English in 1961, Catholicism had two giants in Tasmania.

Suffering ill-health, Cosgrove resigned in August 1958, to be suc-ceeded by a man of comparable import. Eric Elliott Reece, born in 1909, did various manual jobs before becoming a union organiser in 1935. He entered the Assembly in 1946, becoming at once a minis-ter and soon federal president of the ALP. That was a troubled job in these times, and Reece met the challenge, most dramatically at a con-ference in Hobart, in March 1955, when the party split. Dead centre in politics, free from any sectarian incubus, Reece as Premier proved utter in his commitment. He embodied working-class virtue in Tasmanian politics and society. Reece won elections in 1959 (the Assembly's five electorates henceforth again returning seven members each) and did much better in 1964. These were the years of deepest political ease.

The Opposition contributed to Reece's dominance. Tasmania has ever been an intensely political place. Labor men—Cosgrove supremely but not alone—found in politics the elixir of life, occupying a wide mid-dle ground with skilled assurance. Their opponents generally were amateurs, often interested in public affairs as a consequence of being farmers. Such were almost as numerous among Liberal Party Assem-blymen as non-party Councillors. The most notable exception in post-war years, R. C. Wright, soon went off to the Senate. Only in 1960 did the Opposition find, in W. A. Bethune, a leader of any stature, himself a countryman.

A few others of note showed across the political board. R. F. Fagan sat in the Assembly between 1946 and 1974, nearly always second-in-command in Cabinet and true in that role, almost unnatural in his self-lessness. The first female parliamentarian, Margaret McIntyre (Council, 1948) had similar qualities, as shown in her long and creative community service. Her death in an aircraft accident was indeed tragic. Launceston was home both to McIntyre and to Dorothy Edwards, who in 1954 became the first woman to head any Tasmanian municipal government. Four other women had followed McIntyre into parliament by 1960; one of whom, Phyllis Benjamin, later became (Labor) government leader in the Council, an Australian first for her sex. Previous holder of that office was T. G. D. D'Alton—an adventurer, sportsman, philanthropist, and life-affirmer. Enid Lyons had become first female member of federal parliament in 1943 and of Cabinet in 1949. In retirement she wrote reminiscences of charm and value. A. G. Townley entered the House of Representatives in 1949 (beating the premier's son Henry, an able man later to grace the Supreme Court bench). Townley symbolised the impact of ex-servicemen in Australian politics and came to rank among the best of R. G. Menzies' ministers.

The mid 1960s hinted at newer political styles. In the ALP some younger people, often of university background, railed against the power lords. Deepening war in Vietnam steeled such dissidence and even within the broader electorate might have caused the federal Liberal–Country Party Government to do less well in Tasmania than elsewhere at the 1966 elections. One of the government's most tenacious critics over Vietnam was Tasmania's R. H. Lacey, otherwise of classic right-wing Labor type. Vietnam stirred local consciousness—but did not transform it.

Economic matters eased life for both politicians and community. The former must ever invoke progress, prosperity, welfare, and justice. In these times—'the golden age' for the Western European world, as Marxist historian E. J. Hobsbawm has termed it—such cries harmonised with more reality than usual. Individual suffering and social flaws notwithstanding, cheer was the dominant note.

World War II set this pattern. Tasmanians grumbled at not receiving a fair share of the contracts and jobs that it created nation-wide, and these complaints had some justice, but the flow-on was powerful. Booming production at Electrolytic Zinc led a range of mineral-based activities; potatoes of the north-west coast had their time of glory; most vegetable growers enjoyed a heyday; and the well-established textile mills soared in output. Some new industrialisation occurred, and both Hobart and Launceston boasted munition plants. Launceston's railway workshops adapted to produce various tools and equipment. A team led by Professor A. L. McAulay and E. N. Waterworth organised a plant in Hobart that ground optical lenses of superb quality. Debits there were—a flax venture failed, and livestock numbers fell—but the balance was well in credit. Real wages rose and, more importantly, jobs abounded. Unemployment sank towards nothing.

Don Norman's lot was indicative. Born in 1908, able and diligent, with strong family credentials, Norman won his first permanent job only when a brother's enlistment left a space for him to fill. Women found more remunerative and congenial work than ever before—those at the optical plant still celebrated that experience in the mid 1990s. Savings bank deposits rose by 27 per cent in one year, 1941–42. All this and, if Geoffrey Dutton is right, ecstatic sex as well!

A Treasury statement of October 1946 estimated that between 1938 and 1945 production value had risen from £13.44 million to £22.10 million. Factory employment in the same period rose from 13 802 to 19 511, of whom 24 per cent were women, and output had doubled in this sector. 'There has in fact been an industrial revolution in Tasmania during the past decade.' The tone was enthusing—*industrial revolution* stood for wealth and progress, not exploitation and misery. This war fostered a situation very different from the angry schisms of 1914–18.

Euphoria suffused a remarkable paper issued in 1944 by Edward Brooker as Minister for Post-War Reconstruction. (His filling of that role was all the more interesting as he—rarity among Labor politicians—had served in the Great War, as a British Tommy.) The very term *post-war reconstruction* seems to have had particular charisma in Tasmania. On war's outset, the paper declared, government had resolved 'that in the post-war period full-time work should be available to the workers of Tasmania so that the maintenance or "dole" system would not recur'. Now economic planning must 'exploit the potential natural resources of the State to its fullest advantage'. Government works would counter the depression likely to follow immediate post-war boom;

they might employ 60 per cent of ex-servicepeople. The paper offered blueprints for a gamut of socioeconomic advance.

Similar ideas permeated reports from the Department of Labour and Industry, the first of a long series of offices surveying and stimulating these areas. The reports spoke in an almost apocalyptic way of wartime ideas about a 'New Order', but by 1946 said that that idealism had already faltered and that conflict between haves and have-nots was likely to grow both between and within nations. Such prophecies were neither absurd nor wholly false, but scarcely came true in Tasmania. Nor even did Brooker's prophecy about the threat of depression. Rather there was some workaday shift towards a 'New Order'.

Industrialisation's greatest coup was an aluminium refinery at Bell Bay, near the Tamar's eastern head. Discussions between the state and the Commonwealth began during the war, much like those that had launched Electrolytic Zinc. The works opened in 1955, and in 1960 Comalco took the Commonwealth's share in the enterprise. Ten years later, annual output topped 50000 tons. Tasmania could not provide the bauxite for Bell Bay, which disappointed, but mining continued to be important overall. Some novelties varied the old repertoire. Much talk of an iron-pelletising plant at Savage River came good as the period ended. Osmiridium had a brief burst around 1956.

Comalco, employing up to 2000 people, joined other companies—EZ, Associated Pulp and Paper Mills (Burnie), Cadbury's, Patons', Australian Newsprint Mills (Boyer, New Norfolk)—that were large by any standard and proportionally immense in Tasmania. Their geographical range underpinned the eternal vigour of intra-island regionalism. As noted, the two big cities got most of the war factories. That growth continued, with Hobart's Moonah–Glenorchy and Launceston's Mowbray being industrial foci. The former's particular boast was Silk & Textiles Limited, whence came goods of splendid design and colour. The north-west had various complements to APPM. Busy and ugly chemico-metallurgical works lined the coast, while Goliath Cement throve at Railton.

The Hydro-Electric Commission affected Tasmanian life in divers ways, but its key role was to sustain industrial growth, especially that of the ore smelters and paper-makers. Ogilvie had exalted the HEC (its 1936 headquarters in Hobart retain Art Deco splendour), and his successors no less. Reece became known as 'Electric Eric'. Criticisms always met the earmarking of massive loan moneys for the commission, and likewise its distance from parliamentary or even ministerial overview, but they went for little. Head of the commission from 1946 was A. W. Knight. Under him at the commission's peak were 1500 'staff' and 3300 'award' employees. Knight himself had immense talent, and the commission deployed expertise on a scale beyond that in any other area of Tasmanian life. Hydro dams and stations sang their litany: Tarraleah, Waddamana, Tungatina, Liapootah, Wayatina, Poatina . . . Power use climbed sharply by any standard: from 596 641 390 kilowatt hours in 1940–41 to 3 822 000 000 in 1965–66.

While ministers sometimes hushed the fact, primary production always stayed crucial to the economy. Most of the big industrial employers processed Nature's bounty, and the story went further. Farmers had their downs—ex-soldiers on King Island perhaps the lowest—but bigger lifts. The Korean War brought a boom, especially to Midlands woolgrowers. Raising and marketing of vegetables gained further sophistication; the most notable commercial operation (from 1955) was Edgell's at Devonport and Ulverstone. In 1958 the Armed Forces Food Science establishment began at Scottsdale. Fruits did less well, although some pioneers essayed viticulture from around 1958. Forest policy in general and lease-granting in particular caused much heated inquiry in the 1940s, but the industry continued its lucrative and exploitative way. Wood-pulping began at Geeveston in the 1960s. Fisheries were more humdrum, although scallops did extra well around 1960. The primary industries depended much on international trade, now far more vigorous than in the cruel inter-war years. This meant that Tasmania scored above national averages in *per capita* contribution to exports. Politicians boasted about this, but the down side was greater vulnerability to outside forces.

Bureaucratic support to mining and forestry, fisheries and agriculture strengthened, as did the service sector at large. In the thirty years from 1938 state bureaucrats (narrowly defined) rose from 1160 to more than five thousand. Commonwealth public servants boosted such figures but only in a modest way. The Hydro-Electric Commission had no monopoly of bureaucratic talent, although certainly its scale was unique.

Construction was another of the state's key tasks, as transport service was almost as important as electricity in daily life and economic pursuits. Tasmania's traditional pattern of good roads and indifferent railways now intensified. In 1965 Tasmania had a higher proportion of roads for its spatial area, and a higher proportion of sealed to unsealed roads, than did any other state. One great event was the opening in 1963 of the Murchison Highway, which linked the north-west and the west. In 1964 the high-level Tasman Bridge across the Derwent was opened, followed in 1968 by the Batman Bridge on the Tamar. Expansion of air travel was yet more dramatic. Already by 1949 each day saw sixteen in–out flights; in 1963 an Electra flew from Hobart to Melbourne in fifty-five minutes. Launceston's new airport of 1965 was splendidly attractive and situated. Roll-on ferries, most famously the *Princess of Tasmania* from 1959, crossed Bass Strait.

Better transport spurred tourism: attractions stayed much the same, but visiting them became faster and more comfortable. In 1959–60 visitor numbers reached 174000; the past year's increase of 36000 being was about the number brought by the *Princess*. The Licensing Board had long pressured hoteliers and now reiterated that 'if Tasmania is to become the haven and paradise for tourists, a role for which she has been so richly endowed by nature, licencees must understand the true meaning and significance of "service"'. The Licensing Board had some effect, but itself proclaimed that a bigger breakthrough came with motels. Government support for tourism included the establishment in 1961 of a School of Hospitality.

Assisting the state's prosperous ease, as well as marking its limitations, was federal largesse. The Commonwealth Grants Commission, designed to help poorer states, dated back to Lyons's prime ministership and continued into the 1970s. The nature of Federation always had entailed such action, and now Tasmania made the most of it. Some islanders felt demeaned thereby, more mainlanders angered, but all without effect. Every premier (and Dwyer-Gray also as treasurer) proved skilful in working the process, behind them an outstanding public servant, the head of Treasury, K. J. Binns. Not that affection for the federal centre warmed: in the early 1940s first the Legislative Council and then the electorate rejected moves for greater Commonwealth powers, and in 1948 another similar referendum (concerned especially with price-fixing) went the same way. Tasmanian protests about not getting war contracts illustrated a stream of such complaints, some well founded. On becoming Treasurer in 1958 Reece modified this pattern, saluting Commonwealth aid with gallantry.

In September 1966 Treasury issued a revealing economic survey. 'Secondary production is the main sector of the economy', went the characteristic cry, '[it] employs the most people and has the greatest record of production'. The turning point, argued this statement, was not so much war time as the early 1950s. Tasmania now ranked fourth in the state league as to *per capita* factory production and growth rate of factory employment, where job numbers had reached 32 580; further, 'it seems certain that Tasmania is entering a phase of more rapid development'. The value of secondary production was $167.25 million; farming's figure was $69.023m; forestry, fishing, mining, and trapping together scored $34.045m.

The paper estimated population at 366 024, an increase of 8 per cent over six years. Through that period employment had grown by 18.3 per cent, keeping unemployment at the national level of 1.3 per cent. Men held 81 300 paid jobs as against women's 29 400, and the gap was closing. Notwithstanding the stress on industrialisation, Treasury recognised that the greatest rate of increase was in public and community service. (In the year 1968–69 that sector grew by 15.4 per cent.)

Personal income stood at 84.8 per cent of the Australian average, the paper further told, as against 80 per cent in 1948–49; that Tasmania had a higher proportion of children in the population than other states modified such differentials. Average annual income was $1149— it had been $393 in 1948–49—and consumer prices had not much more than doubled meanwhile. Such indicators as retail sales, bank deposits, life insurance, and motor registration were cited to confirm a story of growing bounty. The final series perhaps had greatest resonance: by 1967 Tasmania had 365 vehicles per thousand people against the nation's 354.

Further demographic statistics embellish the picture, to a point. Between the censuses of 1947 and 1954 the average annual growth rate of Tasmania's population exceeded the nation's: 2.65 per cent to 2.46 per cent! Thereafter figures were 1.82 (national, 2.26) for 1954–61, and 1.18 (1.91) for 1961–66. As remarked, the rate of natural increase stayed relatively high: 25.5 per thousand to the nation's 22.7 through the 1950s (both dropped thereafter). The state's higher rurality largely determined this pattern, although, as almost everywhere, rurality was declining too. Out-migration from Tasmania prevailed less than usually, and the island had some share in that great Australian fact of the times: big immigration from overseas, albeit below the national norm. The latter point applied even as to Britons, and more so for others. Census figures for 1966 (which had 371 410 as their total for the state) declared 18 551 residents born in the United Kingdom; 3367, the

Netherlands; 2016, Germany; 1567, Poland; 1448, Italy; 4466, continental Europe elsewhere; 2561, other exotic places. Many others came and went. In 1951, 3800 'displaced persons' lived in Tasmania, but many of them had left by 1966. The new migration had a force in other ways beyond figures. Tasmanians became aware of various ethnicities, and only sterile spirits would find no resulting enrichment. However, there were some of those, and not many citizens joined Good Neighbour groups or otherwise offered positive welcome. Even so the immigrants of these years met a happier response than had generally been the case in the past.

Post-war 'DPs'—Balts, Poles, Germans—did grinding labour, especially on Hydro works, so underpinning the economy. Their life echoed that of colonial convicts, with a similar pattern of perseverance as against disintegration in the outcome. The Dutch overall had less a rugged and more sociable experience. Many of them kept to old-world styles, sustaining Reformed churches, living in neighbourhoods together, and finding common work, especially in the building trades. Higher proportions than elsewhere took Australian citizenship.

Baltic peoples went beyond all in maintaining patriotic allegiance, upholding their nations' right to freedom throughout the decades of Soviet rule. Perhaps yearning for homeland news was desperate enough to cause some among them to join the Europeans whom Ralph Gibson, having a Tasmanian stint as part of his Communist service, remembered as customers at the Party's Hobart bookshop. Balkan angers disrupted the soccer fields of Hobart in the early 1960s and doubtless many less public places as well.

Poles also cherished patriotism, strengthened by Catholic and ex-service ties. Often having to take jobs much below their qualifications, and many never marrying, the earlier Poles suffered much alienation. But sociologist Jan Pakulski has argued that the longer side of that story has been communal strength, which not only celebrates Poland's past but also assists 'a high level of integration with social and political organisations of the Anglo-Australian majority'.

That took time—and so we could ask whether the account belongs to the next chapter rather than this. The answer is that it belongs to both, as for the migration issue at large. Some biographical snippets can appear now, others later. Two Europeans who first came to Australia in rejection of pre-war Fascism but settled in Hobart after 1945 were Edith Emery and Claudio Alcorso. Both long sustained their social beliefs and otherwise contributed much, Emery as teacher and artist, Alcorso as manager of Silk & Textiles, vigneron, patron of the arts, creator of Moorilla, a beautiful estate. Emery and Alcorso both wrote autobiographies. So did Elizabeth Godfrey and Eleanor Alliston, whose accounts of life-building in post-war years—one on Hobart's surburban frontier, the other on a Bass Strait island—affirm that upper-bourgeois Britons retained spirit and style. As well, Alliston wrote Mills & Boonery.

'The impression is left that a great opportunity was missed', W. A. Townsley has written of the years after 1945. Townsley is no Cassandra and recognises the many positive gains of the period. Yet he finds politicians neither able nor much concerned to fuse heightened economic and technical capacity with such zest as to create new ideals. Was life too easy, sapping any such drives, while the efficacy of Labor's machine further stifled innovative assertion?

Such disappointment as Townsley's has most meaning in relation to social policies. Concerning the status of women, for example, an act of 1966 recognised the principle of equal pay in the public service, but a more ambitious bill earlier had foundered in the Council. For a long time calls had sounded to replace Hobart's convict-relic gaol, and in 1960 at last that happened, but the new one was already outmoded by the time it opened. In 1964–65 Professor J. McB. Grant served as Royal Commissioner inquiring into restrictive trade practices. The inquiry ruffled many feathers, but the effect was to pass responsibility for action to the Commonwealth. And these are episodes in which government at least did something! Townsley has his point. Yet when attention moves to traditional reform areas—above all, the trinity of housing, health, and education—the record is stronger. As to each, government played a decisive (although not exclusive) part.

Tasmania had a long history of many substandard, overcrowded dwellings. The war intensified such problems as little material was available for domestic work. Shortages deepened after 1945, with more babies and immigrants on one hand and bigger expectations on the other. Feelings rose very high. Statutes of 1946 and 1952 pressured landlords to make space available at moderate rents, but the need was for massive house-building. Amidst problems and controversy, it came. One statistic tells that in the year 1949–50, 2852 dwellings were completed state-wide as against 700 in 1939; nationally the figure then rose from around 40 000 (Tasmania's share was 1.75 per cent) to 55 485 (5.2 per cent). Completion numbers reached a phenomenal 3999 in 1951–52. Such intensity dwindled, and talk of housing shortage persisted, but this area did see a great catch-up in Tasmania. Near-universal provision of electricity in new houses enriched their comfort. Suburbanism reached its apogee, and many Tasmanians had their holiday 'shack' as well.

The government built up to 30 per cent of all dwellings (in 1950–51), and the Housing Commission—to use the agency's most durable name—was central to many lives. By the late 1960s it owned more than ten thousand properties, which was a high proportion of the total housing stock by Australian standards. Considerable tasks of social welfare and control were entailed. Commission homes and estates heeded notions of amenity and planning. The state's Agricultural Bank had a complementary role, being a major source of those long-term, low-interest housing loans that graced these years.

In 1940 the infant mortality rate fell below the national average. While this situation did not always continue, and while the state's experience was but part of a much broader one, life did become healthier. Doctors from Britain contributed much to professional practice. The mid 1960s decision to establish a medical school at the University of Tasmania resulted from hard advocacy by various community forces. It was to bring great benefits, albeit—as with so many aspects of medicine—becoming ever more expensive. From the outset, women were notable among the school's graduates. Norelle Lickiss later became the university's first female professor (in community and social medicine).

Public health continued to attract able practitioners. The campaign achieving most apparent success was that against tuberculosis. Regular X-rays were compulsory from 1949. Cases dropped steadily and deaths faster, while the X-rays did further good by detecting other troubles. A somewhat similar campaign against hydatids was all the more important because in Tasmania infection rates were very high and, by their nature, difficult to stem. Dr T. C. Beard—one of the British medico-migrants, himself resident at Campbell Town—publicised the issue from 1962. Bureaucrats and farmers gathered in support. By the late 1960s infection rates in tested dogs had dropped tenfold and human disease had been duly curtailed. (There was shock in 1996 when several dogs tested positive.)

Tasmanian teeth had long been horrible, and the 1960s changed this too. Dental care was the one sector of the schools' health service then to flourish, and the establishment of a school for dental nurses in 1966 promised further advance. The school later disbanded, but by 1987 statistics told that Tasmanian children had fewer caries than other Australians. Further contributing to improvement was fluoridation of drinking water. State and local governments started moving towards this policy in the 1950s. They met vocal and tenacious opposition: some straight scientific, other more civil-libertarian, expressed in arguments ranging from high metaphysical to frontier fundamentalist (many from the north-west and western districts). Justice M. P. Crisp sat as Royal Commissioner on the matter in 1967–68. His consequent report brimmed with interest and learning:

> The evidence has ranged from the prehistoric Tasmanian aboriginal to the Eskimo, from Tristan da Cunha to the Punjab, from the laboratory marvel of a fluoride-free diet fed to germ-free rats to the tuckshops of Australian school children, from Fascism to Communism, though strangely the trail ended with Zionism, from ions to aeons, volcanoes to kettles, from null point potentiometry to the social habits of the edentulous . . .

Crisp upheld fluoridation, and a confirmatory act was passed in 1968.

Goitre was another old Tasmanian ill. The period saw intensification of countermeasures, mainly provision of iodine supplements. Only vestiges of the trouble survived.

Notifications of venereal disease stayed low, but concerning them a bureaucrat opined in 1968 'that periods of moral stringency are followed by periods of attempts to gain more permissiveness, and it seems that we are in the latter phase of the pendulum swing'. Tasmania was never particularly chaste (few places have been), but indeed the contraceptive pill now busied such swinging. Births fell as couplings rose. The latter were at perhaps their highest-ever rate in these years of the pill's novelty, if not so decisively as talk might suggest.

The period had rare importance in the history of government schooling. By national comparisons a high proportion of Tasmanians attended state as against independent (private) schools. This continued, and population boom magnified the effect. So too did raising the school-leaving age to 16, via an act of 1942 proclaimed in 1946. A decade later total state enrolments were 70 per cent higher than in 1936, with an annual increase of some 3000 through the early 1950s. The next years saw rapid growth of 'comprehensive' high schools. Their construction

146

became a key public works activity, and their curricula were designed to accommodate varying abilities. The latter shift endangered the academic meritocracy in which older high schools had gloried, but as yet that threat was chimerical. Meritocracy continued in the matriculation colleges, which began in the early 1960s. Thereby all grade 11 and 12 pupils came together in the larger centres, taught by specialists.

Education as a profession gained dignity and appeal in further ways. It benefited much from returned servicemen and (like medicine) from British immigrants. After 1946 the University of Tasmania had a faculty of education, while not only did Hobart's teachers' training college continue but also another developed in Launceston. Government paid studentships for intending teachers through their tertiary studies. Security and advancement seemed certain.

As noted, government bounty did at length go to independent schools but only in the late 1960s, and the interim tempered the schools' resilience. Nearly all continued, with little change of tempo. Friends' School, Hobart, had the experience—rare for any organisation—of having one notable leader, E. E. Unwin (1923–43), being succeeded by another, W. N. Oats (to 1973). These men were among several Quakers who contributed to public life in characteristic ways, above all by working for international peace and welfare.

A closer view can find flaws in children's education. Increased numbers and building delays meant that conditions were often difficult, sometimes barbaric. All the pedagogic talent in creation could not make every pupil industrious and tractable, a truth that became more evident as effort grew to disprove it. Nor did such effort bring Tasmania's retention rates to the national average. Matriculation colleges, their virtues notwithstanding, narrowed the space of educational opportunity. Some recipients of tertiary studentships found it a tyranny that they had to serve the Education Department for years or else repay moneys advanced.

The Faculty of Education was but one indicator of the university's post-war growth. This advance owed something to the determination of the Chancellor, Chief Justice Sir John Morris, although even he could have done little without the inflow of money now coming, especially from federal sources. Good funding and good students resulted especially from the Commonwealth Reconstruction Training Scheme (for ex-servicepeople). The first Professor of Education was C. D. Hardie, who had studied philosophy at Cambridge with that avatar of modern thought, Ludwig Wittgenstein. Near-contemporary professorial appointees were geologist S. W. Carey, of surpassing dynamism and to win fame for his world-leading theories as to 'the expanding earth'; and economist G. G. Firth, fresh from Canberra think-tanks that were planning a socially just Australia. Botanist H. N. Barber soon followed. He then began brilliant work on the genetics of eucalypts, which won him election to the fellowship of London's Royal Society (1963), the first so distinguished for Tasmanian-based research since R. C. Gunn in 1854. Barber's staff included Winifred Curtis, who was one early exception to masculine dominance in the university. Older departments of note were mathematics, whose three members around 1950— E. J. G. Pitman, J. C. Jaeger, and M. L. Urquhart—were each eminent; and physics, where work ranged from optics to astronomy, biology to theory, and where Professor McAulay set the rare pattern of most staff having Tasmanian background.

Great talent prevailed among university students of the 1950s, surely because the affluence of this time gave unprecedented scope for talent to flourish. Pertinent names will appear throughout the rest of this book, but three might make the point now. All were youths of mundane island-wide background, educated in those meritocratic state schools: Lloyd Robson (born 1931), author of much notable history, especially about Tasmania; Neal Blewett (1933), Rhodes Scholar, Professor of Political Science at Flinders University, federal minister, Australia's High Commissioner in London; and David Green (1936), holder of the university's chair of geology (1977–93) and of many other posts and honours, including fellowship of the Royal Society.

While achievement grew, the university suffered many troubles in the 1950s, to a degree that modified not only that record but also the broader one of this being Tasmania's time of ease. From a distance, these crises seem a logical and likely outcome of modernisation proceeding in a context where older modes and men retained power. To many, especially newcomers on academic staff, John Morris appeared an autocrat rather than an inspirer, and the university Council yet more reactionary. Dissidents' protest led to Cosgrove appointing a royal commission in 1955, its report supporting them. 'Old guard' feeling grew embittered.

In March 1956 came the dismissal of S. S. Orr, Professor of Philosophy since 1952 and vehement against the university's power-brokers. Orr allegedly had engaged in sex with a female student, and other criticisms of him went around. Students divided in judging him as a teacher; his research record was scant. The dismissal went to law. Both the Supreme Court of Tasmania and the High Court of Australia upheld it, which merely steeled Orr and his supporters. To many, especially outside Tasmania, Orr's fate smacked of the island's ugliest traditions. The Federation of Australian University Staff Associations backed his cause. A latter-day feminist has interpreted this support as largely driven by male academics' sexual claims over students, and certainly the association saw the case as vital in securing professional tenure and status. Not until 1966 was meagre reconciliation found. The chair was duly filled by W. D. Joske.

One cluster of support for Orr was that of Anglican, Catholic, and Presbyterian churches. The episode belonged with broader ecumenicism. This found expression in the local World Council of Churches, a notable figure in its story being the Anglican Bishop, G. F. Cranswick.

The Orr case was hideous, yet otherwise the university's advance did continue. Both the medical school and the Faculty of Agriculture began in the 1960s. Good staff kept coming, although in these days of high academic mobility they often moved along. All six people appointed between 1960 and 1962 to the relevant departments in time became fellows of the Australian Academy of the Humanities, a record unlikely to be bettered anywhere, whenever.

Formal adult education outside the university had its turbulence earlier and with happier aftermath. The long-established Workers' Educational Association lost its centrality to an Adult Education Board, constituted in 1949. Pioneer chairman was the ubiquitous John Morris, who found greater play for his dynamism here than at the university, especially after the appointment as director of K. G. Brooks in 1953. The board created a wide scope for itself in these pre-television years, sponsoring much more than routine classes. Edmund Hillary shone brightest of its stars, but at just one summer school (1955) speakers included Vance and Nettie Palmer, A. E. Floyd, H. V. Evatt, and M. L. Oliphant. The board embraced live theatre, which generally did well in the post-war years.

A visit by the Old Vic company, led by Laurence Olivier and Vivien Leigh, was a great highlight (1948), the more so as Olivier helped to clinch a campaign to save and revive Hobart's historic Theatre Royal. A National Theatre and Fine Arts Society had State Government backing and achieved good things before running aground. Specialist societies enriched film-going, ever a mainstream entertainment.

Tasmania benefited vastly from the musical entrepreneurship of the Australian Broadcasting Commission, most obviously through visits of world celebrities and through an agreement of 1948 with the State Government to sustain the Tasmanian Symphony Orchestra. The orchestra advanced far under the baton of Thomas Matthews (1961–68), and its crescendo has long continued. In 1964–65 the Education Department launched a Conservatorium of Music. Rex Hobcroft and Jan Sedivka were its distinguished directors.

The passions of new-beat music that swept the western world from the later 1950s had local force: Jerry Lee Lewis, Fabian, and Louis Armstrong were other musical celebrities to visit Tasmania. Huge crowds saluted them and related activity. Square-dancing had tremendous vogue. Supreme local figures in the whole story were Tom Pickering and Ian Pearce. They had started playing jazz together at Hutchins School in the 1930s and were still gigging sixty years later, but the 1950s were their heyday.

Art schools in both Hobart and Launceston continued feisty. Jack Carington Smith headed both from time to time. Winning the Archibald Prize for portraiture in 1963 confirmed his leadership of the island's artists. Many worked in that area, women prominent among them, with Edith Holmes perhaps the most notable. Public sculpture made its mark in Hobart through Lyndon Dadswell's wall-reliefs at the Commonwealth Bank (1954) and Tom Bass's madonna and child at St Mary's Catholic cathedral (1962).

A stirring story of cultural success lay in the creation of the State Library of Tasmania. In the late 1930s a Free Library Movement had burgeoned. It called for light in a gloomy area where the only relief was an old-style subscription library in Launceston. With war's outbreak the movement was quick to establish a 'camp library service' among troops, who, Treasurer Dwyer-Gray forecast with delight, 'will bring the love of reading and literature back to civilian life'. There followed an archetypal outside-expert inquiry and in 1943 an act, which established the library by coordinating current bodies and extending their work through state and municipal funding. The plan was optimistic and the problems were many, but change did prevail. Again John Morris led the van. 'New services to the Gaol, nursery schools, youth clubs, and study groups have been instituted', went the State Library's 1945 report; 'the inauguration of sessions of documentary films added to the continuing success of the winter evening recitals of recorded music, public lectures, displays of books, and exhibitions of art'. Public expenditure had grown sixfold in the two years between 1943 and 1945.

The Tasmanian Museum in Hobart and the Queen Victoria Museum in Launceston also expanded, if more modestly. They, not the university, backed some research into the Tasmanian Aboriginals. The QV took a large and creative part in Launceston's intellectual life. Both museums interacted with the Royal Society of Tasmania, which had its centenary in 1943. Field naturalist groups aided more popular, hands-on inquiry. The Australian and New Zealand Association for the Advancement of Science held fine Tasmanian congresses in 1949 and 1965. Every registrant at the latter received from the State Government a masterly *Atlas of Tasmania*, edited by University of Tasmania geographer J. L. Davies. At the 1991 congress, their successors received tourist brochures, and no new Atlas has appeared.

Establishment of a state archives authority in 1949 augured well for the study of local history. The office soon employed three young men— R. C. Sharman, P. R. Eldershaw, and G. T. Stilwell—not only excellent in that work but also pioneers of the Tasmanian Historical Research Association (1951). The Patron was E. M. Miller, then ending his thirty-nine years teaching of philosophy and psychology at the university, author of the mighty *Australian Literature from Its Beginnings to 1935* (1940) and about to add *Pressmen and Governors: Australian Editors and Writers in Early Tasmania*. THRA's most famous meeting came on 28 May 1952 when K. M. Dallas—iconoclast academic and sailor in Tasmanian yachts and the Royal Navy—argued that Britain's decision to settle New South Wales derived from concerns for sea power and trade rather than for 'dumping' convicts. Another enduring fame for the association was to publish N. J. B. Plomley's *Friendly Mission: The Tasmanian Journals and Papers of George Augustus Robinson 1829–1834* (1966), so crucial in advancing knowledge of the Tasmanian Aboriginals. Research into Tasmanian history quickened at the university. The National Trust, established in 1960, deepened interest in 'heritage in stone'. Museums like that about pioneers at Burnie and folk at Narryna in Hobart worked to complementary effect.

The eternal debate about convictism and its legacy took an interesting twist in 1941 with publication of B. C. Smith's *Shadow Over Tasmania*, which presented transportation as so successful in redeeming potential criminals that latter-day Tasmanians should feel no shame in descent from them. Premier Cosgrove endorsed this 'bright, common-sense' approach. *Shadow* sold bountifully over many years, but otherwise attitudes appeared to stay much the same, which reflects that confused schizophrenia (very naturally) besetting the matter. Twenty-four years after *Shadow*, Robson's first book, *Convict Settlers of Australia*, drawing on the marvellous Tasmanian archives, said much the same as had Smith but in scholarly mode. Van Diemen's Land, wrote Robson, had offered the not-so-petty thieves that most convicts were 'a golden opportunity to make good. It could be done and it was done'.

Probably the Tasmanian who wrote and sold the largest number of books in these years was children's author Nan Chauncy, who deployed the island's geography and peoples. Local initiative made a pleasant film, *They Found a Cave* (1962), from one of her works. Marie Bjelke-Petersen and N. W. Norman still lived on Hobart's eastern shore. Their pre-war books did well in the world's middle-brow markets. She invoked romance, with much passionate Tasmaniana; he wrote of Central Australia and its peoples of all races with loving sympathy and called on his compatriots to find identity and inspiration there.

Yet of course gifted Tasmanians often sought the Big World. Two scholars who had graduated from the University decades earlier, philologist John Orr and physicist Philip Bowden, respectively won fellowships of the British Academy and London's Royal Society. In London F. M. Alexander continued to teach his method of bodily posture, which promised liberation of all kinds of creative energy. Oliffe Richmond, who turned 21 in 1940, was already sculpting somewhat in the manner of Henry Moore in a Hobart garden-shed. He was later to work with Moore and so build a notable career. Loudon Sainthill's settings were a glory of the post-war London stage. The 1940s saw Errol Flynn's peak as swashbuckling film hero and fornicator. Also in Hollywood lived Merle Oberon. Was she once little Mary O'Brien of Hobart, child of a Chinese domestic, or did her Asian-style beauty descend from an Indian prostitute, and her tales of Tasmanian background seek to dispel that heritage (even from her own consciousness)? Whatever, Oberon visited Tasmania shortly before her death in 1979.

An embodiment of modern culture flew into Hobart early in 1946: Hal Porter, immediately to teach at Hutchins School, in the longer term to meditate upon the island. Porter made some close friends, enjoyed drinking with ex-service chaps, gave much vitality to the city as a producer of plays; but all such pleasures were marginal. In Hobart he found 'evil . . . moving as naturally as blood through veins, an impulse drugging enough to blot guilt from the mind'. Some would judge that evil lay within Porter rather than around him, but his perception underlay a powerful *oeuvre* of fiction, verse, and autobiography. Porter's novel, *The Tilted Cross* (1961), counterparts Marcus Clarke's *His Natural Life*. His reports of, say, a schoolboy riot at Hutchins (King's Birthday 1946) or of libertinism among Hobart's 1950s intelligentsia fascinate no less.

Gwen Harwood came south just before Porter and stayed until her death fifty years later. Through the first twenty years or so she rarely left suburban Hobart (and Australia never), but constantly nurtured her genius, rooted in deep riches of European literature, music, and philosophy. Similar in intellectual and creative capacity was James McAuley. Until his death in 1976, Tasmania was home to two great poets, each writing of the place with gripping intensity.

The Penguin Book of Australian Verse, as first published in 1958, ordered contributors by age. Last to appear were Christopher Koch (born 1932) and Vivian Smith (1933). Both were 'old Tasmanian', graduates of Hobart High School and the University of Tasmania, marvellously read, destined to maintain creativity towards the century's end. Also appearing in 1958 was Koch's *Boys in the Island*, supremely *the* modern Tasmanian novel, parallel in time and nature with Patrick White's *Tree of Man*, although Porter was a more direct influence. By 1958 Koch already had travelled in Asia, so preparing for his *Across the Sea Wall* (1965), which is less Tasmanian than *Boys*, but also a marker in Australian cultural history.

Sport ever kept its place in popular delight. Foul weather dimmed an interstate Australian Rules football carnival in 1947, but thirteen years later came one of Tasmania's rare defeats of Victoria at that game. Yet a Melbourne-bred newcomer who arrived in the state at just that time found Tasmanians lackadaisical in spectating. Rather they participated—in many sports, but notably in yachting, hunting, shooting, fishing, all preserves of privilege by Old World norms. For many, bushwalking sustained body and spirit, even soul. Had these styles something to do with the remark (as told by Townsley) in 1957 by British academic Denis Brogan: 'to him Australians looked as if they did not belong to the land on which they walked, excepting the Tasmanians'?

If not the greatest of spectators, Hobartians enjoyed an event launched in 1945 and soon bringing international fame, the Sydney–Hobart yacht race. Running between Boxing Day and New Year, it prompted much cheer and carousing in those easiest of days. Yet summer could bring other, and more profound, messages.

9

Post-modern flux: 1967–96

September and October 1966 brought lush growth to southern Tasmania, and summer turned ultra-dry. The first days of February 1967 blazed hot, and smoke clouded the sky. On Tuesday the 7th gale-force northerlies spread the inferno deep into Hobart itself. Deaths numbered sixty-two. Every kind of property was devastated, and more than a thousand homes burned. The day will remain forever in the memory of those who endured it. What Lloyd Robson elsewhere called 'old Tasmanian carelessness' contributed to the disaster, and arson too had its place, but the root problem was that of a small polity having to manage sizeable and challenging terrain. The contrasts of nature were stark: a normally temperate region suffered extremes of heat and wind; wooded gullies and steeps—symbols of Tasmania's beauty—fed the terrible flames.

Various circumstances softened the fires' aftermath. Deeds of courage and survival balanced those of death and suffering. From mainland Australia and beyond came much material aid. Controversy arose as to relief policies (especially whether they should discriminate between victims with and without insurance), but unity and resolve were dominant. That helped recovery from the devastation of the fires, but longer retrospect makes them the most appropriate marker of that pervasive change that came upon Tasmania around 1970.

Change is eternal, and the final third of the twentieth century has told that rule worldwide. *Post-modernity* is an overused term but a necessary one. Considering Tasmania's limits and isolation, with many strains of self-sufficient continuity, its share in this transformation is notable. 'Tasmania possesses too much history,' Peter Conrad, fiercest of all the place's critics, has written, and the fires renewed that pattern. 'History' means problems. *Angst* long had tinctured Tasmanian life,

and it now swelled again. Standards and aspirations that post-war ease
had promised to crystallise began to waver, even to dissolve, while others challenged for hegemony. Paramount among the latter was eleva-
tion of nature, its putative rights and power. Consequent issues came
to dominate politics and many sociocultural affairs. The fires set a context, if ambiguously, even for that theme.

Changes in the economy were crucial to this new scenario, both in
themselves and by impelling further drives. While the early 1980s saw
the lowest ebb, the period overall came to resound with constriction
and crisis. The knowledge that grimmer counterparts of the situation
existed elsewhere in the world did little to ease local pain. Social tensions and problems branched out.

The decline of industrial manufacturing loomed large. Employment
in this sector fell sharply. At its peak, one in four of the workforce had
been engaged in industrial manufacturing, but the figure declined to
fewer than one in seven. Job numbers shrank from a high in the late
1960s of around 36 000 (by one calculation, 32 000 by another) to
24 000 and less. The change in the value of manufacturing output was
far less, staying near 20 per cent of overall product, very much the
Australian average. Despite fears of closure, most of the industrial giants
stayed, but that was not true in textiles, and many smaller industries
did fold their tents, or just fold. The surviving giants managed with many
fewer workers. A parliamentary committee of 1982–83 found that in
the past decade employment at Associated Pulp and Paper had shrunk
by 2000 while production rose 40 per cent, and Electrolytic Zinc's figures were similar. While such efficiencies were imperative for survival,
they exacted heavy human and social cost. A similar pattern prevailed
at Mount Lyell, underlining the continuity between mining and manufacturing industries. Here talk of catastrophic closures was even more
persistent, but again not quite fulfilled. Mount Lyell itself proved the
great stayer, although copper smelting ceased there in 1969 after nearly
seventy-five years. There were no finds to re-create the minerals surge
of a century before. Gas from Bass Strait delivered something, but not
to that level.

Industrialisation yet had its achievements. Pre-eminent was that of
Robert Clifford and his Hobart firm, International Catamarans, which
came to employ many hundreds of skilled workers in producing craft
for world markets. Blundstone's had made footwear for Tasmanians

since around 1870, and more than a century later their boots became international high fashion. Southern Aluminium, established in the 1980s close to Comalco at Bell Bay, produced car wheels in vast numbers, especially for Japanese customers.

One reason for dating Tasmania's new age from the late 1960s is that thereafter woodchips became a significant export. Forest policy had many earlier stirs, but (as will be seen) now came qualitative change. Chips helped the industry to remain important: Tasmania employed a sixth of the nation's forestry workers. Other land-based industries saw greater variation. Pastoralism steadily diminished, although superfine wool from the Midlands ever fetched astronomical prices, and the locally bred Cormo sheep found international buyers. Traditional farming could still sponsor success stories, as was most evident in the autobiography of B. A. Farquhar, who battled from childhood on a small holding outside Scottsdale to become a great proprietor of the region, famous in his praise for earthworms.

Those traditional Tasmanian pursuits, pome and berry fruit-growing, declined still more than pastoralism, albeit with some traces of revival from the late 1980s. Many orchards became hobby lots for exurbanites. Vegetables held better; in the north-west potatoes still throve, especially the Kennebec, which helped to meet the nation's voracity for fries and chips; while onions had a more novel success story. Production of gourmet foods was much vaunted. Vineyards sprang up throughout warmer areas, and local wines won high esteem and prices. Dairy produce belonged here, King Island's most insistently. Essential oils and drugs were other high-intensity crops to deliver good returns. Opium poppies were among them, while in 1992 parliamentarians learned that Tasmanian cannabis 'is much sought after'.

Exploitation of the seas echoed colonial times. Shell-fish predominated. In the 1970s abalone made fortunes for some fishermen and boosted exports. Then came intense cultivation of oysters, mussels and, above all, salmon. As with gourmet foods, marketing made much of the island's 'clean, green' image, another link with the nature debate. Deep-sea fishing, for tuna especially, had some importance. Hobart became a port for Japanese fleets, which were most numerous in the late 1970s. The crew bought Chanel perfume in such quantity as to make local sales among the world's highest.

Despite whirls of reshuffling, downsizing, and golden-handshaking, the state bureaucracy remained a considerable employer, more than offsetting lower-than-national levels in Commonwealth and municipal service. Thus in 1994 around a third of all employees were in government work, the highest proportion in Australia. Personal service jobs also loomed large, but not so as to balance shortfalls in finance and banking. The latter situation (as did the scarcity of other jobs) owed much to the impact of technology, which fostered centralisation of services in mainland capitals. Takeovers and shakedowns multiplied throughout business. However, space still offered for local speculators. The most notorious was one Colin Room, who caused the loss of much Tasmanian money entrusted to him and then escaped overseas for years before returning to trial and spending 1988–92 in gaol.

Stringency of federal aid cut at employment and the broader economy. Greater rigour was constant from the mid 1970s, whichever party held power in Canberra and whichever allocation system prevailed. Again reality was not always as bad as rhetoric threatened. Such comfort was cold, but it was some kind of reward that Tasmania now drew less on national coffers. A louder boast remained that the island had more than its share of national exports. However, both pertinent figures and the assumptions underlying such pride became fuzzier. Of course exports did matter. Japan as a market loomed yet larger and quicker for Tasmania than the nation generally.

Tourism easily scored as the major sector of growth. By the 1990s it provided nearly 10 per cent of gross product and yet more of employment. The island's beauty and historic sites received more boosting than ever. The industry easily could seem to offer salvation, bringing in a more genial way such 'tertiary service' bounty as had gaol provision throughout colonial days. Convictism served the economy again by providing many of the historic sites. Establishment of the state's National Parks and Wildlife Service in 1972 strengthened the bureaucratic underpinning of tourism. The Whitlam Federal Government of 1972–75 cherished heritage matters, and henceforward Canberra funded many related projects, notably at Port Arthur.

Also drawing tourists were casinos at Hobart (built in 1973) and Launceston (1982). The former led the nation in being approved by law. The blessing of the law was sanctioned by a plebiscite (1968), in which chief opposition came from Protestant moralism, still carrying force. There was continuity on the successful side of the debate too, for the casino belonged in a tradition most evident in Tattersalls' history. This episode stained Eric Reece a little; his government had been largely free from drink and gambling odium. The casinos were big and bold, providing high-quality accommodation and much entertainment. Such was the necessary thrust of tourism. Restaurants multiplied, and the School of Hospitality flourished as did few other institutions. Varied benefits spun off and around, glossing life. Yet anti-casino voters could remark that gambling addiction grew, while many more customers were locals (and fewer mainland or Asian high-flyers) than propaganda had forecast.

Whatever tourism might do, modesty of growth remained the basic economic fact. By 1994 population had risen to but 472 400, a minimal increase. Outmigration (largely to mainland Australia) continued to climb, and there was little counterflow. Breaking long norms, the rate of natural increase fell below national averages: Tasmanians no longer had relatively more children. Economic torpor entailed many problems, most obviously job scarcity and decline of property values. Unemployment rose above 10 per cent in the early 1980s and still further ten years later. The teenage figure exceeded 40 per cent. Total employment struggled above 200 000 in 1990 and then fell; many new jobs had long been seasonal and part-time. Males suffered particular decline in employment. All this indicated polarisation between haves and have-nots. Karl Marx's theories seemed more cogent as the regimes around the world that professed them crumbled into absurdity and horror.

Trade union membership (in relation to all employees) stayed higher in Tasmania than elsewhere, probably because much employment was in big plants and the public sector. New-style management could evoke fierce protest. The supreme instance was at Burnie's Associated Pulp mill, where production rates had risen to high levels and which earlier had been a proud site of welfare capitalism. Militant protest against further controls and cuts unrolled through mid 1992. Each side claimed final victory, but hurt and hate went deep. Around that same time police arrested fifty-six Hobart stevedores who stopped the unloading of a trawler allegedly manned by scabs. Electrolytic Zinc was another plant where once welfare capitalism flourished but now strife blew. White-collar and service unions, nurses and teachers among them, appeared to be particularly ready to strike.

Young male suicide was the most terrible indicator of social trauma seemingly related to economic distress. Less extreme but more visible alienation of youth prompted drunken violence in the cities. Street-begging became obtrusive. Around 1980 reported drug cases exceeded a thousand annually. By then police reports already spoke more generally of 'blatant disrespect towards the property and possessions of others', and pertinent offences more than doubled afterwards, to 37 653 in 1991–92.

Just as traditional Tasmanian birth rates had been higher than the rest of the nation, so divorce rates had fallen below, but by the mid 1990s they had become the highest of any state. The rate of marriage continued to decline. In 1969 the state's Welfare Department noted that many young single mothers were keeping their babies and taking jobs to do so, whereas a Legislative Council committee in 1984 suggested that single mothers were sustained by pensions. The Welfare Department also spoke (not apropos of single mothers) of 'growing numbers of family crises, parental irresponsibility, and social inadequacy'. Domestic life was hard in straitened times. In 1967 the state housing authority had two tenants on social benefit; in 1989 there were 2320.

Yet the same report that told those figures also cited one client's tribute:

I have been in my house for ten months now . . . and I'm very happy with it. This is my first real home since I left my parents' place when I was sixteen. Thanks to you, my children have their own bedrooms and a big backyard to play in and keep them safe. I also have my garden . . . thanks very much.

Difficulties and torpor were never all the truth. Tasmanians still knew how to make pragmatic hedonism out of moderate things. Some statistics were positive: household incomes kept rising, even in the 1980s (overall) by about a tenth, some two-thirds of the national average. Ownership of white goods and prevalence of liquor licences were national highs at least some of the time, as also (in the early 1990s) was the ratio of cars to humans. New houses kept crowding towns, beach, and bush, much beyond population growth. Did the world ever know so much domestic space for each body? While men dropped from the workforce, women gained much ground, notably in tourism and public service, and their participation rate of about 50 per cent in the 1990s was little below Australian norms.

Perhaps, after all, Tasmanians were showing that people could be happy within a steady-state economy. A longer perspective might see its stagnation, above all absence of population pressure, as a mighty boon. But no consensus prevailed on such issues. Instead they were part of that controversy over nature that now had come to grip the island.

To nature conservationists—*Greens* became the convenient word—the relative failure of industrialisation in Tasmania seemed to prove the grotesquerie of policies founded on it, all the more so because allegedly industry exploited the earth, forest, and seas; while dams that provided the electricity essential for industry raped lakes and mountains. Greens felt that, while wrong by any standard, such practice was all the more abominable amidst Tasmania's surpassing beauty. Against such views, others insisted that the very constriction of the economy demanded all the more striving for new development. Was not the logic of conservation an ever-diminishing, impoverished Tasmania? Did not opposition to hydroelectricity prove the Greens' hypocritical absurdity, since it was a self-sustaining and clean energy source, its use a wonderful conjunction of nature's bounty and human skill?

The conservation issue dominated Tasmanian politics throughout these years, if not quite so much as the following narrative might imply, yet with the result that Greens won much influence both outside and within parliament. They benefited from the fact that the House of Assembly is elected by proportional representation, a system championed by that pre-eminent nineteenth-century liberal, A. I. Clark. The Greens fulfilled Clark's ideal in building a political culture in which parliamentary representatives had intimacy with constituents: Clark wanted a legislature brimming with such representatives for various interests. However, he wanted also an executive with strength based on direct popular legislation, as distinct from the Westminster model in which the sanction for government was majority support in the lower chamber of parliament. Tasmania's structure followed Clark in having proportional representation in the Assembly, but stayed with Westminster notions of responsibility. That situation, with other aspects of the Tasmanian electoral system, had led in the past to many precarious governments, and now that pattern intensified. Politics fluxed, perhaps towards transformation.

In May 1967 the Hydro-Electric Commission announced plans for massive damming of the Gordon River catchment in the island's southwest. Hints of this design had stirred conservationist alarm for years, and now it deepened. At issue was beautiful Lake Pedder. Earlier the HEC had spoken of protecting it, but now drowning was forecast. While protest grew, the 1967 drought (one cause of the bushfires) worsened. A result was for Tasmania to lead the nation towards daylight saving, but that was minor. Both the HEC and Reece's government lost standing as dams drained to 16 per cent capacity. Power for industry and homes was rationed. Commission plans for the Gordon won parliament's approval, against criticism within and without.

Labor Party affairs added to Reece's troubles. Argument over Brian Harradine and his alleged subversion gathered venom with the years, and Vietnam-inspired radicalism also grew. Reece continued in his courses. As the May 1969 elections approached, he invoked the recent past as Tasmania's 'Golden Age of Development'. Such a case had returned the ALP since 1934. Something more crucial than apparent had changed: the government lost. A clue perhaps lay in this being the first time when anyone born since World War II had voted.

Walter Angus Bethune still led the Liberals and so became Premier, the first scion of 'old gentry' landowners to attain the position for nearly a century. To hold office Bethune had to coalesce with Kevin Lyons, who, as the son of Joseph and Enid, had his own Tasmanian heritage. Earlier Lyons had broken from the Liberals to form the Centre Party. He long had questioned the Hydro-Electric Commission's claims, and generally the Liberals—with their rural and professional bias—had never been so thoroughly committed to industrialisation as was Labor. Nevertheless, the flooding of Pedder began.

Bethune had some ministers with his own ability and diligence. His government built a fair record—the Parks and Wildlife Service was one result already mentioned, and others will follow. However, Lyons never subordinated his ambitions for leadership, and on that reef the government broke. Bethune resigned in March 1972, facing doom at the consequent elections. In this campaign the United Tasmania Group, a precursor in environmental politics throughout the world, was active. Its inspirer was Richard Jones, botanist and pioneer of environmental studies at the University of Tasmania. In southern electorates the UTG did well enough, without winning any seats. Reece returned to office with a good majority, doubtless confident that the electorate had learned lessons which would long keep him leader of Tasmania.

That was not to be. The gap between Reece and the newer world now widened. One to make that point has been Kevin Kiernan, a worshipper of Pedder who yet tells of casual talk with Reece after a

Green demonstration. The Premier was contemplative: 'Look at that little girl feeding the seagulls . . . How warm the sun feels.' That demonstration would have been among the many that disputed Pedder's flooding, completed in 1972.

An Environmental Protection Act of the following year mollified little. Pedder and conservation became issues dividing Reece both from Whitlam's Federal Government and from local Laborites who venerated Whitlam. State ALP conferences grew rabid, with charges that the leadership had bribed Lyons to defect from Bethune provoking much drama. Caucus pushed some youngish, ambitious dissidents into Cabinet. Reece had no ease with them, nor with the older M. G. Everett, who had some potential to 'Whitlamise' Tasmanian Labor. After several brushes with the Premier—their differences over Lake Pedder were especially bitter—Everett went to the Senate in 1974. Trade unions remained quick to lambast all the politicians, Reece included. Fate added its blow in January 1975 as the *Lake Illawarra*, coming up the Derwent, crashed into the Tasman Bridge, disabling the bridge for nearly three years. This was a less profound disaster than the fires, but its political damage went deeper.

In February 1975 the ALP state conference resolved that henceforth pre-selection be denied politicians older than or approaching the age of 65. Reece's year of birth was 1909: Oedipal urges had triumphed. The Premier soon resigned, and W. A. Neilson—who had not manoeuvred against him—succeeded. First elected in 1946, then aged 21 and a postal clerk, Neilson had qualities and aspirations but was also vulnerable and difficult. Labor retained office in the polls of late 1976.

The Tasmanian Wilderness Society formed that year. Its was especially concerned with the island's south-west. Among its leaders was R. J. (Bob) Brown, a doctor who had come to Tasmania in 1972, and soon after denounced Pedder's flooding as 'world epitome of man's destructiveness'. Brown was to become central to the Green story. Sympathetic media coverage encouraged many to find him charismatic. Environmental sensitivity grew with proof that industry—predominantly Electrolytic Zinc and Australian Newsprint Mills—had polluted the Derwent. The University of Tasmania's Professor of Chemistry, Harry Bloom, led this charge.

The cares of office became very heavy for Neilson, and he resigned in November 1977. His successor was D. A. (Doug) Lowe, Catholic and tradesman by background, young and thoughtful. The world's virtues could scarcely have sustained Lowe through the travails ahead.

In late 1978 the Hydro-Electric Commission proposed further dams in the south-west, embracing the Franklin and lower Gordon Rivers. Controversy stormed. Opinion polls showed majorities strongly against the HEC. Within Cabinet and caucus relations between commission and government ranked high among various disputes. Most ministers were as youthful as Lowe; ambition and determination raged among them. At general elections in mid 1979 the government won with an ease that in retrospect seems odd, and which gave Lowe little respite. A constitutional imbroglio forced a by-election for all seats in the Hobart-centred electorate of Denison. Among those returned was N. K. Saunders, standing as a Democrat. The Australian Democrats were long to retain local standing and to uphold conservation, if not so fervently as the Greens. Within Labor, parliamentarians included, attitudes to conservation ranged widely—from Reecean developmentalism to quasi-Green—and with increasing vehemence all round. Ministerial shuffling fomented differences rather than soothed them.

Anger at the HEC's plan for the south-west rose higher. The National Parks and Wildlife Service joined the dissidence, and the Wilderness Society proved masterly in its orchestration. The issue attracted interest far beyond Tasmania (even in Buckingham Palace). A high conservationist stance came more easily to outsiders than to many locals. In mid 1980 the government opted for a hydro scheme ('Gordon above Olga') that would save the Franklin. Lowe promoted this scheme, which, for many, proved his vacillation. Gordon-above-Olga passed the Assembly but halted in the Legislative Council. Employees and supporters of the HEC, Reece and Bethune among them, counter-organised.

In September 1981 Labor caucus determined on a plebiscite to choose between the dam proposals. Pro-development forces pushed that decision, humiliating Lowe. Ever more complex and perfervid factionalism forced him from leadership of party and government early in November. H. N. Holgate, a former journalist, became Labor Premier. As the plebiscite date of 28 November approached, conservationists urged an informal vote to express hostility to all hydro schemes. Final, confused, results went 47 per cent for the HEC plan, 8 per cent for the above-Olga scheme, and 45 per cent informal.

When parliament resumed, Lowe, Saunders, and another Laborite,

Mary Willey, joined the Opposition in a vote of no confidence against the government. A consequent election in May saw a mighty anti-Labor swing, probably impelled by blue-overall votes. Lowe duly wrote a powerful account, *The Price of Power*. One of his ministers, T. G. Aulich, found melodramatic fiction (*The River's End*) the appropriate mode for his narration. Amanda Lohrey, political scientist and spouse of yet another Labor minister, invoked the *Zeitgeist* in *The Reading Group*, a novel of high quality and so distressing to Aulich that he brought action to halt its sale.

The new Liberal Premier, Robin Trevor Gray, was an agricultural consultant who had moved from Victoria to Launceston in 1965. More forceful than any incumbent since Reece, Gray had an able team, and, as the early 1980s recession lifted, it seemed that a pro-growth government was pushing towards success. However, extraordinariness soon resumed.

Environmentalism had a large part in this. Gray's first statute, passed with full Labor support, authorised the Franklin dam. When work commenced, Greens opposed it with physical confrontation. Bob Brown became a national figure and in early 1983 an Assemblyman, filling the place of N. K. Saunders, who had become a senator. Supporters of development, including many industrial workers in western Tasmania, felt increasing hostility for the Greens. This gap between commonalty and idealistic intelligentsia had something of that which prevailed during the governorship of Franklin himself.

Federal pressure secured a Green victory. Prime Minister Malcolm Fraser accepted the environmental case sufficiently to nominate the south-west as a World Heritage area. The nomination proceeded against the opposition of Fraser's fellow Liberals in Tasmania. However, Fraser did not attempt to block the dam's construction, so giving his opponent R. J. Hawke an opportunity. Taking that opportunity helped Hawke to win the 1983 election. His Labor government moved against damming the Franklin, and the High Court duly confirmed this federal sovereignty.

Gray fulminated, and then directed the Hydro-Electric Commission to shift operations northward (evidently Tasmania's damming age was to close with their completion). Federal compensation enlivened the state's economy. Feeling between conservationists and developers remained high, and now forestry became the flashpoint. Woodchipping aroused much Green animus, and again federal power backed that stand. Legislation and 'agreements', notably of 1985, brought little peace. Gray increased his vote at the 1986 election, but another Green joined Brown in the Assembly. Soon conservationists and lumbermen fought at one crucial site, Farmhouse Creek. Logging the Lemon-thyme forest evoked more anger; extension of the World Heritage area was involved. On top of all this burst proposals for a pulp mill at Wesley Vale in northern Tasmania. Conservationists saw the proposals as threatening gross pollution. Christine Milne emerged as leader of this environmental cause. A parent, erstwhile teacher, and locally reared, she became a Boadicea. At the 1989 polls Milne and two further Greens—making one in each electorate—were elected to the House of Assembly.

With Labor holding fourteen seats, Gray had lost his majority. Labor and Greens (led by Brown) formed an 'accord' whereby the latter promised hypothetical support for a Labor government in return for guarantees that the mill would not proceed and the environment generally would receive protection. Weeks of crisis saw Governor Sir Phillip Bennett deny Gray's call for a dissolution. When parliament resumed in late June, Greens and Labor acted together, sustaining the accord. Bennett commissioned Labor's leader, M. W. Field, to form a government from that party.

During the crisis one of Labor's new parliamentarians, J. G. Cox, was offered a bribe to switch allegiance and so keep Gray in office. The briber was E. A. Rouse, owner of Launceston's *Examiner* and other media interests, and possessed of sometimes creative drive. The bribe had its logic. Gray stood for growth against Green intellectualism and intransigence; moreover, environmentalism was strongest in the island's south, for which Rouse—giving Tasmania's regional jealousies as sharp an edge as they ever had—felt little liking.

Cox having reported the matter, Rouse stood trial in April–May 1990 and received a three-year gaol sentence. Many thought that lenient, making it easier for Field to appoint a royal commissioner, Judge J. W. J. Carter of Queensland, to inquire into the matter. Carter's report spoke of Rouse's 'lust for ever greater power and influence', and lamented that some Tasmanians had exculpated him. The inquiry considered that Gray's 'conduct and behaviour was improper and grossly so', but not criminal.

Lloyd Robson's final words in his 'big' *History of Tasmania* hailed the Labor–Green accord: 'Fragile though it might be, it raises possibilities of a radically different future. The ghosts of Tasmania's past have not been laid to rest, but it is possible to go forward with hope.' Michael Field, Labor's leader since 1988, like Christine Milne, was youngish, a graduate and teacher, hailing from the north-west. A member of Lowe's government, he had survived that shambles without dishonour. As Premier and Treasurer Field promised to eschew 'the old political game of deals and pandering to vested interests'. The new government indeed showed brave in reclaiming public accounts from Gray's promiscuity with loan moneys. The economy glimmered.

That soon waned, as did the accord generally. Are not such arrangements doomed to failure? For good and ill, the Greens were still more determined than Labor to end 'the old political game' and so resisted its compromises. Swelling animosities between the two groups vitiated the government. At the February 1992 elections Labor won fewer votes than it had for decades, whereas the Greens kept their five seats.

The Liberals returned, under R. J. Groom, who had earlier been a federal minister under Fraser. Groom capped the long story whereby distinguished sportsmen entered Tasmanian politics. Among them he no doubt ranked below Darrel Baldock as a footballer (who didn't?) but was tops as a politician, although in office he lacked the decisiveness that had exalted him on the field. The economy languished; nevertheless his term was relatively quiet. Even conservation issues receded a little. One cause and effect was Bob Brown's move towards federal politics from 1993, culminating in his election to the Senate in 1996. He supplanted R. J. Bell who had well maintained the custom of Tasmania having a Democrat voice in the Senate. Christine Milne became leader of the parliamentary Greens.

At the February 1996 polls the Liberals lost their majority, and the Greens lost one seat. Groom gave way as Liberal leader to capable businessman A. W. Rundle, the ninth person to be premier in twenty-five years. Rundle emulated Field in treating with the Greens, between whom and Labor bitterness yet prevailed. The new situation perhaps went beyond that of 1992 in suggesting the decay of party rigidities. Compared with the current worldwide collapse of various regimes this change was minuscule, but flux nevertheless.

Notwithstanding the Greens' lost seat and whatever might happen afterwards, environmentalism had proved central in this generation's affairs. As will be seen, the impact went beyond electoral politics. The movement captured many Tasmanian hearts and minds, incorporating and vitalising radical impulses broadly of a kind that had much play in the world since the 1960s. Elsewhere their crucible often was hostility to the Vietnam War, but here the rivers and forests mattered more; conversely, Green sympathy burned wide, but perhaps nowhere else with such relative heat. Theorists could see meaning and dignity in the situation.

> It is at the international frontier [wrote P. R. Hay of his Tasmania] . . . In an integrated global economic and cultural 'market' geographically focused and dominated by a few centres of activity, it becomes ever more likely that a movement embodying a new radical social vision will emerge in the peripheries, from where the new world order will be at its most evident, most obvious, and most readily comprehended.

Various thinkers with a Tasmanian base lifted conservationist debate to high levels. Hay (a political scientist, who worked in government during the accord), Robyn Eckersley, and Warwick Fox all developed eco-centric theory. Their association with the University of Tasmania's Department of Geography and Environmental Studies honoured the legacy of Richard Jones (who died in 1986). They were among contributors to *The Rest of the World is Watching* (1990), a scintillating collection of Tasmanian essays, edited by Cassandra Pybus and Richard Flanagan, themselves significant in the discourse. Earlier B. C. Mollison had developed in Tasmania both the theory and the practice of his 'permaculture'.

The Greens proved exciting and impressive, but always the question recurred: were they *right*? Among them was a rift between the ecocentrists and those, outstandingly Richard Flanagan, who put humanity first, albeit stressing nature's centrality to human fulfilment. This tension never became virulent, scarcely overt, yet it could seem irreducible. It pertained to fundamental issues concerning how Green ideals might function. The novelist Amanda Lohrey extolled the Green stance as 'no longer utopian versus gothic—subdue the wilderness or be subdued by it—but a narrative that leaves behind enlightenment paradigms, both scientistic and romantic, to argue for a post-modern position that can be encapsulated in the slogan—use the social to sustain the wilderness and the social will be sustained by it.' Such words could arouse, but what policies did they offer those concerned with the future of their children and their investments? On another tack, it might seem absurd to suggest that Tasmania, with its several constrictions and catastrophes, should lead the world into new light. Perhaps everyone of common sense might be able to rest assured that by the mid 1990s the state had various environmental acts and agencies, with 26.8 per cent of its land mass—far beyond national figures—under protection, and likewise a heavy swag of National Estate sites, historic, natural and Aboriginal.

Then the argument swings around. Isn't the Greens' whole point that Tasmania's erstwhile constrictions and catastrophes are the very qualifications for it to break free from the past and lead into a new world? Unless society accepts something like Lohrey's *dicta*, so giving them a chance to work against whatever odds, will not all progeny and property dissolve into nightmare?

Aboriginal Tasmanians have received little mention since this book's early pages, which signifies their marginal and muted place in the record between the mid nineteenth and the mid twentieth centuries. Greater change occurred from the 1960s in this realm than in any other. The people best called Palawa now built an achievement comparable with those of their ancestors by living further south than any other humans more than 20000 years ago and surviving the formation of Bass Strait more than 10000 years ago. Since the 1870s many Europeans had spoken of the Aborigines as having been obliterated. The tone of such remarks was often compassionate, but now to Palawa ears they complemented killings and deaths of the past in reflecting the European will to expunge Aboriginality. Defying that fate, the Palawa became active and vital. The 1961 census reported thirty-eight Aborigines in Tasmania; that of 1966, fifty-five; whereas by 1994 their official number was 10 113. Aboriginality became a palpable fact of everyday Tasmanian life. This story accorded with decline of European hegemony worldwide, and certainly with Australian trends, but had a dimension of particular force. It might seem a surpassing instance of that self-invention (or 'construction') that post-modern theory saw as permeating all society and culture, but its ultimate source was humanity's yearning for decent esteem.

Every Palawa's genes were largely Caucasian. Palawa language long had ceased to be in customary use, and other cultural remains were scant. To critics such facts vitiated the Palawa cause, exposing it as a rort for benefits and favours; from another perspective, they made its vigour all the more amazing. The past that Palawa constructed gave minimal place to European forefathers and kin, flouting positivist truth. However, as many forerunners of post-modernism have glimpsed, myth does better than positivism in sustaining group cohesion and purpose.

Mutual rejection of positivism forged one affinity between Greens and Palawa, and there were others: Greens had to rally with all whom imperial capitalism had scourged. Yet some counter-tensions and ambiguities existed, most evident as to 'wilderness'. Greens revered Tasmania's south-west as wilderness, yet also cited early Aboriginal residence there as strengthening the case against Gordon–Franklin dams. Palawa insisted that the south-west was no wilderness but a site of Aboriginal creativity. Palawa leader Michael Mansell contributed to *The Rest of the World is Watching*, accepting the Greens as allies, but conditional on their recognition that his people's territorial rights surpassed those of all Europeans, including environmentalists and archaeologists.

Nor was the Palawa movement altogether united and harmonious. Faction and advancement occurred in their politics, no less than among Caucasians. Regional, historic, and family ties were all influential. Any person's identification as Palawa required (along with more objective criteria) acceptance by the community, and this could foment troubles.

Over the years Tasmanian politicians and philanthropists had spared occasional thought and word for 'half-castes' and 'Islanders'. Sometimes the people spoke for themselves. Governor Sir James O'Grady had reported in the late 1920s that Cape Barren Islanders proclaimed they were 'descendants of the original owners of Tasmania' and accordingly that 'all the white people . . . are usurpers'. Yet to stress an earlier stream of proud assertion—as Palawa and their sympathisers tended to do—is to muffle the force of recent change.

An academic might identify as the turning point in this story the publication in 1966 of G. A. Robinson's journals (especially as their editor, N. J. B. Plomley, went on to further profound scholarship in the field), but there are other possibilities. In 1967 Tasmania joined the nation in overwhelmingly approving full constitutional rights for Aborigines in a referendum. Probably more importantly, that same year the state's Education Department forsook plans to close its school on Cape Barren. This proposal complemented ideas long harboured in some official circles to drive local 'half-castes' into the broader community. Now the Reverend James Colville, of the Methodist Church, energised the state branch of an Aboriginal Advancement League, which had had a shadowy existence in the north-west since the 1950s. Colville and other Methodists fostered Islander assertion while upbraiding Europeans. *In the Name of God, Stop the War* cried a manifesto by Colville in 1971.

Abschol, which provided aid for higher education to Aborigines, operated nationwide from 1961 but had little effect in Tasmania until late in the decade. Then it gathered various support: from Communist lawyers Derek Roebuck and P. W. Slicer, for example, and Bill Mollison, future guru of permaculture, who earlier had worked on Flinders Island as a CSIRO scientist but now was with the University of Tasmania's psychology department. In the early 1970s Mollison strove to identify all Tasmanians qualified for Abschol, and so began to construct vast genealogies. This proved a profound impetus. Some mainlanders came to Tasmania on Abschol: one of them, Harry Penrith, spoke for the local cause, presaging his future fame as Burnum Burnum. The Palawa movement was to owe more to its own university graduates than did counterparts nationally.

In August 1971 Abschol organised a conference of Islanders who resolved that 'we do not wish the Tasmanian Government to dilute and breed out our people and our cultural heritage'. The next year saw the establishment of the Tasmanian Aboriginal (Information) Centre, destined to spearhead Palawa assertion with skill and tenacity. The Whitlam Government encouraged Aboriginality in various ways. Roslyn Langford, Morgan Mansell, and Roy Nicholls joined consequent national councils. Langford linked Tasmanian feeling with the land rights movement that now developed.

In 1976 Palawa claims and feeling achieved the release of Trugannini's bones from the Tasmanian Museum and their subsequent disposal. Return of skeletal material from throughout the world became a major Palawa thrust, and often succeeded. Another aftermath of the Trugannini episode developed when notable film-maker Tom Haydon— advised by Rhys Jones, distinguished for his Tasmanian archaeology— produced *The Last Tasmanian* (1978). Palawa denounced the film's intended message as a variant of genocide, the more fiercely as Jones had proposed that by 1800 the Tasmanians had suffered such genetic and cultural exhaustion as to doom their future, irrespective of European contact. (Similar ideas echoed in Tim Flannery's most interesting essay in neo-Malthusianism, *The Future Eaters* (1994), but then made no waves.)

Concern for land rights strengthened. During a royal visit in 1977 Michael Mansell confronted the Queen on this matter, and Neilson's government appointed a study group to ponder it and related issues. While the Aboriginal Centre declined to cooperate, the study group issued a penetrating report. It used the term Palawa—if not so spelled, nor with the effect of impelling the term to general use even twenty years later. The report proposed a land trust as the key means to advance. A bill went forward, but too many politicians were still continuing the war, and it aborted.

The movement developed a militant edge. On 16 January 1984 Palawa occupied Oyster Cove, fateful site of their past. Mansell went to Libya in 1987, evidently not to seek money from Colonel Gaddafi, as critics alleged, but to proclaim Palawa wrongs to the world. The Labor–Green accord included reference to such matters. The mainstream bureaucracy came to include an Aboriginal Affairs Office while the Tasmanian Land Council formed among Palawa. In 1991 another land rights bill provoked some fervent advocacy, but the Legislative Council blocked it again. May 1992 saw Palawa occupy Risdon Cove, and in mid year Mansell dominated national moves for Aboriginal sovereignty. The Mabo case added more drama.

Yet, as with conservation, some relaxation then appeared. Perhaps this made it easier for Groom, who had become somewhat sympathetic since the 1980s, to introduce yet another land rights Bill in his government's last weeks. It passed; Palawa achieved control over various sites including Risdon and Oyster Coves, and a trust would facilitate future transfers. Unanimous goodwill prevailed neither within nor between races, but grand Palawa matriarch Ida West declared, 'I feel very happy', and she mattered.

The movement had its cultural dimension. Ida West, embodying a style that had sustained Aboriginality through the darkest years, wrote a most impressive autobiography. Jim Everett was not only active in direct politics—joining Mansell in upholding sovereignty, for example—but also wrote fiction and verse. 'Every Aborigine is a poet', Karen Brown declared, and herself made the point. Folk-style collections of story and rhyme have appeared. The state Education Department, acting with the community's advice, brings Palawa-Aboriginal material before pupils generally. Mudrooroo is not Palawa but his novel, *Doctor Wooreddy's Prescription for Enduring the Ending of the World* (1983), invoked that heritage.

While several Palawa engaged in European-style academic study, there remained tensions *vis-à-vis* that tradition. In 1995 Palawa pressure secured the 'freezing' of much material gathered by La Trobe University's archaeology department, pre-eminent in the Tasmanian field. Plomley's work received little Palawa admiration.

Other Caucasian scholars have taken stances closer to those of the Palawa. Julia Clark's work as anthropologist at the Tasmanian Museum belonged here, as did that of Lyndal Ryan, author of the important *Aboriginal Tasmanians* (1981; republished 1996). Henry Reynolds, of Tasmanian birth and education, has achieved renown since the appearance of his book, *The Other Side of the Frontier* (1981), which interpreted European–Aboriginal contact in terms of putative Aboriginal perceptions. Reynolds, long resident in Queensland, drew primarily from mainland material in *Frontier*, although Tasmaniana had its place. In *Fate of a Free People* (1995) Reynolds tilled this soil deeper, arguing that the Tasmanians' response to settler incursions in the 1820s was so effective as to force George Arthur to sue for peace and offer a kind of treaty envisaging future Aboriginal rights over land. The Europeans' dishonouring of that promise, went Reynolds's argument, strengthened the current Palawa case.

Ultimate issues as to the Palawa are as grand and intractable as those relating to nature conservation. However, it seems that a working compromise could come more easily in this field than the other. Minorities of either ethnicity probably will always feel aggrieved, but others might rub along in passive peace. This is a flat note on which to end a strange and potent story, but better that than war.

Economics, politics, Palawa: these issues had a thematic coherence that now wanes. The following pages tell of a wide range of Tasmanian achievement. *Tasmanian* itself is used loosely, without excessive regard for birth or length of residence.

Lance Barnard stands first among important politicians outside the earlier narrative. Deputy leader to Whitlam on the ALP's victory in December 1972, and the Prime Minister's sole Cabinet colleague in the following heroic weeks, Barnard was archetypal middle Australia. That was appropriate to representing the Launceston-centred electorate of Bass, and Barnard's subsequent ostracism within the Whitlam regime signed its ruin, made plain in mid 1975 when Barnard accepted an ambassadorship and Bass went Liberal. By then K. S. Wriedt was Whitlam's

Minister for Primary Industry and Senate leader, tough tasks both. R. C. Wright (1968–72) and Neal Blewett (1983–93), both mentioned previously, contributed as federal ministers. Wright was ever a sharp critic of both ally and foe; Blewett succeeded in the most difficult portfolio of health. Barnard's successor in Bass was K. E. Newman, whose own fair record gave way to that of his wife Jocelyn, minister in John Howard's first team.

Justin O'Byrne of Launceston held a Senate seat from 1946 to 1981 and was Senate president in 1974–76, both evidence of vigour and integrity. O'Byrne had been among those who challenged Brian Harradine within the ALP. That saga ended in 1975 as Harradine resigned, to uphold Catholic social justice long thereafter as an independent Senator. Another veteran was G. W. A. Duthie, whose tenure of Wilmot (Lyons)—1946–75—far outstripped Tasmanian records for the House of Representatives. Duthie's *I had 50 000 Bosses* (1984) illuminated grassroots politics. Genial populism touched his style and even more so that of Bruce Goodluck, who burgeoned as a community leader on Hobart's eastern shore after the Tasman Bridge fell. He held volatile Franklin in the House of Representatives 1975–93 and then entered the State House of Assembly in 1996.

The governorship gained weight from 1973 when held by Australians: Stanley Burbury, James Plimsoll, Phillip Bennett, and Guy Green. Ex-soldier Bennett proved commanding in the Gray–accord crisis; Plimsoll, bachelor and erstwhile diplomat, traversed countless interests; Burbury and Green (the latter locally born) ascended to the position after long Tasmanian careers. All four were knights of the realm, but their appointments told the fading of the Britannicism that Lloyd Robson and others saw as Tasmania's scourge. Despite what the *Mercury* said on Singapore's fall, and despite Japan having early become Tasmania's trading focus, the old loyalty had stayed alive for many. The republican debate aroused only a little feeling, either way.

Burbury and Green had each been Chief Justice immediately before becoming Governor. An interesting appointment to the judicial bench in 1991 was that of P. W. Slicer, earlier noted as a Palawa upholder and Communist. No woman joined the judges, but in 1994 Helen Lambert became first female stipendiary magistrate and the youngest appointee ever. The profession lost its ultra-masculinity.

Politics had more marked gendering as other women emulated Milne and Newman. Labor's Frances Bladel won esteem as a member of the Assembly after 1986. The 1996 elections returned ten women to the thirty-five-member Assembly, which is perhaps as big a change as any these pages relate. In municipal affairs L. P. (Doone) Kennedy reigned as Lord Mayor of Hobart (1986–96) in non-feminist womanly mode. A Women's Electoral Lobby formed in 1972, strengthening feminist consciousness. It proved durable, as did various older organisations of comparable aims. The bureaucracy had an office for the status of women from 1989. For some hard-pressed mothers the new patterns of employment that favoured such as themselves must have been an ambiguous boon, but they underlay basic changes in gender relationships. Women gained some higher public service jobs, notably apropos of culture and welfare. Feminist ideas and attitudes advanced. Cassandra Pybus, writer on Green and Aboriginal matters, also reinterpreted the Orr case as driven by the sexual rapacity of male academics. Kay Daniels, of the university's history department, won national recognition for blending gender concerns with broader radical perspectives. A graduate from the same department, Marilyn Lake, became central in Australian feminist historiography.

The women's movement had a lesbian touch, linking with larger homosexual issues. Conservation again interplayed: Bob Brown was homosexual, and Rodney Croome—chief Tasmanian publicist in this cause—linked the crusade for homosexual rights with Green and Palawa surgence as complements in a transforming radicalism. Dennis Altman, another University of Tasmania graduate, enhanced Australian thinking in this area much as did Lake for feminism and Reynolds for Aboriginality. Altman's novel, *The Comfort of Men* (1993), imagined a Tasmania wherein repression of homosexuality fused with wider brutalism. Elsewhere Altman himself recognised how different Tasmania had become since the 1950s, but the Legislative Council resisted pressure dating back almost that long to acknowledge the legality of homosexual acts. Meanwhile Stephen Biddulph, yet another of the university's graduates, had Tasmania as his base as he preached a doctrine of masculinity—proud, sensitive, and heterosexual.

Animal liberation found no great Tasmanian theorist but in Pamela Clarke a formidable doer. Hostile especially to battery-rearing of fowls, Clarke won publicity by embarrassing politicians in somewhat the manner of Britain's pre-1914 suffragettes. Avoiding gross fanaticism and ridicule, her cause had some success.

Homosexual deeds were not legitimated, but otherwise governments did something for civil rights. One body to take the van in this and allied matters was the Law Reform Commission. From the mid 1970s the commission proposed various channels of codifying and updating practice and statutes. Perhaps the most notable result was a Small Claims Tribunal, in which law was demythologised. Bethune's government moved towards establishing an ombudsman. Legislative Councillors were chary and for years a committee among them took on the function of ombudsman. A more formal structure did not prevail until 1979. A Freedom of Information Act (1991) likewise worked to some effect. Probably of greater overall benefit were consumer protection measures, again launched in the Bethune days.

Economic stagnation meant that these years saw but little expansion of ethnic/immigrant history. In 1991, 87.5 per cent of Tasmanians claimed Australian birth as against the nation's 75.5 per cent. Numbers of Asian students rose, although even that merely amplified a tradition from the 1950s. Small refugee groups came but largely went so that, for example, Tasmania had very few Vietnamese residents. However, there was a South American presence, and from 1978 a Hmong group gave local multiculturalism its most exotic touch. All the while, older immigrants were spending their lives. Most immigrant autobiographers cited in the previous chapter lived throughout this later period, and others of like background made their marks. Hendrik Petrusma, for example, was active in Hobart business, sport, philanthropy, and politics. Launceston offered two early post-war immigrants who founded their fame as supermarketeers: Roelf Vos went on to become a commercial tycoon, and Ananais (Jimmy) Tsinoglou became the city's mayor (1987–90).

The collapse of the Tasman Bridge shaped the careers of both Bruce Goodluck and of catamaran-builder Robert Clifford, the latter doing much to provide a ferry service in the disaster's wake. Curtailment of car use was a central fact of eastern shore life through the months ahead. Some theorists hoped that the effect would be urban planning that might force a permanent move in this direction, but such was not to be. By the end of 1975 a Bailey bridge 788 metres long—'believed to be the largest of its type ever built'—offered respite, and in time not only did the Tasman reopen but also the Bailey had a permanent successor. The *Lake Illawarra* still lies on the river bed, nudging the Tasman's pylons. Seven of its men and five motorists died.

Among the latter group was an erstwhile secretary–confidante of

Marie Bjelke-Petersen. The latter's nephew Joh attended that funeral, so upholding a tie with Tasmania that long pre-dated his many years as Premier of Queensland. Subsequently he was to spend much time on the island. Another celebrity to retire to Tasmania was Peter Wright, formerly a whiz of British intelligence and author of the famous *Spycatcher*. Tasmania's cheaper housing and other amenities attracted a fair number of older people, many adding much more than money to their new communities.

Close to the bushfires in proving human endurance was the saga of the *Blythe Star*, a vessel in state service. In October 1973 it disappeared, presumably off the west coast. Search found no trace, and hope withered. In fact the *Star* had rounded the south coast before sinking, and eight crew rafted for eight days to come ashore on the Tasman Peninsula. There the hero of the episode died; the others survived.

Darrel Baldock and Ray Groom were not alone as stars in Victorian football. Peter Hudson equalled the season record of 150 goals in 1971, and around then Ian Stewart thrice won the outstanding player award and Royce Hart played in four premiership-winning teams. Later years saw mainland recruitment of Tasmanian talent become more systematic, which sapped the island's competitions and made them more vulnerable to troubles consequent on sport becoming big business. In cricket the converse happened as the state's acceptance into national competition made it attractive to mainland players frustrated at home. Tasmania performed creditably, winning the one-day competition in 1978–79; hero of the match was Jack Simmons, a Lancastrian devoted to Tasmania. Outstanding among local players was David Boon, a key batsman for Australia through a decade around 1990. As his career waned, fellow Launcestonian Ricky Ponting promised similar glory. Max Walker never played for Tasmania, but he was its best bowler, and throughout Australia his books (some said) outsold even God's. Stephen Randell proved a cricket umpire of the highest calibre.

Woodchopping continued to be the most distinctive of Tasmanian sports. It was appropriate that world championships should go in the 1960s to Doug Youd, scion of 'the world's greatest chopping family', and in the 1990s to David Foster, vast in cheer as in body. Tasmanian topography always gave cycling an extra nuance: Danny Clark won the island's first individual Olympic medal (silver) in 1972, Michael Grenda (in a team) the first gold in 1984. Oarsman Steven Hawkins followed Grenda in 1992. Lindsey Goggin emulated Boon in national distinction, thrice winning the Australian women's golfing championship. Beverley Buckingham led her female counterparts worldwide by leading the local jockeys' table in 1981–82. A swimmer, Melissa Carlton, excelled among disabled athletes, achieving gold at the 1996 Paralympics. Women helped to bring crowds and interest to basketball around 1990.

The mid 1980s saw opening of a state Institute of Sport, a top-level velodrome outside Launceston, and a rowing course at Lake Barrington, on which the world titles of 1990 were held. Against these advances there prevailed (and not only in football) problems arising from increasing costs on one hand and the island's economic and demographic constraints on the other. Even basketball's popularity wilted under these burdens. Horse-racing's triumphs—locally bred Halwes won Sydney's top trotting race in 1968, and Piping Lane the Melbourne Cup in 1972—receded into a misty past, and the sport languished as alternative forms of gambling multiplied.

An obvious change in relation to matters of the mind concerned tertiary education. Consequent upon John Gorton's plans as prime minister the Tasmanian College of Advanced Education was established in the 1970s. While stressing applied and pragmatic studies, the college yet competed with the university. That it was sited in Hobart sharpened this competition, and drew criticism from interests outside the capital. With considerable anguish the college was restructured, with some parts joining the university and the core moving to Launceston (1979). The college received much support there and developed as a quasi-university. It was renamed the Tasmanian State Institute of Technology in 1985. Amalgamation with the university became a matter of hot debate, and federal pressure hastening the outcome, which proceeded during the early 1990s. The emphasis of the Launceston campus on business and management remained, although work advanced in fields as diverse as aquaculture and Kierkegaardian philosophy.

Amalgamation was not alone in disrupting old-style university concerns. Federal oversight, with stress on quantitative outputs and market competition, seemed inexorable. Post-modernism's challenge to Western intellectual traditions posed difficulties of varying yet complementary order. Withal, in the 'old' university geology, physics, chemistry and mathematics continued strong, with agriculture and Antarctic sciences joining them. Benefit accrued from transfer to Hobart through the 1980s of CSIRO laboratories in oceanography, fisheries, and forestry, and of the federal Antarctic division. Work in the university's departments of psychology and geography and environmental studies has been mentioned already. Social sciences, accounting, and law came to attract large numbers of students. Notable in this area was the department of sociology from which came penetrating study of the post-modern world. The history department, by contrast, won acclaim in mediaeval studies. The appeal of history—like the other humanities as well as the 'hard' sciences—waned for students.

John Gorton's ambition to upgrade technical education through new colleges largely misfired, but over time 'technical and further education' became an increasing if inchoate part of the world of learning. Federal pressure prompted universities to credit approved TAFE courses towards their degrees. Tasmania went these several ways. The Australian Maritime College, founded in Launceston and funded by the Commonwealth, taught a variety of appropriate courses in a way that probably brought it closer to the Gortonian ideal than any other Australian institution.

The quest for relevance and output affected especially state secondary education. The sector boasted of a 'revolutionary' thrust carrying all towards year 12. In truth many stayed as pupils only because no jobs offered, a situation that diminished the incentive to learn. Computers might supply loads of data, but questing intelligence did not necessarily follow. State schools combined teaching and palliation with more success than logic might have promised, and erstwhile matriculation colleges served their communities by making courses widely available, but meritocratic standards had to fade. Independent schools had so much the more opportunity, and they took it. Public funding, social polarisation of wealth, and continuing readiness of many parents to make financial sacrifice all helped these schools to grow, or at least to survive.

As ever, religious groups had provision of education high among their roles: Catholics, Anglicans, Quakers, Calvinists, Lutherans, and Adventists all did so. The task was never easy. The Catholic sector especially was beset by tensions as its leaders sought to rationalise. The older churches had further problems. Anglicans had happier experience than Catholics with their schools, but otherwise they seemed close to crisis, and the uniting of other Protestant churches was more often a factor of weakness than strength. Independent congregations—

not always small—better met the times. Ethnicity continued to sustain religious practice. At another level, Green environmentalism had traits of spirituality and charisma-centred faith, and the alternative communities that dotted Tasmania—down the Huon–Channel, around Deloraine, Stanley, Derby—a touch of eremite asceticism.

A sublime creation of secular culture was Peter Sculthorpe's music. It drew from nature and history, occident and orient (young Peter having listened with delight to the instruments of Chinese market gardeners outside Launceston). Unlike Sculthorpe, Donald Kay remained in Tasmania. His compositions yet more deliberately evoked its landscape. Stuart Challender, chief conductor of the Sydney Symphony Orchestra from 1987 until his death in 1991, was outstanding among performance musicians. At home the Tasmanian Symphony Orchestra won acclaim as a 'treasure'. Graeme Murphy's passion drove him from Mathinna (Eric Reece's birthplace) to marvels of dance. Folk and other popular music had phases of immense activity, culminating in annual festivals at Longford in the earlier 1980s and important in many 'alternative' contexts.

Gwen Harwood and James McAuley remained supreme throughout their lives, elevating much other achievement in poetry. Coming to approach them in iconic status was poet, novelist and academic Margaret Scott, who told of the alienation she felt in the early years of her migration to Tasmania in 1960 and her later discovery of endless inspiration there. Sarah Day, a poet and teacher, was a younger woman of English birth who crossed two worlds, while Vicki Raymond moved from Tasmania to flourish as a poet in Britain. Of several poets to sympathise with the Green cause, P. R. Hay had perhaps the greatest power. Graeme Hetherington and Timothy Thorne often wrote in sombre tone, the former invoking Tasmanian history and his own childhood as he did so. Thorne found the resilience to be active in Launceston's cultural life, notably as publisher and director of an annual poetry festival. Vivian Smith's *oeuvre* continued to show Tasmanian elements; the anthology of Tasmanian verse that he and Margaret Scott edited, *Effects of Light* (1985), is enchanting.

Richard Davey is the only playwright to measure against all these (and more) poets. Active from the mid 1970s, Davey drew much from Tasmanian, including Aboriginal, history, to build a major corpus in this most challenging field. Presentation of his plays lifted local theatre; one was mounted at Strahan, site of its plot. High costs meant that fully professional drama was rarely offered to Tasmania. Local enthusiasts met the challenge, their number sometimes close to exceeding audiences (a version of the non-spectating syndrome already noticed apropos of sport). The balance seemed to shift in the 1990s, as it deserved to do.

Amanda Lohrey's *Reading Group* (1988) followed *The Morality of Gentlemen* (1984), the latter inspired by her family's absorption with the Hobart waterfront and its politics, specifically the Hursey case. The two titles established Lohrey as peerless among Australian writers of political fiction, and her third novel, *Camille's Bread* (1995), signalled yet greater achievement. As noted, Lohrey upheld the environmental cause. That loyalty also suffused Richard Flanagan's *Death of a River Guide* (1995), a novel of profound intent, seeking to confront Tasmania's past agonies and to strengthen its people in resolving them, thereby achieving liberation. An older writer of Green sympathy was James McQueen, whose *Hook's Mountain* (1982) told of one man's attachment to one Tasmanian place. McQueen has otherwise written of Tasmania with passion and insight. Perhaps a hint of melodrama has caused his work to achieve less than due acclaim. All the while Christopher Koch kept at work. His major new books of Tasmanian provenance were *The Doubleman* (1985) and *Highways to a War* (1995). The latter is to be complemented by another, carrying back into the Vandiemonian past. Koch, McQueen, Flanagan, Lohrey—did ever so small a place fire such a blaze?

This account already has used several Tasmanian autobiographies, including the most remarkable, Peter Conrad's *Down Home* (1988). In his thirties Conrad, born in Hobart in 1948 of working-class parents, became a cultural analyst of international repute. *Down Home* presents Tasmania in darkest terms, 'Gothic' and demonic. Doom descends from Aborigines and convicts to such people as Conrad's own relatives—empty, inert, caring naught for their place or its history. Conrad exemplifies that, for many, Tasmanian birth has seemed fate's blow, to be escaped and even reviled. The space between Conrad and Flanagan (both Rhodes scholars) is meet for contemplating all Tasmanian experience.

Two other autobiographers might be juxtaposed with Conrad. Barney Roberts has spent virtually all his life (outside war service) as a farmer in the north-west. That region has inspired several fine memoir–histories, but none so rich in evocation and moral force as Roberts's *Where's Morning Gone?* (1987). Roberts has written verse and further prose; his son Bruce continues similar in life and art. No less different from Conrad is Marjorie Bligh. Born of Midlands rural poor, Bligh's *Life is for Living* (1986) gives rare insight into that *milieu* and many another aspect of grassroots Tasmania. Bligh's title suggests her worldview, and other books—ranging from household hints to history—have developed it. Some readers find Bligh the epitome of crass philistinism, hers a life following the absurd art of Barry Humphries's Dame Edna Everage; others will judge Bligh's *Life* and the rest so authentic and impermeable as to disarm such judgment. Enid Lyons, a fellow resident of Devonport, was writing a preface for Bligh's current work when she died.

Studies and writing about many areas of Tasmanian life proceeded. The Royal Society's *Papers* moved towards 150 years of serial publication; from 1967 the Commonwealth Statistician issued *Yearbooks*, which, at their (earlier) best, were first class; maps from the state cartography service never failed to meet such a standard; the Centre for Regional Economic Analysis continued a long association between government and that stream of academic learning. Manifold examples could continue, but a historian must give most space to history.

Convictism always fascinates, and debate on it continues to fluctuate. The 'commonsense' verdicts of B. C. Smith and young Robson retained support, but other analysts felt that such commentary hid the vicious cruelty of Britain's imperial rule. Robert Hughes was not so far to the Left as most who took this stance, but his *Fatal Shore* (1987) thereby had all the more effect, bringing colonial Australia, Van Diemen's Land much included, vividly before world notice.

Notwithstanding that debate, the passage of time allowed easier acceptance of the convict past. Notable in the process were P. F. Bolger's *Hobart Town* (1973) and Marjorie Tipping's *Convicts Unbound* (1988). Genealogy had at least as big a following in Tasmania as it now acquired worldwide. Convict ancestry was no matter for shame to its devotees but rather a matter of delight in the promise of rich documentation. Most famous of Tasmanian family hunters was Germaine Greer, who found not convictism but bastardy and other fascinations, as she told in her *Daddy, We Hardly Knew You* (1989).

Historical research proceeded through many channels: academic and amateur, documentary and oral, private and public. Major syntheses came from Robson and his erstwhile teacher, W. A. Townsley. 'There appears a virtually unslakeable thirst for knowledge of the past', judged

Robson in 1985, 'no doubt impelled in part at least by the increasing anonymity of Tasmanians as individuals as they are caught up like everyone else in the computer age, automation and high technology which mark a new industrial revolution.' The Tasmanian Historical Research Association continued active, but now many groups shared this field. The university likewise sustained a pattern dating from the 1950s. Its history department established a Centre for Tasmanian Historical Studies in 1984, and several other departments embraced historical work.

The Tasmanian Writers' Union, founded in 1979, organised many activities, most famously an annual writers' festival in Hobart. Its contemporary and complement was the literary journal entitled (by 1996) *Island*. From 1975 the government sustained the Tasmanian Arts Advisory Board (later Arts Tasmania), which became the most effective instrument of official help to culture. The Tasmanian Trades and Labor Council included arts patronage in its activities. One project sought to heal wounds inflicted on Burnie by the Associated Pulp strike.

An historian of Australian art might rank as Tasmania's greatest fame of this time the fact that Lloyd Rees (1895–1988) spent his final years there, painting gloriously almost to the end. Jack Carington Smith's legacy endured, notably in a watercolour school led by Max Angus and Patricia Giles. Who else to name from a myriad of talent? Geoffrey Dyer's landscapes had a sombre power very different from that of the watercolourists, if varying from them no more than did the island's different topographies among each other. David Keeling vested suburban and rural vistas with cool, quizzing surrealism. The university's art schools included practitioners and critics of note; post-modernism prevailed among them, most remarkably in Peter Hill's creation through imagination and technology of a 'Museum of Contemporary Ideas' ('based' in New York), which achieved notice from international media and thus reality.

At the Hobart art school were photographers Anne McDonald and David Stephenson. The island's beauty long had inspired landscape photography, a tradition sustained by Green publicity and distinguished work. Olegas Truchanas and Peter Dombrovskis both depicted the wilderness in wondrous ways, and both died there. Still more famous was photojournalist Neil Davis, noted for his coverage of the Vietnam War, who likewise perished as he had lived, covering an attempted coup in Bangkok; his life was echoed in the protagonist of Koch's *Highways to a War*. Tim Bowden, Davis's biographer, was one of several Tasmanians who contributed much to other styles of journalism. Older names were Denis Warner and Clive Turnbull, while the next generation offered Bowden, Helene Chung, Charles Wooley, and Martin Flanagan.

From his Tasmanian studio Stephen Walker created fountains and statues that enriched many Australian places, Hobart above all. Peter Taylor's sculpture made splendid use of local timbers. Furniture of highest quality came from several artists, Kevin Perkins and John Smith among them. Potters, weavers, and metalsmiths could all claim like achievement. Craft had a place in the state's economy, art schools, and many lives, especially throughout exurbia.

Craftspeople brought wares to Hobart's Salamanca Place market each Saturday. Many other goods and services were offered there. Behind the market ran a range of buildings, most of handsome style and colonial vintage. They housed an intimate theatre, galleries, boutiques, and bookshops—in number and quality made possible by tourism. Much coffee was drunk; Salamanca Place caught all-day sun but anyway around 1990 *al fresco* became Tasmanian fashion. Among buskers perhaps the most tuneful was a Chilean group, Arauco Libre. Across one way Hmong sold their fruit and vegetables. Then came Stephen Walker's statue-fountain of Abel Tasman, and beyond that Parliament House. On its lawn gathered many a meeting, often of sociopolitical protest. Palawa might be there, Greens very likely so. Such was Tasmania. As its numerical share in the world became ever more minute, the place seemed increasingly a microcosm.

Epilogue: Death and life

On the idyllic Sunday afternoon of 28 April 1996 a gunman killed thirty-five people at Port Arthur. That such an outrage could happen —at the site remarkable for convict suffering in the past and for tourist vitality in the present—through the deed of a fellow citizen chilled many hearts, especially but not only in Tasmania. Evil walked our home-place, in a manner conforming to such analyses as those of Hal Porter and Peter Conrad.

Burdens fell on many beyond the bereaved. Workers and visitors at the settlement, police and medical personnel, these and others proved valiant. At a memorial service in Port Arthur's old church on 3 May these words sounded:

> Today we have gathered to reclaim this place for the people, to reclaim it
> for peace, to reclaim it as a place of safety and play and laughter.
> Today we stand together to refuse evil the right to take this place
> from us.
> Today we are here to say we will not allow our fear to take anything else
> from us.
> Today we stand united to say that violence and hate should have no place
> in our society.
> Today we stand against the use of weapons that destroy and maim.
> Today we stand to say that this community will survive; that our
> community will go on, and will continue to share its beauty and peace
> with all who come to visit this area.

The statement could have meant more for no one than Walter Mikac, who had lived with his family at nearby Nubeena and whose wife and two young daughters died in the tragedy. Mikac's suffering entered Tasmanian consciousness.

In the months ahead Mikac transcended his grief and worked for reform of gun laws, which was now pursued by governments throughout Australia. The matter provoked local feeling. Even as to guns, even at this time, there worked that old, tough Tasmanian determination to hold what one had. Some politicians were ready to endorse such feeling. Gun owners doubtless abhorred the killings as much as anyone, indeed with a particular edge. After delay, legislation did pass parliament.

The words spoken at the Port Arthur service give a lead to those who contemplate the past. Evil and tragedy pervade all events, Tasmania's history very much included. But to give ground to those dire forces in any way, even by conscious risk of exaggerating their force, is itself dire. The role of evil and tragedy must be loathed and contested, made subordinate to that of achievement and ideals. This must be the final credo of a history of Tasmania written at the time of the Port Arthur tragedy.

References

This *Short History of Tasmania* [first edition, 1985] is based on depatches transmitted between the governors of Van Diemen's Land/Tasmania and the Colonial Office, *Journals and Printed Papers* of the Parliament of Tasmania, newspapers, periodicals and theses held in the Morris Miller Library of the University of Tasmania. Also used were:

Australian Dictionary of Biography, Melbourne, 1966 to date, Melbourne University Press, Melbourne.

Bennett, S. C., *Federation*, Cassell, Melbourne, 1975

Davies, J. L. (ed.), *Atlas of Tasmania*, Lands and Surveys Department, Hobart, 1965

Davis, Richard, *Eighty Years' Labor: The ALP in Tasmania, 1903–83*, Sassafrass Books and the History Department, University of Tasmania, Hobart, 1983

Green, F. C. (ed.), *A Century of Responsible Government 1856–1956*, Commonwealth Parliamentary Association and Tasmanian Historical Research Association, Hobart, n.d. [1956]

Lake, Marilyn, *A Divided Society: Tasmania during World War I*, Melbourne University Press, Melbourne, 1975

Murphy, D. P. (ed.), *Labor in Politics: The State Labor Parties in Australia 1880–1920*, University of Queensland Press, Brisbane, 1975

Robson, L. L., *A History of Tasmania*, Volume 1: *From the Earliest Times to 1856*, Oxford University Press, Melbourne, 1983

Smith, Vivian, *Tasmania and Australian Poetry*, University of Tasmania, Hobart, 1984

Tasmanian Historical Research Association, *Papers and Proceedings*, 1951 to date

Tasmanian Year Book, Commonwealth Bureau of Census and Statistics (and successor agencies), Tasmanian Office, Hobart, 1966 to date

Townsley, W. A., *The Government of Tasmania*, University of Queensland Press, Brisbane, 1976

Lloyd Robson

References

In preparing the second edition of this book (1997), I have drawn from several of these same sources where chronologically appropriate. My text indicates further items I have used, sometimes with such detail as to make any further citation redundant. An exception to that rule must be volume 2 of Robson's *History of Tasmania*. The other secondary work of comparable value is W. A. Townsley, *Tasmania . . . 1945–1988*. Readers might note that *The Rest of the World is Watching* (edited by Pybus & Flanagan) includes cited work by Croome, Hay, Kiernan, Lohrey, and Mansell. For the rest, chapters 8 and 9 have drawn on the following:

Alcorso, Claudio, *The Wind You Say*, Angus & Robertson, Sydney, 1993

Alliston, Eleanor, *Escape to an Island*, Heinemann, London, 1966

Bowden, Tim, *The Way My Father Tells It*, ABC Books, Sydney, 1990

Brooks, K. G., *An Affirming Flame*, William Legrand, Hobart, 1987

Bull, T. I., *Politics in a Union: The Hursey Case*, Waterside Workers' Federation with Alternative Publishing Cooperative, Sydney, 1977

Daniels, D. W., 'The assertion of Tasmanian Aboriginality', Master of Humanities thesis, Department of History, University of Tasmania, 1995

Davis, Richard, *Open to Talent: The Centenary History of the University of Tasmania*, University of Tasmania, Hobart, 1990

Dutton, Geoffrey, *Out in the Open*, University of Queensland Press, Brisbane, 1995

Eckersley, Robyn, *Environmentalism and Political Theory*, UCL Press, London, 1992

Emery, Edith, *A Twentieth Century Life*, Artemis, Hobart, 1995

Farquhar, B. A., *Bert's Story*, Regal, Launceston, 1990

Fox, Warwick, *Toward a Transpersonal Ecology*, Shambala, Boston, Mass., 1990

Gibson, R. S., *My Years in the Communist Party*, International Bookshop, Melbourne, 1966

Godfrey, Elizabeth, *A Patchwork Quilt*, Fitzroy Press, Hobart, 1980

Hagger, A. J. & others, *The Tasmanian Economy*, University of Tasmania and Centre for Regional Economic Analysis, Hobart, 1989

Hobsbawm, E. J., *Age of Extremes*, Michael Joseph, London, 1994

Julian, Roberta, 'The Dutch in Tasmania', Doctor of Philosophy thesis, Department of Sociology, University of Tasmania, 1989

Lyons, Enid, *So We Take Comfort*, Heinemann, London, 1965

——*The Old Haggis*, Heinemann, Melbourne, 1969

——*Among the Carrion Crows*, Rigby, Adelaide, 1972

Norman, Don, *A Tasmanian Life*, D. Norman, Sandy Bay, Tas., 1987

O'Brien, Eileen, 'Tasmania transformed or transportation revisited?: Immigration to Tasmania, 1945–1955', Master of Humanities thesis, Department of History, University of Tasmania, 1992

Pakulski, Jan, *Polish Migrants in Hobart*, Department of Sociology, University of Tasmania, Hobart, 1982

Parkin, Ross, *Into the Smother*, Pacific Books, Sydney, 1963

Phillips, D. M. & Sprod, M. N., *Making More Adequate Provision: State Education in Tasmania 1839–1985*, Education Department of Tasmania, Hobart, 1985

Pybus, C. J., *Gross Moral Turpitude: The Orr Case Reconsidered*, Heinemann, Melbourne, 1993

Pybus, C. J. & Flanagan, R. (eds), *The Rest of the World is Watching*, Sun Books, Sydney, 1990

Robson, Lloyd, *A History of Tasmania*, Volume 2, *Colony and State from 1856 to the 1980s*, Oxford University Press, Melbourne, 1991

Townsley, W. A. *Tasmania: Microcosm of the Federation or Vassal State? 1945–1988*, St David's Park Publishing, Hobart, 1994

West, Ida, *Pride against Prejudice*, Australian Institute of Aboriginal Studies, Canberra, 1984

Michael Roe

Index